CHOICES IN LIFE

Roy K. Lintz

authorHOUSE®

AuthorHouse™
1663 Liberty Drive
Bloomington, IN 47403
www.authorhouse.com
Phone: 1-800-839-8640

First published by AuthorHouse 05/23/2011

ISBN: 978-1-4567-6504-0 (sc)
ISBN: 978-1-4567-6503-3 (hc)
ISBN: 978-1-4567-6505-7 (e)

Library of Congress Control Number: 2011908269

Printed in the United States of America

Table of Contents

— 1 —

What's Important

I once heard that a person should do three things in life. Have a child, plant a tree and write a book. Why? The answer is that we are only on this planet for a short time and one day we will all die. Life is all about the choices we make during this lifetime. Nothing in this life is forever, one day it will end. What happens after this life - do we really know? Leave a child, tree and book when you go. What matters is not what you take with you, but what you leave behind. Perhaps life really is all about the choices we make during this lifetime.

Role Models

I had two great parents growing up as a kid. My Dad was the bread winner of the house and Mom was the person that stayed home to rise the kids, all four of us, a brother and two sisters. My Dad taught me to work hard for the dollar, be on time and make your own choices. That is what a man does in life. My Mom ensured that we understood that family is important to your life no matter what you do or become in life. She was always there to ensure we got onto the school bus and there to meet us at the end of the school day. My Mom always had dinner on the table when my Dad arrived from work and we all had a family dinner together. My Mom loves pictures of the family, they are all over the house. At the end of the day, what you have is your family by your side and to always have time for your family.

I was lucky to be coached by a good man in my high school years. His name is Max Ramey. Sports was the X factor for keeping me in school during those years. The older I get, the more I see his guidance from the basketball court to life. Every basketball player wants to put the ball in the air and score points. The score tells us the winner or loser. But the real truth is determined before the ball is in the air. It's all about the preparation and choices prior to the ball going in the hoop. All the time, all the hard work and all of the Coach's guidance during practice and choices we make. Once the ball is in the air, it's out of your hands. Life is just like his basketball practices. He was both my Coach and Role Model during those very important years of high school. Plus, all of his long and hard practices both on and off the basketball court.

Soldier

The life of a battlefield Soldier is a challenge and choices are made. Most goes through a mental process before taking a life. The person between the sites of your weapon becomes a target, not a living person. By changing your behavior and way of thinking enables you to take that life. Telling yourself that it's for the betterment of your overall cause. A Soldier on the battlefield is expected to defeat the enemy or your opponent. It comes down to you or your opponent, life or death. It's human nature to want survival for yourself and your buddy next to you. Therefore, this mental process becomes somewhat like a security blanket enabling you to accomplish your mission at hand and be able to live with yourself. But how will we be judged at the end for taking lives for what we believe to be the betterment of our overall cause? In the overall picture, is it ever right to take another's life away?

At the end of the day, were you successful, did you make the right choices? Did you obtain your goals and objectives? Did you hit your 25 meter target? True leadership is not about your position, it's all about the action that you took or did not take, your choices. Did you get done today the goals and objectives that was most important to you? If you did, great job, keep up the good work. If you fell short, you must ask yourself why? What can you do to get better for tomorrow? Have a plan, make a plan and put that plan into action. Find a way, get the important things in your life done; just get it done. Make them a priority as you go about your daily life. You will become happier with yourself and your overall life itself will improve. Who am I? What am I living for? Are

2

you making the right choices for you as a person. Your objective must be very clear in your mind.

Dream

Take your dream plan very seriously. If you spend the time well and expend the effort, it will change your life forever. Start by committing your dream to paper today. If you don't know the destination, there's no way you'll ever be able to chart a course to get there. If your dream is vague, take some time to think it through. Your goal should be well defined before you proceed beyond this point. But at times, you just need to move forward, not really knowing where you are going.

Don't just dream about what you would like to be, become intimate with it. Get to really know it, and you'll be well prepared when you start making your game plan. You'll have all the information you need to determine what you'll have to get done and how long it may take. Hopefully, your research efforts will help you to get on with making your dream come true. Being very careful and honest with yourself, do you have the brains, the aptitude and the talent to make your dream come true? You either do or you don't. Are you making the right choices? The point here is simple. Make sure that you really have the right stuff to make your dream come true. Assuming you have the brains, aptitude and talent, you can obtain everything else. Education, training and practice are keys. It's now only a matter of determining what you need and how long it will take to get it. This will comprise the formulation of your game plan and choices ahead of you in life.

I developed the book cover of my second book or the Custom Cover Illustration. My intent or basic concept was a tree in the center with a single red apple which stands for knowledge. Moses on the left side with a Bible in one hand and a wooden walking stick in the other for faith; Einstein on the right side with the equation E=MC2 in the background for reason. What do we mean by faith and reason? What are the most important issues in your life? We live in a complex society and cultural conditions affect the nature of an individual or community. Are you a person of God? Does God exist now or in our past? If you believe in God, is God dead or alive? The choices are yours to make, nobody else, only you. I discussed many issues that are important to

3

leadership, faith, reason and just plain getting things done. The focus was on what constitutes common sense by way of leadership, faith and reason in life.

This current book is based on choices and my wife developed this book cover. What do we mean by choices we make in life? That's the focus in this book. Perhaps it's the way things in life really are – it is what it is. What are the most important issues in your life? Are you making the right choices for you? I see choices as what is important to you as a person within our society. We live in a complex society and cultural conditions affect the nature of an individual or community. It's also the study of society and of individual relationships in and to society, and the environment in which we live. Are you a person of God? I have decided to write about one person's view of choices in life. I will discuss many issues in this book that are important to choices and just plain getting things done based upon own choices. It's important that we find ways to improve upon activities as we travel though life.

Strategy implementation may be the most important factor shaping management today. How do we measure strategy? Is our organization decentralized and closer to the customer - customer driven? Become a more customer focused organization, one that understands its customers better and deliver what they want. The ability to execute strategy can be more important than the strategy itself. Intangible assets have become the major source of competitive advantage. Experience has repeatedly shown that the single most important condition for success is ownership. We will discuss what true ownership is all about and how to obtain it.

A strategy map is the cornerstone, shared service synergies, strategic learning and strategic awareness. Individual strategies must be linked and integrated. The competitive landscape is constantly changing, so strategies must constantly evolve to reflect shifts in opportunities and threats. Strategy must be a continual process. It requires that all employees understand the strategy and conduct their day to day business in a way that contributes to the success of that strategy. The first job is to make the need for change obvious to all; importance of teamwork in executing strategy. In many cases you can link personal objectives to the strategy. Learning and growth are priorities to create a climate that supports organizational change, innovation and growth.

To be a great leader, you must have a dream. Again, I want you to take your personal dream plan very seriously. If you spend the time well and expend the effort, it will change your life forever. Being very honest with yourself, do you have the brains, the aptitude and the talent to make your dream come true? Focus on the dream. Make a habit of keeping a copy of your action plan with you at all times. This will help you to make the right choices. Life is too short to be saddled with doing something you don't like. People must realize that they are in their most productive years and that it's all going to end someday. Are you old or young? Old or young, you have today and at the end of the day, it's gone, never to return again. Therefore, what is your focus today? Are you working toward the most important issues in your life? You hear people talk about the good old days. Well today is that good old day, right here, right now, today.

Attitude

Attitude is a little thing that helps you get the most out of life and be successful regardless of what the odds might be. The only thing winners are up against is their own attitude and choices. Attitude is very important for a leader, because attitude and choices are everything. By having a personal mission statement helps us to have the right attitude and make the right choices. Our outlook must be that the glass is always half-full and never half-empty. We must focus on a strong finish. However, be realistic about strengths and weaknesses. Remember that little changes and a positive attitude can make a huge difference in regards to health and wellness.

Our society may over use the term leadership. There are three basic styles of leadership; directing, participating and delegating. Choosing the correct style of leadership requires you to understand the four factors of leadership. Anyone can do almost anything with unlimited resources. The true leader finds a way to do great things with limited resources. Leadership is action, not position. No matter what kind of leader you have been in the past, you can decide to be a new and different leader, a better leader tomorrow. A great leader will provide purpose, direction and motivation. The four major factors of leadership are always present and affect the choices we make and when we should make them. They are the led, the leader, the situation and communications.

Counseling is a fundamental responsibility of every leader. Leaders at all levels have a responsibility to assist and develop subordinates. Counseling requires that a leader's actions demonstrate knowledge, understanding, judgment and ability. Of a leader's traits or characteristics in promoting effective counseling, a caring attitude is the most important. There are as many approaches to counseling as there are counselors. But there are three basic approaches used in counseling, directive approach at one extreme, nondirective approach at the other and combined approach in the middle. What choices are you making and are they the right choices?

A great leader must be able to set goals and have good time management skills. Goals give a sense of direction and purpose, force us to plan ahead and give us a clear understanding of what is expected. Self-disciplined people know how to set a goal, define the steps to accomplish the goal, and take each step, even though each one might be more painful than the one before. It's all about own choices. Such planning refreshes your outlook and reinforces your determination to move forward. You are happier in life if you know what your goals are? Find out what you really want out of life. Make a game plan for your dream. Map out a plan to make it happen and then go out into the world and get it done. The choice is yours to make.

The essence of the secret lies in a change of mental attitude. The life of inner peace, being harmonious and without stress; is the easiest type of existence. A primary method for gaining a mind full of peace is to practice emptying the mind. Each day, empty your mind of fears, hates, insecurities, regrets and guilt feelings. To prevent unhappy thoughts from sneaking in again, immediately fill your mind with creative and healthy thoughts. Another effective technique in developing a peaceful mind is the daily practice of silence. Insist upon no less than a quarter of an hour of absolute quiet every twenty-four hours. Go alone into the quietest place available to you and sit or lie down for fifteen minutes and practice the art of silence.

It's suicide to go through life being passively shoved around by an employer who decides your earnings, exact hours you will work, vacation time or whether you'll even have a job. A person must take control of their own life. You can too. Choice is a gift, but you must exercise this gift. You can have all that you want. You need only make up your mind and take action. Life is not a spectator sport. All the knowledge in the world won't help you if you don't take action. Dreams only come true if the desire is great enough. Why not see what you can really do, how far you can go? Why not become the most you can and really live life instead of just watching it pass by.

Stress

One of the biggest killers in our present world is stress. One of the primary factors in stress and one of the main reasons we don't enjoy life are that we worry about everything. A strong leader will find a way to deal with the stress that is in our daily lives. Education allows you to work smarter, not harder. Get plenty of rest, exercise regularly, eat well and watch you diet and keep a clean conscience. What choices are you making? Highly recommend getting a complete physical examination to rule out any medical problems that could be contributing to stressed-out feelings and again every five years. Other factors, such as poor nutrition, bad eating habits, inadequate rest and lack of exercise, can contribute to a run-down, sick and tired feeling.

Stay healthy. Only then do you have the equipment, the brainpower and physical power necessary to recognize, analyze and manage problems. Staying healthy involves inheriting the right genes (you can't do much about this one), exercise, diet and attitude. Don't work yourself to death. Today people are sacrificing themselves in the workplace. They tolerate immensely harmful symptoms such as anger, chemical dependencies and loneliness in a blind pursuit of self-fulfillment through career success. People live to work – work – work – and more work. We should work to live the life we want and support our priorities during our lifetime on this planet. This is your choice.

A good marriage is very important to good health. The key is to stay engaged and be willing to enter the relational dance that healthy marriages must maintain, even when it's painful. Be sure you are in control of your discussion so that a small hurt to you doesn't end up killing the relationship. Resolution comes when you choose to forgive and forget. This is a choice. People who get even never seem to find a way to get ahead. As mature individuals, we eventually stop focusing on what was and what might have been and get on with what is and what is to be. It is what it is, now move on in your life. Sometimes our hurts are based on our perceptions of life. By carrying bitterness in our hearts toward those who have wounded us, we hurt ourselves most of all. When physical and emotional health is the goal, forgiveness is not an option, it is a requirement.

Communication is one of the biggest problems in relationships today. Listening makes effective leadership possible. Don't use the absence of involvement as an excuse for not living a full life. Don't blame another for your lack of fulfillment. Take responsibility for your own life, this is your choice to make. Do what you can to change yourself in ways that will help you live a balanced life. Any price you pay that forces your family to take a back seat is too high a price. The wise professional invests in family first.

You see quite a few people whose marriages are ruined when their mates say that they can't put up with their work anymore because they're constantly unhappy with their job or business. That's sad, it shouldn't really happen. You can't really tell someone else what to do with their personal life. They have to decide for themselves, that is a choice.

On a limited basis, stress can help you response to a special challenge, but your health will begin to break down if the body becomes chronic or you do not allow sufficient time to relax or regroup. Learn how to handle the stress in your life. Take some time off from work and your family. Spend some time for you, re-look your life from time to time. Are you making the right choices? Reconsider how you view stress and stop trying to get rid of it all. Work to make your life more interesting, take up a new challenge or give your life some excitement in sports, hobbies or other leisure activities. If you drink gallons of caffeine, smoke countless cigarettes or use drugs or alcohol to relieve stress, these substances will eventually create more stress than you bargained for. The more you take, the more you need. Occasional use to relieve stress can quickly turn into stressful dependency.

Believe

Believe in yourself. Have faith in your abilities. Without a humble but reasonable confidence in your own powers, you cannot be successful or happy. A sense of inadequacy interferes with the attainment of your hopes, but self-confidence leads to self-realization and achievement. An appalling number of people are made miserable by an inferiority complex, but you need not suffer from this trouble. You can develop faith in yourself. To build up feeling of self-confidence, practice suggesting confidence concepts to your mind. It is possible, even in the midst of your daily work, to drive confident thoughts into consciousness.

Apparently lack of self-confidence is one of the great problems besetting people today. In a university a survey was made of six hundred students in psychology courses and the students were asked to state their most difficult personal problem. Seventy-five percent listed lack of confidence. Perhaps the same large proportion is true of the population in general. Everywhere you encounter people who are inwardly afraid, who shrink from life, who suffer from a deep sense of inadequacy and insecurity, and who doubt their own powers. Deep within themselves they mistrust their ability to meet responsibilities or to grasp opportunities. They do not believe that they have it in them to be what they want to be and so they try to make themselves content with something less than that of which they are capable. Thousands upon thousands go crawling through life on their hands and knees, defeated and afraid.

When I get up in the morning, I have two choices, to be happy or unhappy. I just choose to be happy. People are just about as happy as they make up their minds to be. You can be unhappy if you want to be. It is the easiest thing in the world to accomplish. Just choose unhappiness. Go around telling yourself that things aren't going well, that nothing is satisfactory and you can be quite sure of being unhappy. But say to yourself, things are going nicely. Life is good. I choose happiness and you can be quite certain of having your choice. To become a happy person, have a clean soul, eyes that see romance in the commonplace, a child's heart and spiritual simplicity. Believe in something biggest then yourself.

Many leaders commit the error of separating leadership from relationships. This happens when people step into leadership positions and assume that everyone will follow them because of their position. Some leaders wrongly believe that their knowledge alone qualifies them to lead others. People don't care how much you know until they know how much you care. We cannot separate leadership from relationships.

Leaders help themselves by developing good relational skills. If you don't have time to do it right, when will you have time to do it over?

People don't follow others by accident. They follow individuals whose leadership they respect. When people get together for the first time as a group, take a look at what happens. As they start interacting, the leaders in the group immediately take charge. They think in terms of the direction they desire to go and who they want to take with them. At first, people may make tentative moves in several different directions, but after the people get to know one another, it doesn't take long for them to recognize the strongest leaders and to follow them. In time, people in the group get on board and follow the strongest leaders. Either that or they leave the group and pursue their own agendas. Something to remember, once respect is lost, it's almost impossible to earn respect back. Once it's gone, it's gone forever.

The place to start empowering people is by evaluating them. With inexperienced people, if you give them too much authority too soon, you can be setting them up to fail. With people who have lots of experience, if you move too slowly you can frustrate and demoralize them. Sometimes when leaders misjudge the capabilities of others the results can be comical. As we now know, Albert Einstein had one of the greatest minds of all time. For example, Albert Einstein applied for admittance to the Munich Technical Institute and was rejected because he would never amount to much. As a result, instead of going to school, he worked as an inspector at the Swiss Patent Office and with his extra time he refined his theory of relativity. Remember that everyone has the potential to succeed. Your job as a leader is to see the potential, find out what he lacks, and equip him with what he needs.

Wisdom can be a leader's best friend, especially in times of decision. Suppose you find yourself in a meeting in which a crucial decision must be made. The people in the room reaches an impasse and everything stops. Who will become the most influential person in that room? The answer is the one with the wisdom to draw a conclusion that not only works, but which receives the blessing of everyone in the room.

As a leader, you are responsible for understanding and directly transmitting values to your people. Ethical responsibilities such as beliefs, values, norms and character are keys to an ethical decision making process. Whether you like it or not, you are on display at all times. Your actions say much more than your words. Subordinates will watch you carefully and imitate your behavior. You must accept the obligation to be a worthy role model and you cannot ignore the effect your behavior has on others. You must be willing to do what you require of your people and share the dangers and hardships. No matter what, work hard to always do the right thing.

We have explored the environment, spread across the face of the globe, developed concepts and ideas. We have built settlements, machines, languages and societies. We have emptied our waste in, on and around this big blue planet of ours that we call home. We have added strange new man-made chemicals to this planet. No one knows exactly how great the ultimate consequences of these changes may be. Actions undertaken in the sudden glare of a crisis will not provide a long-term solution to problems that have been slowly building for many decades. Just as a crash diet cannot correct an overweight problem of many years standing. What is needed is a change in daily habits. A commitment to the health of our planet in the face of increasing population pressure and rising expectations of all humanity must be our focus point. Will our society provide the leadership that is needed to keep our planet alive, so the human race will live to see another day?

Do you live a good or evil life? Do you believe in God? Must you have God in your life to live a good life? What really happens when our life comes to an end? Do you believe in the Holy Bible? Have you read both the Old and New Testaments? If not, should you if you believe in God? Or is God all based upon faith or a frame of mind? If you believe in God, then you must believe in the other – the Devil, Satan, the major spirit of evil and ruler of Hell. But what if there is no God or Devil, only this lifetime. How would you live your life?

There was a time when all of my friends were graduating from high school. I left the high school lifestyle by entering the United States Military and made it a career. My generation is slowly but relentlessly moving through the decades after our life's dream. It occurs to me that a time will soon come when my high school friends will be dying. Why should we work ourselves into an early grave, missing those precious moments with loves ones who crave our affection and attention? Once you get out from under the constant pressures of making a living, you will wonder why you drove yourself so hard for all those years.

Therefore, what do you really want from life? You don't want to ask yourself how did I get to where I am which is so far from where I am supposed to be? The destiny of your future is in your hands, that's why one person can make a difference. Are you making the best choices for you as a person and the people that you truly care about?

Spend a lot of time on your research. Who am I? What am I living for? Your objective must be very clear. Don't just dream about what you would like to be, become intimate with it. Get to really know it and you'll be well prepared when you start making your game plan. You'll have all the information you need to determine what you'll have to get done and how long it may take. Hopefully, your research efforts will help you to get on with making your dream come true.

I want to drive this point home again. Being very careful and honest with yourself, do you have the brains, the aptitude and the talent to make your dream come true? You either do or you don't. The point here is simple. Make sure that you really have the right stuff to make your dream come true. Assuming you have the brains, aptitude and talent, you can obtain everything else. Education, training and practice are keys. It's now only a matter of determining what you need and how long it will take to get it. This will comprise the formulation of your game plan. It may take many years, a sacrifice of time from pleasurable activities for a while, a surrender of present finances and lifestyle. Your dream will not come easily. You must be prepared to go after it with all you've got. Don't look for or depend upon luck. Remember that luck requires you to be well prepared when opportunity knocks.

Try to clear your mind of all your daily problems, such as earning a living, paying the mortgage or figuring out what you're going to eat next. Try to get a clear picture in your mind. Not the day-to-day stuff, but who you really are and how you got to where you are today. Reflect on all that is good and bad in your life. It's important that you get a firm grip on reality and how you got to this point in life. Age and experience tend to change a person's outlook on life. Are you just going through a mid-life crisis? Don't make a major change in your life just for the sake of change. Your dream should be something you really want, not just an escape from the present.

Your strategy is the logic through which you hope to achieve your dream. Try not to compare yourself to other people and their progress in life. You are unique. Try to build a healthy attitude, confident of what you want to do with your life. As you start building your personal game plan, try to start on a self-improvement program of proper diet, rest and exercise. Concentrate on eliminating or reducing bad habit at this time. Dedication, concentration and positive thinking will help you make a plan that will work for you and lead to a happier and fuller life. Look at your choices that you are making. Focus on the dream. Be persistent, diligent and committed. Remember that this program is designed for a lifetime. Make a new plan for next year starting from the beginning. Even if your dream goal, supporting goals and other goals are the same, it's beneficial to rewrite your plan each year to help you keep a sharp focus on your progress.

Make a habit of keeping a copy of your action plan with you at all times. Review your goals daily, review your performance and see if your behavior matches your goals. Those who have made their dreams come true will tell you that it took time, effort and most importantly, a strong determination to stay with it. Don't give up, you may slow down from time to time, but don't give up. The people who are unwilling to invest time and effort into achieving their dreams probably won't succeed in obtaining their dreams.

A major newspaper reported that the average life span of a man after full retirement is only two years. Over 95% of people die broke after working over 40 years of their lives. Don't work hard for a living, work smart for a lifestyle. Merely making large amounts of money is not the answer if you are looking for any real security. Ask a high paid professional of this world that is about to drop dead from exhaustion. No matter how much you make, you have to keep working all the time to make more money and buy more things that you really don't need or the money stops coming in.

Remember, life is too short to be saddled with doing something you don't like. A lot of people never decide what they want to do. They may want something easier, and nothing is easy, but if they know what they want to do, they should do a little advance planning. I can't think of anything worse than being miserable at what you're doing, but I also say, stay at something long enough to find out enough about it to know whether you really like it or not. You've got to have patience. I think I'll stay in the workforce for many years to come. I just enjoy working with people, helping people and it's fun for me, but you must work at the things that you enjoy. Once the fun stops, it's time to look for something else in life to do.

You need support, encouragement, but more than anything else, you need the determination to do it, to leave security behind at times and take a chance. You'll never know, unless you try. Just go for it. If you've got a dream, make a plan to make it happen. COL Sanders of Kentucky Fried Chicken (KFC) never retired. At age 75 (in 1965) he was just getting started with KFC. This is a great example that we are in our most productive years, now, today, right now. Don't think that you are too old to start something new. Take on your dream. What do you really want to do in life? Don't wait, get started today.

People must realize that they are in their most productive years and that it's all going to end someday. It's much better to spend those years doing the things that makes you happy. Some people flourish in an environment where everything is provided for them and they are told what to do. If this is you, and you are happy, that's great, that's what you should do in life. You have to be self-driven and self-motivated to obtain your dream. If you want to be successful, you have to discipline yourself. If you love what you're doing, it's not really considered work. Take a chance on your dream. What's the worst possible thing that could happen if you fail? It's alright to slow down from hurting and bleeding for a little while, but you must get back up to face another day. You just go back and start again. If you're willing to work hard and believe in yourself, you'll be successful and obtain your dream.

— 2 —

Leadership Styles

What is leadership? Leadership is the process of influencing others to accomplish the mission by providing purpose, direction, and motivation. What do we mean by providing purpose, direction, and motivation? Let's take a look at each term, but before we do that, I was required to write my Leadership Philosophy as I attended the United States Army Sergeant Major Academy. This is what I wrote and I still believe it today:

As your Sergeant Major, you have the right to know what my priorities and expectations are. My intent is that we have this understanding early and use it as a point of focus. Feel free to question me about this at any time. The Army is a "PEOPLE BUSINESS". We all have the right to excellent, dedicated leaders who treat their personnel with dignity and respect. Insist on high goals and standards for your unit. Develop and maintain effective management systems, which maximize the efforts of all members of your organization. Effective Army leaders lead from the front, set the example both morally and professionally. I understand that while mission is always first, our personnel will accomplish it. If we do not take care of our personnel, we will not be able to accomplish our many and varied missions. The four major factors of leadership are always present and affect the actions you should take and when you should take them. They are the led, the leader, the situation and communications. True leaders will lead people and manage things. Work hard, but work smart. Work with synergy, it means that the whole is greater than the sum of its parts. One plus one equals three or more. I will expect you to conduct yourself as a highly trained, SELF-

DISCIPLINED and COMPLETELY COMPETENT WINNER. You can, and should, expect the same out of me.

Influencing Others

Purpose gives people a reason why they should do difficult things under sometimes dangerous and stressful circumstances. You must establish priorities, explain the importance of missions, and focus people on the tasks so that they will function in an efficient and disciplined manner.

Direction gives people an orientation of tasks to be accomplished based on the priorities set by you the leader. The standards you establish and enforce will give your people order; real training will give them confidence in themselves, their leaders and each other.

Motivation gives people the will to do everything they are capable of doing to accomplish a mission, it causes people to use their initiative when they see the need for action. Motivate your people by caring for them, challenging them with interesting tasks, developing them into a cohesive team, rewarding successes and giving them all the responsibility they can handle. Effective leaders use both direct and indirect influence to lead. You will probably influence your people mainly in a direct manner, but others above you may use more indirect methods.

As a military leader, I developed some basic rules to follow during my years of military service. My leaders and Soldiers had a copy of these rules posted in their offices. It only covers one page and I focused on two words **"BE PROFESSIONAL"**. My basic rules are as follows:

B – Be honest, always do the right thing.

E – Effective Management Systems, do things right the first time.

P – People business, take care of your people and they will meet mission.

R – Read daily for self-improvement.

O – Open mind; observe all the way around you, 360 degrees.

F – Focus on dignity and respect to all.

E – Encouragement to all, even your bad personnel.

S – Support the Boss and Chain-of-Command.

S – Set the example and be the example.

I – If you want it done, check it.

O – Obligations, meet them all.

N – Never quit, you may slow down, but never quit.
A – Always train to win.
L – Loyalty to country, family, organization and personnel.

The above rules are very simple, but very hard to follow through on day after day. As a leader in our society we must do many things. We are always being watched, both in our goods times and bad. We have a choice to do the right thing or wrong thing. The real question is, will we do what is right or make the choice to do something else?

Assessment

Development leadership assessment is a process used to improve a person's ability to lead. It involves comparing performance to a standard or performance indicator, giving feedback and developing a plan to improve leadership performance. It is an essential element of your leader development responsibilities. Just as you need your leader's coaching, your subordinates need your help to improve their leadership performance. You have two leadership assessment responsibilities. Assess your own leadership performance; identify your strengths and weaknesses, and work to improve yourself. Assess your subordinate's leadership performance, give them feedback and help them overcome their weaknesses.

The goal of leadership assessment is to develop competent and confident leaders. Leadership assessment should be a positive, useful experience that does not confuse, intimidate or negatively impact on leaders. It should be decided what leadership skill, knowledge or attitude you want to assess. Make a plan to observe the leadership performance. Observe the leadership performance and record your observations. Compare the leadership performance you observed to a standard of performance indicator. Decide if the leadership performance you observed is exceeded, or is met, or is below the standard or performance indicator and give the person feedback. Help the person develop an action plan to improve leadership performance.

Normally, leadership assessment will not lead to improved performance unless it includes an action plan designed to change undesirable performance and reinforce desirable performance. The leader and the subordinate must design the action plan together. Agree on the actions necessary to improve leadership performance. Review the action plan frequently to see if the subordinate is making progress and to determine if the plan needs to be changed.

Naturally, when assessing your own leadership performance you have to modify the steps. First, examine your performance in a particular situation. Then, compare your performance to a leadership standard or performance indicator. Finally, decide how you can improve your leadership performance. You may want to discuss your self-assessment with your leaders, peers, subordinates and others. A complete and accurate leadership assessment includes feedback from six sources; the person himself or herself, leaders, peers, subordinates, close friends and family members, and trained leadership assessors.

It will not always be possible to get feedback from all of these sources, but each of them can give valuable information about a person's leadership performance. If you can get feedback from all six sources, you will have a complete picture of the person's leadership performance.

Factors of Leadership

When assuming a leadership position, you should consider the four factors of leadership that is a large part of the military (the led, the leader, the situation and communications). Direct your initial efforts to determine what is expected of your organization. Determine who your immediate leader is and what is expected of you. Determine the level of competence and the strengths and weaknesses of your subordinates. Identify the key people outside of your organization whose support you will need to accomplish the mission. The four major factors of leadership are always present and affect the actions we should take and when we should take them. They are the led, the leader, the situation, and communications.

The first major factor of leadership are the people you are responsible for leading. All people should not be led in the same way. A person with a new job or task normally needs closer supervision than a person who is experienced at that same job or task. A person with low confidence needs your support and encouragement. A person who works hard and does what you know must be done deserves your praise. A person who intentionally fails to follow your guidance may need to be reprimanded.

You must correctly assess your subordinate's competence, motivation and commitment so that you can take the proper leadership actions at the correct time. You must create a climate that encourages your subordinates to actively participate and want to help you accomplish the mission. Key ingredients to develop this relationship are mutual trust, respect and confidence.

The second major leadership factor is the leader. We must have an honest understanding of ourselves, what we know and what we can do. You must know your strengths, weaknesses, capabilities and limitations so you can control and discipline yourself, and lead your people effectively. You must continuously ensure that each person is treated with dignity and respect. Assessing others may be easier than looking honestly at ones self. If you have difficulty assessing yourself, ask your leader what he would like to see you change about the way you lead your people or in how you support him. Do not put him on the spot. Give him time to think of specific suggestions and then meet with him to talk about them. You can also seek the counsel of your peers or ask an experienced subordinate how well he thinks you issue orders or provide needed information. Consider all these points of view and then work on improving yourself.

The situation is the third major leadership factor. All situations are different, leadership actions that work in one situation may not work in another. We learn to manage and lead by exception based upon the given situation. To determine the best leadership action to take, first consider the available resources and all factors. Then consider the subordinate's level of competence, motivation and commitment to perform the task or mission. In one situation you may have to closely supervise and direct a subordinate's work. Another situation may require you to encourage and listen to ideas. In still another, you may need to both direct and encourage a person to ensure he can accomplish a task. The situation also includes the timing of actions. Confronting a subordinate may be the correct decision, but if the confrontation occurs too soon or too late, the results may not be what you want. You must be skilled in identifying and thinking through the situation so you can take the right action at the right time. What if you take the wrong action? It happens, we all make mistakes. Analyze the situation again, take quick corrective action and move on. Learn from your mistakes and those of others.

Communication, the fourth major leadership factor, is the exchange of information and ideas from one person to another. Effective communication occurs when others understand exactly what you are trying to tell them and when you understand precisely what they are trying to tell you. You may communicate what you want orally, in writing, through physical actions, or through a combination of all of these. You must recognize that you communicate standards by your example and by what behaviors you ignore, reward, and punish. The way you communicate in different situations is important. Your choice of words, tone of voice and physical actions all combine to affect people. Leadership is more than setting the example and bravely leading the charge. The ability to say the correct thing, at the appropriate moment and in the right way, is also an important part of leadership. Effective communication implies that your people understand you. Since people listen to leaders who listen to them, you must work hard at understanding exactly what your people are saying to you. Good listening is hard work but you can learn. Do not interrupt when others are speaking. Look at the person speaking; listen to what is said and also to how it is said since emotions are an important part of communication. If you listen to your subordinates, they will listen to you.

The four major leadership factors are always present in every situation, yet they affect each other differently. The most important factor in one situation may have little importance in another. You must constantly consider all four factors of leadership and choose the best course of action. Mistakes happen when leaders fail to consider all four leadership factors and see how they affect each other and mission accomplishment. Self-assessment, study and experience will improve your understanding of the four major factors of leadership. Leadership style is the personal manner and approach of leading by providing purpose, direction and motivation. It is the way leaders directly interact with their subordinates.

Leadership Style

Effective leaders are flexible in the way they interact with subordinates. They deal with subordinates differently, changing the way they interact as a subordinate develops or as the situation or mission changes. Your manner and approach of leading will obviously depend on your training, education, experience and view of the world. You have to be yourself, yet flexible enough to adjust to the people you lead and to the missions you are assigned.

Some say they admire a certain leader because he always seems to know exactly what to do in a particular situation. Or they admire a leader who knows just the right words to say at the right time to ensure the mission is accomplished and people are cared for. Experience has taught you that you should not deal with all people the same. You know it is not effective to deal with a new person the same as you would deal with an experienced person. For years, when people talked about leadership styles, they thought about two extremes, an autocratic style and a democratic style. Autocratic leaders used their legitimate authority and the power of their position to get results while democratic leaders used their personality to persuade and involved subordinates in solving problems and making decisions. Thinking like this fails to consider the possibility of a leader using different styles and flexible enough to be autocratic at times and democratic at other times or to combine the two extreme styles at still other times. Leadership is about action, not position. Let's look at three basic styles of leadership; directing, participating, and delegating.

A leader is using the directing leadership style when he tells subordinates what he wants done, how he wants it done, where he wants it done and when he wants it done and then supervises closely to ensure they follow his directions. This style is clearly appropriate in many situations. When time is short and you alone know what needs to be done and how to do it, this style is the best way to accomplish the mission. When leading subordinates who lack experience or competence at a task, you need to direct their behavior using this style. They will not resent your close supervision. You will be giving them what they need and want. In fact, asking inexperienced subordinates to help you solve complex problems or plan an operation would be frustrating for them. Some people think that a leader is using the directing style when he yells, uses demeaning language or threatens and intimidates subordinates. This is not the directing style. It is simply an abusive, unprofessional way to treat subordinates.

A leader is using the participating style when he involves subordinates in determining what to do and how to do it. The leader asks for information and recommendations, however, he still makes the decisions. He simply gets advice from subordinates before making the decision. This style is appropriate for many leadership situations. If your subordinates have some competence and support your goals, allowing them to participate can be a powerful team building process. It will build their confidence and increase their support for the final plan if they help develop it. If a leader asks subordinates to recommend a course of action, he is using the participating style of leadership. He still makes the decision but considers information and recommendations from his subordinates first. Do not be concerned that asking a subordinate for advice or using a subordinate's good plan or idea shows weakness. The opposite is true; it is a sign of strength that your subordinates will respect. On the other hand, you are responsible for the quality of your plans and decisions. If you believe an idea one of your subordinates offers in not a good one, you must reject the idea and do what you believe is right, regardless of pressure to do otherwise.

A leader is using the delegating style when he delegates problem solving and decision-making authority to a subordinate or to a group of subordinates. This style is appropriate when dealing with mature subordinates who support your goals and are competent and motivated to perform the task delegated. While you are always accountable to your leader for the results of any task you delegate, you must hold your subordinates accountable to you for their actions and performance. If a leader tasks an experienced and motivated subordinate to plan, organize and run with a course of action, he is using the delegating style of leadership. Some things are appropriate to delegate, others are not. The key is to release your subordinate's problem solving potential while you determine what problems they should solve and help them learn to solve them.

Choosing the correct style of leadership requires you to understand the four factors of leadership. You, the leader, must size up every situation and subordinate, the led, carefully to choose the right style. Consider how competent, motivated, and committed those you lead are at the task, the situation, you want performed. Have they done it before? Where they successful? Will they need your supervision, direction, or encouragement to accomplish the mission to standards? The answers to these questions will help you choose the best leadership style and manner to communicate so that your people will understand your intent and want to help you accomplish the mission.

As a leader you want to develop and train your subordinates so that you can confidently delegate tasks to them. The delegating style is the most efficient of the three leadership styles. It requires the least amount of your time and energy to interact, direct and communicate with your subordinates. Because it is the most efficient style, it is in your best interest to use the delegating style with as many of your subordinates and as much of the time as possible, but before you can use the delegating leadership style, you must train and develop your subordinates.

An inexperienced subordinate needs your direction. You must tell him what needs to be done and how to do it. After he gains some competence, and if he is motivated and shares your goals, you can reduce the amount of supervision you give to him. Encourage him, ask him for advice and allow him to participate in helping you make plans and decisions. With time, experience and your skillful leadership, this person will gain even more competence and become even more motivated and committed to helping you accomplish your missions. When you have trained and developed a subordinate to this level of competence and commitment, use the delegating style of leadership.

As missions change or as new tasks are assigned, you will need to continue to be flexible in the leadership style you use. Even though you have successfully used the delegating leadership style with a subordinate, you may need to temporarily return to the directing style of leadership if you give him an unfamiliar or a new task. Because the subordinate is unfamiliar with the task, you will need to tell him what to do and how to do it. As the subordinate gains competence, confidence and motivation in this new task, you can gradually shift your style again to the participating or delegating style. By assessing the leadership needs of your subordinates, you can determine what leadership style to use.

Do not confuse emotion or anger with styles of leadership. A leader frustrated with a poor program in his company might angrily say to his subordinate leader that this program is terrible. I do not have the answer, but you are going to develop a plan to fix it. Nobody is leaving this office until you all develop a plan and agree on it. He is using a delegating style because after he identifies the problem, he gives his subordinate leader complete freedom to develop the plan. There is not one best leadership style. What works in one situation may not work in another. You must develop the flexibility to use all three styles. Further, you must develop the judgment to choose the style that best meets the situation and the needs of the subordinate.

One of the most common mistakes a leader can make is to misjudge the level of their personnel. If the leader doesn't work with each person according to where he is in his development, the person won't produce, succeed and develop. According to management consultant Ken Blanchard, all team members fit into one of four categories with the type of leadership they need:

1- Personnel that need direction. These personnel don't really know what to do or how to do it. The leader needs to instruct them every step of the way.
2- Personnel who need coaching. These personnel who are able to do more of the job on their own will become more independent, but they still rely on you for direction and feedback.
3- Personnel who need support. These personnel are able to work without your direction still may require resources and encouragement.
4- Personnel to whom you delegate. At this stage, personnel can be given a task and you can be confident that it will be done. They only need you to lead. Provide them with vision on the front end and accountability on the back end. They will multiply your efforts toward success.

Attitudes

One thing I've found is that many times leaders take themselves much too seriously. I have meet people who have too much doom and gloom in their attitudes. They simply need to lighten up. No matter how serious your work is, there's no reason to take yourself seriously. If any person had a reason to take his job and himself seriously, it would be the President of the United States. Yet it's possible for even people holding that position to maintain their sense of humor and keep their egos in check. If you tend to take yourself too seriously, give yourself and everyone else around you a break. Recognize that laughter breeds resilience. Laughing is the quickest way to get up and get going again when you've been knocked down.

When things go wrong, the natural tendency is to look for someone to blame. You can go all the way back to the Garden of Eden on this one. When God asked Adam what he'd done, he said it was Eve's fault. Then when God questioned Eve, she blamed it on the snake. The same thing happens today. The next time you experience a failure, think about why you failed instead of who was at fault. Try to look at it objectively so that you can do better next time. People who blame others for their failures never overcome them. They simply move from problem to problem. To reach your potential, you must continually improve yourself. You can't do that if you don't take responsibility for your actions and learn from your mistakes.

Vision is everything for a leader. It is utterly indispensable. Why is this? It paints the targets, sparks a fire within and draws them forward. It is also the fire for others who follow those leaders. Show me a leader without vision and I'll show you someone who isn't going anywhere. At best, they're traveling in circles. One of the most valuable benefits of vision is that it acts like a magnet, attracting, challenging and uniting people. The greater the vision, the more winners it has the potential to attract. The more challenging the vision is, the harder participants fight to achieve it.

Educators in the United States have been seeking ways to increase students' test scores. One popular theory states that the best way to improve children's ability is to puff up their self esteem. Because high achievers tend to have high self esteem. However, researchers have found that simply building children's egos breeds many negative traits, indifference to excellence, inability to overcome adversity and aggressiveness toward people who criticize them. I place high value on praising people, especially children, but I also believe that you have to base your praise on truth. I use this method with everyone, including myself. No matter where I fail or how many mistakes I make, I don't let it devalue my worth as a person.

Being a winner is not in a gifted birth, in a high IQ or in talent. The winner's edge is in attitude, not aptitude. Unfortunately, many people resist that notion. They want to believe that talent alone is enough, but plenty of talented teams never amount to anything because of the attitudes of their players. Take a look at how various attitudes impact a team made up of highly talented players. If you want great results, you need good people with great talent and awesome attitudes. I have a sign posted on my door in my office at work. This is what you see as you enter into my office:

ABILITIES + ATTITUDES = RESULT
Great Talent + Rotten Attitudes = Bad Team
Great Talent + Bad Attitudes = Average Team
Great Talent + Average Attitudes = Good Team
Great Talent + Good Attitudes = Great Team

Committed to Helping

Every day parents and spouses leave their families in the pursuit of success. It's almost as though they're traveling down the road of life and then they realize they've left members of their families behind. The tragedy is that many value their careers, success or personal happiness more than they do their families. They decide that it's too much work to go back, so they just keep traveling down this road of life, but what many are now realizing is that the hope of happiness at the expense of breaking up a family is an illusion. You can not give up your marriage or neglect your children and gain true success. When you have a strong family life, you receive the message that you are loved, cared for and important.

Nothing speaks to others more loudly than generosity from a leader. True generosity isn't an occasional event. It comes from the heart, touching their time, money, talents and possessions. Effective leaders, the kind people want to follow, don't gather things just for themselves. They do it in order to give to others. The only way to maintain an attitude of generosity is to make it your habit to give your time, attention, money and resources.

Security provides the foundation for strong leadership. When we feel insecure, we drift from our mission whenever trouble arises. We must feel secure when people stop liking us, when funding drops, when morale dips, or when others reject us. If we don't feel secure, fear will eventually cause us to sabotage our leadership.

Not everyone you influence will think the same way you do. You have to help them not only believe that they can succeed, but also show them that you want them to succeed. Once people recognize and understand that you genuinely want to see them succeed and are committed to helping them, they will begin to believe they can accomplish what you give them to do.

As the leader of a team or an organization, you set the tone for communication. A leader's communication must be consistent, clear, and courteous, but leaders must also be good listeners. Ultimately, poor listening leads to hostility, miscommunication and a breakdown of team cohesion. How are your listening skills? Give yourself a 360 degree review. Ask for feedback concerning your ability and willingness to listen from your boss or mentor, your colleagues and your subordinates. If you don't get good grades from all of them, then quiet down, listen up and work to become a better communicator.

A great lesson I've learned over the years is that the people closest to me determines my level of success or failure. I had identified potential leaders and developed them. My intention in developing leaders had been to help them improve themselves, but I found that I was also benefiting greatly. Spending time with them had been like investing. They had grown and at the same time I had reaped incredible dividends. That's when I realized that if I was to make it to the next level I was going to have to extend myself through others. I would find leaders and pour my life into them, and as they improved, so would I.

One of the mistakes people make is that they focus too much attention on their dream and too little on their team, but the truth is that if you build the right team, the dream will almost take care of itself. If you really want to achieve your dream, not just imagine what it would be like then grow your team, but as you do so, make sure your motives are right. Some people gather a team just to benefit themselves. Others do it because they enjoy the team experience and want to create a sense of community. Still others do it because they want to build an organization.

If you don't get what you want, it is a sign either that you did not seriously want it or that you tried to bargain over the price. How badly do you want to reach your potential and fulfill your purpose in life? There's a cost with everything in life. It will take passion on your part to keep growing, leaning and trading up. I've found that you have to make tradeoffs throughout life in order to succeed and only through wise exchanges can you reach your potential. The problem many unsuccessful people have is that they haven't worked to develop much in their lives that are worth trading. You can only make a trade when you've got something of worth that someone else wants.

One of the most common obstacles to success is the desire to cut corners, but short cuts never pay off in the long run. If you find yourself continually giving into your moods or impulses, then you need to change your approach to doing things. Cutting corners is really a sign of impatience and poor self discipline, but if you are willing to follow through, you can achieve almost anything. The best method is to set up standards for yourself that requires accountability. Any time you suffer a consequence for not following through; it helps you stay on track. Once you have your standards in place, work according to them, not your moods. That will get you going in the right direction. Self discipline is a quality that is won through practice.

Have you been wronged? If so, you're faced with a decision. Are you going to spend your time and energy on what should have been, or are you going to focus on what can be? Even when truth and justice are on your side, you may never be able to right your wrongs. Continually fighting for your rights will just make you resentful and angry. Those are all destructive emotions that tap our energy and make us negative. When people focus on their rights, they're often looking backwards rather than forward. When we stop worrying about our rights, it focuses us in the right direction and releases us to move forward on the journey that we call life. We recognize the wrongs, but we forgive them, and focus on what we can control. When we do that, it increases our energy and builds our potential.

Too many people simply fall into a comfortable niche in life and stay there rather than pursue goals of significance. Leaders can't afford to do that. Leaders must ask themselves whether they want survival, success or significance. The best leaders desire significance and expend their time and energy in pursuit of their dreams. The idea is that if you had anything you wanted; unlimited time, money, information, staff, what would you do? Your answer to that question is your dream. Acting on your dream adds significance to your life. Therefore, what are you waiting for?

Without a challenge, many people tend to fall or fade away. You must have a long range vision to keep you from being frustrated by short range failures. Vision helps people with motivation. That can be especially important for highly talented people. We should ask for more than we can accomplish. Only people who can see the invisible can do the impossible. That shows the value of vision, but it also indicates that vision can be an elusive quality. If you can see vision for your team, then your team has a reasonably chance at success. Vision gives team members direction and confidence, two things they can't do without.

Building Potential Leaders

If you desire to influence another person, the way to start is by nurturing them. At the heart of the nurturing process is genuine concern for others. As we try to help and influence the people around us, we must have positive feelings and concern for them. If you want to help people and make a positive impact on them, you can't dislike them. You must give them respect and always be kind. You may be wondering why you should take on a nurturing role with the people you want to influence, especially if they are employees, colleagues, or friends. You may be saying to yourself, isn't that something they can get at home and with their family? The unfortunate truth is that most people are desperate for encouragement. If you become a major nurturer in the life of another person, then you have an opportunity to make a major impact on them.

Just about anyone would agree that growing is a good thing, but relatively few people actually dedicate themselves to the process. Because growth requires change, and change is hard for most people, but the truth is that without change, growth is impossible. Most people fight against change, especially when it affects them personally. Everyone thinks of changing the world, but no one thinks of changing himself. The ironic thing is that change is inevitable. Everybody has to deal with it in their lives. On the other hand, growth is optional. Making the change from being an occasional learner to someone dedicated to personal growth is tough. It goes against the grain of the way most people live. Most people celebrate when they receive their high school or college degree and think that learning is over. I'm done with studying. That kind of thinking will only make you average, nothing more.

All the training in the world will provide only limited success if you don't turn your people loose to do the job. The way to do that is to give them responsibility, authority and accountability. For some people, responsibility is the easiest to give, but what is difficult for some leaders is allowing their people to keep the responsibility after it's been given. Poor managers want to control every detail of their people's work. When that happens, the potential leaders who work for them become frustrated and don't develop. Rather than desiring more responsibility, they become indifferent or avoid responsibility altogether. Once responsibility and authority have been given to people, they become empowered to make things happen, but we also have to be sure that they are making the right things happen. That's where accountability comes into the picture.

It's a fact that you will get knocked down in life, but the length of time you remain down is important. In life, you will have problems. Are you going to give up and stay down, wallowing in your defeat or are you going to get back on your feet as quickly as you can? When you fall, make the best of it and get back on your feet. Learn what you can from your mistake, and then get back in the game. Failure is the opportunity to begin again more intelligently.

Leaders in some organizations don't recognize the importance of creating a climate conducive to building potential leaders. To see the relationship between environment and growth, look at nature, look at the shark. The reason is that sharks adapt to their environment. If you catch a small shark and confine it, it will stay a size proportionate to the aquarium in which it lives. Sharks can be six inches long yet fully mature, but if you turn them loose in the ocean, they grow to their normal size. The same it true of potential leaders. Some are put into the organization when they are still small, and the confining environment ensures that they stay small and under developed. Only leaders can control the environment of their organization. They can be the change agents who create a climate conducive to growth.

Every good coach has a game plan. He's got one not only for each individual game, but a plan for the development of the whole team over the course of the current and upcoming seasons. Once the game plan has been drawn up, he then communicates it to his team on an almost continual basis. The process must begin with communicating the game plan. That is the key to productivity, but it must continue with the exchange of information. When there is interactive communication between the team leader and his people, it empowers them to succeed.

Many organizations today fail to tap into their potential. Because the only reward they give their employees is a paycheck. The relationship between employer and employee never develops beyond that point. Successful organizations take a different approach. In exchange for the work a person gives, he receives not only his paycheck, but he is also nurtured by the people he works for. Nurturing has the ability to transform people's lives. The acronym BEST is a reminder of what people need when they get started with an organization: **B**elieve in them; **E**ncourage them; **S**hare with them; and **T**rust them. Nurturing benefits everyone. Who wouldn't be more secure and motivated when their leader believes in them, encourages them, shares with them and trusts them (BEST)? People are more productive when they are nurtured. Even more important, nurturing creates a strong emotional and professional foundation within workers who have leadership potential. Later, using training and development, a leader can be built on the foundation.

Encourage Change and Growth

In this world of rapid change the leader must be out in front to encourage change and growth to show the way to bring it about. Managers usually are more skilled in the technical requirements of change, whereas leaders have a better understanding of the motivational demands that the followers need. In the beginning, the skills of a leader are essential. No change will ever occur if the psychological needs are unmet. Once change has begun, the skills of a manager are needed to maintain needed change. A good exercise when you face change is to make a list of the logical pros and cons that should result from the change and another list indicating the psychological impact. Just seeing this on a sheet of paper can be clarifying.

While every leader needs financial and human resources to reach his or her goals, commitment should always precede those resources.

When a leader demonstrates a commitment to the mission and goals of the organization, a whole stream of events begin to flow. The key is commitment. Once a leader definitely commits, all manner of unforeseen incidents, meetings, personnel, and material assistance begin to stream forth.

As you look for potential leaders, you need to realize that there are really two kinds of leaders; those who attract followers and those who attract other leaders. People who attract and team up only with followers will never be able to do anything beyond what they can personally touch or supervise. Look for leaders who attract other leaders. They will be able to multiply your success. In the long run, you can only lead people whose leadership ability is less than or equal to your own. To keep attracting better and better leaders, you will have to keep developing your own leadership ability.

Mind Set

Have you discovered the differences between problems and facts? Problems are things we can do something about. We can solve problems. Facts are things we can do nothing about; therefore we do well not to worry about them. We should apply energy only to those things we can change. When we do, we can feel peace and act with poise, because we no longer beat our heads against an unbreakable wall. Delegation is the most powerful tool leaders have. Delegation increases individual productivity according to the number of people to whom leaders can delegate. It increases the productivity of their department or organization. Leaders who can't or won't delegate create a bottleneck to productivity.

If a team is to reach its potential each player must be willing to subordinate his personal goals for the good of the team. Some sports teams seem to embrace this mind set. The attitude of subordination and teamwork into the fabric of everything they do. Notre Dame does not put names of the players on their jerseys. Lou Holtz said "at Norte Dame, we believed the interlocking Norte Dame was all the identification you needed". If your priority is the team rather than yourself, what else do you need? Winning teams have players who put the good of the team ahead of themselves. They want to play in their area of strength, but they're willing to do what it takes to take care of the team. They are willing to sacrifice their role for the greater goal of the team.

Every leader ought to build an inner circle that adds value to him or her and to the leadership of the organization. But choose well, for the members of this inner circle will make you or break you. You can tell a lot about which direction your life is heading by looking at the people with whom you've chosen to spend your time and share your ideas. So who belongs in the inner circle? You need people that are creative, loyal, wise, intelligent, people who share your vision and with influence and integrity. You don't need yes people; they will not increase your overall value. The short answer in adding people to your inner circle is your instincts, follow them.

When we give our people authority and responsibility, we must also give them the tools they need. Giving responsibility without resources is ridiculous, it is incredibly limiting. If we want our people to be creative and resourceful, we need to provide resources. Tools include much more than just equipment. Be willing to spend money on things like books, tapes, professional conferences, etc… Fresh ideas from outside an organization can stimulate growth. Be creative in providing tools. It will keep your people growing to do the job well.

Keep away from people who try to belittle your ambitions. Small people always do that, but the really great ones make you feel that you too can become great. How do most people feel when they're around you? Do they feel small and insignificant, or do they believe in themselves and have great hope about what they can become? The key to how you treat people lies in how you think about them. It's a matter of attitude. What you believe is revealed by how you act. Hope is perhaps the greatest gift you can give another person as the result of nurturing. Even if people fail to see their own significance, they still have a reason to keep trying and striving to reach their potential in the future.

People often associate commitment with their emotions. If they feel the right way, then they can follow through on their commitments, but true commitment doesn't work that way. It's not an emotion; it's a character quality that enables us to reach our goals. Human emotions go up and down all the time, but commitment has to be rock solid.

Team Sport

If you continually invest in your leadership development, the inevitable result is growth over time. Although it's true that some people are born with greater natural gifts than others, the ability to lead is really a collection of skills, nearly all of which can be learned and improved, but the process doesn't happen overnight. Leadership is very complicated. It has many factors; respect, experience, emotional strength, people skills, discipline, vision, momentum, timing, and the list goes on and on. As you can see, many factors that come into play in leadership are intangible. That's why leaders require so much seasoning to be effective. It is the capacity to develop and improve their skills that distinguishes leaders from their followers. Successful leaders are learners. The learning process is ongoing, a result of self discipline and perseverance. The goal each day must be to get a little better, to build on the previous day's process.

If you look at the roster of any successful team, you will see that the starters are always outnumbered by the other players on the team. In pro football, twenty two people start on offense and defense, but teams are allowed to have fifty three players on a team. You find similar situations in every field. In the entertainment industry, the actors are often known, but the hundreds of crew members it takes to make a movie are not. For any politician or corporate executive that you know about, hundreds of people are working quietly in the background to make their work possible. Nobody can neglect the majority of the team and hope to be successful.

All leaders make mistakes. They are a part of life. Successful leaders recognize their errors, learn from them, and then work to correct the faults. True leaders admit to their mistakes and accept the consequences, rather than trying to blame others. Most people don't want to reap the consequences of their actions. You can see this type of attitude everywhere. A leader who is willing to take responsibility for their actions and be honest with their people is someone they will admire, respect, and trust. That leader is also someone they can learn from.

To be an empowering leader, you must do more than believe in emerging leaders. You need to take steps to help them become the leaders they have the potential to be. You must invest in them if you want to empower them to become their best. Empowering people takes a personal investment. It requires energy and time, but it's worth the price. If you do it right, you will have the privilege of seeing someone move up to a higher level. When you empower others, you create power in your organization.

If your team members believe in the goals of the team and begin to develop genuine trust in one another, they will be in a position to demonstrate true teamwork. Notice that I mention the team members will be in a position to demonstrate true teamwork. That does not necessarily mean that they will do it. For there to be teamwork, several things must happen. First, team members must genuinely believe that the value of the team's success is greater than the value of their own individual interests. Second, personal sacrifice must be encouraged and then rewarded by the team leader and the other members of the team. As this happens, the people will identify themselves more and more with the team. They will recognize that individualism wins trophies, but teamwork wins super-bowls and wins the war on the battlefield.

Criticism

Leaders can bank on two truths. First, they will be criticized. Second, criticism always changes them. Unhappy people tend to attack the point person. How a leader deals with the circumstances of life tells you a lot about their character. Crisis doesn't necessarily make character, but it certainly does reveal it. Adversity is a crossroads which make a person choose one of two paths – character or compromise. Every time leaders choose character, they become stronger, even it that choice brings negative consequences. The development of character is at the heart of our development, not just as leaders, but as human beings. If you're not making mistakes, than you're not doing anything.

Most people who are dissatisfied and discouraged feel that way because they haven't grasped a vision for themselves. As a leader you can help others discover their dreams. You may already recognize much of the potential of the people you're leading, but you need to know more about them. To help them recognize the destination they will be striving for, you need to know what really matters to them. To know where people truly want to go, you've got to know what touches their hearts.

In the long run, people need to focus a lot of energy on what gives them joy. If you can help people discover their dreams and truly believe in them, you can help them become who they want to be.

Good team leaders never want yes men on their teams. They need direct and honest communication from their people. I have always encouraged people on my team to speak openly and directly with me. Our meetings are often brainstorming sessions where the best idea wins. Often, a team member's remarks or observations really helps the team. Sometimes we disagree. That's okay, because we've developed strong enough relationships that we can survive conflict. Getting everything out on the table and getting everyone involved always improves the team. The one thing I never want to hear from a teammate is, I could have told you that wouldn't work. If you know it beforehand, that's the time to say it. Besides directness, the other quality team members need to display when communicating with their leaders is respect. Leading a team isn't easy, it takes hard work, and it demands personal sacrifice. It requires making tough and sometimes unpopular decisions. We should respect the people who take on leadership roles and show them loyalty.

Character Traits

Leaders must live by higher standards than their followers. Be more concerned with your character than your reputation, because your character is what you really are, while your reputation is merely what others think of you. This insight is exactly opposite of most people's thoughts concerning leadership. In a world of perks and privileges that accompany the climb to success, little thought is given to the responsibilities of the upward journey. Leaders can give up anything except responsibility. Too many people are ready to assert their rights, but not to assume their responsibilities. Two emotions usually follow a great achievement; a sign of relief and celebration. The period after a success can become a dangerous time. Sometimes we feel tempted toward complacency, especially if we lack another goal. We can become satisfied and let down our guard.

What does it take to have the focus required to be a truly effective leader? The keys are priorities and concentration. Effective leaders who reach their potential spend more time focusing on what they do well, than on what they do wrong. If you want to get better, you have to keep changing and improving. That means stepping out into new areas. If you dedicate time to new things related to your strength areas, then you'll grow as a leader. Nobody can entirely avoid working in areas of weakness. The key is to minimize it as much as possible; leaders can do it by delegating.

In a culture that praises individual gold medals and where a person fights for rights instead of focusing on responsibility, people tend to lose sight of the big picture. In fact, some people seem to believe that they are the entire picture. Everything revolves around their needs, goals, and desires. A team isn't supposed to be a bunch of people being used as a tool by one individual for their own selfish gain. Members of a team must have mutually beneficial shared goals. They must be motivated to work together, not manipulated by someone for individual glory. Anyone who is accustomed to pulling together people and using them to benefit only himself isn't a team builder, he's a dictator.

Most people think of charisma as something mystical. They think it's a quality that comes at birth or not at all, but charisma is the ability to draw people to you. Like other character traits, it can be developed. How do you rate when it comes to charisma? Are other people naturally attracted to you? Nobody wants to follow a leader who thinks he is better than everyone else. If you are uncomfortable, others will be too. If people never know what to expect from you, they stop expecting anything. People respect the desire for excellence, but dread unrealistic expectations. People don't want to be rained on by someone who sees a cloud around every silver lining.

Many people discover their dream in a flash of insight after working in an area for years. Some are motivated by an event from their past. People full of themselves usually don't have much room left over for a life changing dream. Discontent is the driving force that makes people search for their dreams. Complacency never brings success. Don't accept what is without considering what could be. When it comes to dreams, truly successful people have enough creativity to think it out and enough character to try it out.

Leaders who navigate do more than control the direction in which they and their people travel. They see the whole trip in their minds before they leave the dock. They have a vision for their destination, they understand what it will take to get there, they know who they'll need on the team to be successful and they recognize the obstacles long before they appear on the horizon. Good navigators always have in mind that other people are depending on them and their ability to chart a good course and the secret to successful navigation is preparation. When you prepare well, you convey confidence and trust to people. Leaders who are good navigators are capable of taking their people just about anywhere.

Team members always love and admire a person who is able to help them go to another level, someone who enlarges them and empowers them to be successful. Players who enlarge their teammates have several things in common. People's performances usually reflect the expectations of those they respect. Players who enlarge others understand their teammate values. That kind of knowledge, along with a desire to relate to their fellow players, creates a strong connection between teammates. An enlarger looks for gifts and talents in other people, and then helps them to increase those abilities for their benefit and for that of the entire team. You cannot give what you do not have. If you want to increase the ability of a teammate, make yourself better.

How many leaders have ruined their lives, their families and damaged the lives of others through immorality? Character has become a crucial issue today precisely because of leaders in political, business, military and religious worlds have failed morally. Leaders need to remember that they influence many others beyond themselves. They also need to realize that replacing fallen leaders is a slow and difficult process. So how can we guard against failing? We must take care not to emphasize the gifts of a leader over his or her character. We have an unhealthy tendency to see and reward the gift more than the character, but both must be developed.

Share Common Experiences

People who build successful teams never forget that every person's role is contributing to the bigger picture. A good example of this involves Winston Churchill. During World War II when Britain was experiencing its darkest days, the country had a difficult time keeping men working in the coal mines. Many wanted to give up their dirty, thankless jobs in the dangerous mines to join the military service, which got much public praise and support. Yet without coal, the military and the people at home would be in trouble. Therefore, Churchill faced thousands of coal miners one day and passionately told them of their importance on the war effort, how their role could make or break the goal of maintaining England's freedom. It's said that tears appeared in the eyes of those hardened men. They returned to the mines to meet their duty. That's the kind of mindset it takes to build a team.

People always project on the outside how they feel on the inside. Have you ever interacted with someone for the first time and suspected that their attitude was poor, yet you were unable to put your finger on exactly what was wrong? Most bad attitudes are the result of selfishness. If one of your teammates puts others down, sabotages teamwork, or makes themselves out to be more important than the team, then you can be sure that you've encountered someone with a bad attitude.

Influence is a curious thing. Even though we make some kind of impact on nearly everyone around us, we need to recognize that our level of influence is not the same with everyone. To see this principle in action, try ordering around your friend's dog the next time you visit. You may not have thought much about it, but you probably know instinctively which people you have great influence with and which ones you don't. One person may think all your ideas are great. Another may view everything you say with a great deal of skepticism. Yet that same skeptical person may agree with every single idea presented by your boss or one of your colleagues. That just shows your influence with him may not be as strong as that of someone else.

Success is within the reach of just about everyone, but personal success without leadership ability brings only limited effectiveness. Success is never final and failure is never fatal, it's courage that counts. A person's impact is only a fraction of what it could be with good leadership. The higher you want to climb, the more you need leadership. The greater the impact you want to make, the greater your influence needs to be. Whatever you'll accomplish is restricted by your ability to lead others. Leadership ability is the lid that determines a person's level of effectiveness. Lower a person's ability to lead, lower the lid on his potential; higher the leadership, greater the effectiveness. Your leadership ability, for better or for worse, always determines your effectiveness and the potential impact of your organization. To reach the highest level of effectiveness, you have to raise the lid on your leadership ability. The good news is that you can, if you're willing to pay the price to make a change.

Have you ever been part of a team that didn't seem to make any progress? Maybe the group had plenty of talent, resources, and opportunities, and team members got along, but the group just never went anywhere. There's a strong possibility that the situation was caused by lack of vision. Great vision precedes great achievements. Every team needs a compelling vision to give it direction. Leaders do not have to be the greatest visionaries themselves. The vision may come from anyone. However, leaders do have to state the vision. Leaders also have to keep the vision before the people and remind them of the progress that is being made to achieve the vision. Otherwise, the people might assume that they are failing and give up. If you lead your team, then you are responsible for identifying a worthy and compelling vision and articulating it to your team members.

Even if some members of a team don't share common experiences or have a personal relationship with each other, they can still posses a cohesiveness that defies the size of the team. What it takes is a common vision and shared values. If everyone embraces the same values, team members can still have a connection to each other and to the larger team. If you are the leader of your team, and if you don't work to help them embrace the values you know to be important, then team members will create an identity of their choosing.

The number of people today who lack a strong sense of purpose is astounding. There is aimlessness in most people's lives. People don't pay any attention to where they are going. They are undecided and will go in any direction. Goals give you something concrete to focus on and that has a positive impact on your actions. Goals help us focus our attention on our purpose and make it our dominant aspiration. The world makes way for the person who knows where they are going.

Leadership that People Respects

Effective leaders are always on the lookout for good people, but who you get is not determined by what you want, but by who you are. In most situations, you draw people who posses the same qualities you do. Every leader has a measure of magnetism. A leader's magnetism may impact others intellectually and emotionally. Magnetism is neither good nor bad in itself; it depends on what a leader does with it. Secure leaders draw both similar and complementary followers. A leader's magnetism never remains static. It is possible for a leader to go out and recruit people unlike himself, but it's crucial to recognize that people who are different will not naturally be attracted to him. Their quality depends on yours. If you think the people you attract could be better, then it's time for you to improve yourself.

Great leaders always have self-discipline. As General Dwight D. Eisenhower stated; there are no victories at bargain prices. When it comes to self-discipline, people choose one of two things. Either they choose the pain of discipline, which comes from sacrifice and growth, or they choose the pain of regret, which comes from taking the easy road and missing opportunities. Each person in life chooses. We must look for two areas of self-discipline in potential leaders. The first is in the area of the emotions. Effective leaders recognize that their emotional reactions are their responsibility. The second area concerns time. Every person on the planet is given the same allotment of minutes in a day, but each person's level of self-discipline dictates how effectively those minutes are used. Disciplined people maximize the use of their time.

As much as we admire solo achievement, the truth is that no lone individual has done anything of value. Daniel Boone had companions as he blazed the Wilderness Road. Wyatt Earp had his brothers and Doc Holiday looking out for him. Even Albert Einstein didn't work in a vacuum. The history of America is marked by the accomplishments of many strong leaders and innovative individuals who took great risks, but those people always were part of a team. A Chinese proverb states that behind an able man there are always other able men. The truth is that teamwork is at the heart of great achievement. One is too small a number to achieve greatness. You can't do anything of real value alone.

A leader's history of successes and failures makes a big difference in their credibility. It's a little like earning and spending pocket change. Each time you make a good leadership decision, it puts change into your pocket. Each time you make a poor one, you have to give some of your change to the people. All leaders have a certain amount of change in their pockets when they start in new positions. From then on, they either build up their change or pay it out. It doesn't matter whether the poor decisions were big or small, when you're out of change, you're out as a leader. Leaders who keep making good decisions and recording wins build up change.

Many people are able to recognize an opportunity after it's already passed them by. That's a pretty easy thing to do in life, but seeing opportunities coming, that's a different matter. Opportunities are seldom labeled, that's why you have to learn what they look like and how to seize them. The best people to take with you on the leadership journey don't simply sit back and wait for opportunities to come to them. They make it their responsibility to go out and find them. Good potential leaders don't rely on luck. The reason so many people never get anywhere in life is because when opportunity knocks, they are looking for luck to come their way and not prepared. Of the people around you, who always seems able to recognize opportunities and does something about it? The people with those qualities are the ones you're probably going to want to take with you on this journey.

People follow men and women whose leadership they respect. The lesser skilled will follow the more highly skilled. In general, followers seek those who are better leaders than themselves. The more leadership ability someone has, the more quickly they recognize leadership, or its lack in others. When groups of people get together for the first time, take a look at what happens. Leaders in the group immediately take charge. They think about the direction they desire to go and whom they want to take with them. At first, individuals may make tentative moves in several directions, but after they get to know one another, it doesn't take long for them to recognize the strongest leaders and to follow them.

Have a Giving Spirit

A true leader is someone who can give correction without causing resentment. If I had to name a single all purpose instrument of leadership, it would be communication. If you can't communicate, you will not lead others effectively. If you lead your team, give yourself three standards to live by as you communicate to your people; be consistent, clear, and courteous. Nothing frustrates team members more than leaders who can't make up their minds. Your team can't execute if they don't know what you want. Don't try to dazzle anyone with your intelligence, impress them with your simple straight forwardness. Everyone deserves to be shown respect, no matter what their position or what kind of history you might have with them. If you are courteous to your people, you set a tone for the entire organization. Never forget that as the leader, your communication sets the tone for the interaction among your people.

Nothing has such a positive impact on a person as giving to others. People who have a giving spirit are some of the most positive people. That's because giving is the highest level of living. They focus their time and energy on what they can give to others rather than what they can get from them. The more a person gives, the better his attitude. Most unsuccessful people don't understand this concept. They believe that how much people give and their attitude about it are based on how much they have, but that's not true. In life, it's not what you have that makes a difference, but what you do with what you have. That's based completely on attitude.

With good leadership, everything improves. Leaders are lifters. They push the thinking of their teammates beyond old boundaries of creativity. They elevate others' performance, making them better than they've ever been before. They improve people's confidence in themselves and others. While managers are often able to maintain a team at its current level, leaders are able to lift it to a higher level than it has ever reached before. The key is working with people and bringing out the best in them.

The ability to empower others is one of the keys to personal and professional success. No matter how much work you can do, not matter how engaging your personality may be, you will not advance far in business if you can't work through others. When you empower, you certainly work with and through people, but you also do much more. Empowering is giving your influence to others for the purpose of personal and organizational growth. It's seeing others' potential, sharing yourself, your influence, position, power and opportunities, with others with the purpose of investing in the lives of others so that they can function at their best. The act of empowering others changes lives, and one of the greatest things about it is that it's a win-win for you and the people you empower. If you empower others by giving them your authority, it has the same effect as sharing information. You haven't lost anything. You've increased the ability of others without decreasing yourself.

Intangible Factors

Leadership intuition is often the factor that separates the greatest leaders from the merely good ones. Some people are born with great leadership intuition. Others have to work hard to develop and hone it. It's a combination of natural ability and learned skills. The best way to describe this informed intuition is an ability to understand them and work them to accomplish leadership goals. Successful leaders see every situation in terms of available resources, money and people. They can sense people's hopes, fears and concerns. They can step back from the moment and see not only where they and their people have gone, but also where they are heading. It's as if they can smell change in the wind. Leadership is more art then science. The principles of leadership are constant, but the application changes with every leader and every situation. That's why it requires intuition. Without it, you can get blindsided, and that's one of the worst things that can happen to a leader.

Connection is absolutely critical if you want to influence people in a positive way. Think of connecting with people and compare it to trains and what happens to them in a train yard. The cars sitting on the tracks have great value because they are loaded with cargo, they have a destination, and they have a route to follow, but they don't have a way of getting anywhere on their own. They have to hook up with a locomotive. Have you ever watched how a bunch of pieces form a working train? It all begins with the locomotive. It switches itself to the same track as the car it's going to pick up, then it backs up to the car, makes contact and connects. Then it repeats the process until the cars are all hooked up and together they start moving toward their destination. The same thing must happen before you are able to get people going with you on any kind of journey. You have to find out where they are, move toward them to make contact and connect with them. If you can do that successfully, you can take them to new heights in your relationship and in the development.

Every game in life has its own rules and its own definition of what it means to win. Some teams measure their success in points scored, others in profits. Still others may look at the number of people they serve, but no matter what the game is, there is always a scoreboard. If a team is to accomplish their goals then they have to know the score. Why is the score so important? Because teams that succeed make adjustments to continually improve themselves and their situations. In preparation, teams come up with a detailed game plan, but as the game goes on, the game plan means less and less, while the scoreboard becomes more and more important. Why? Because the game is constantly changing as we travel the road of life. The game plan tells you what you want to happen, but the scoreboard tells what is happening.

Where does a leader's vision come from? To find your vision, you must listen. Vision starts within. Do you know what your life's mission is? If what you're pursuing in life doesn't come from the depths of who you are and what you believe, you will not be able to accomplish it. Where does inspiration for great ideas come from? From noticing what doesn't work. Discontent with the status quo is a great catalyst for vision. No great leader in history has fought to prevent change. Nobody can accomplish great things alone. Don't let your vision be confined by your own limited capabilities. Have you looked beyond yourself, even beyond your own lifetime as you've sought your vision? If not, you may be missing the true potential of your life.

Having exceptional people on the journey with you doesn't happen by accident. It's true that the greater your dream is, the greater the people who will be attracted to you, but that alone isn't enough. You need to make sure they're compatible with you. Does this person want to go? That can be a hard lesson, because you may want to take everyone. Don't assume that everyone wants what you want. You need to ask whether that person is able to go. There has to be a match between the journey you want to take and their gifts and talents. Can this person make the trip without me? If so, make friends with them and try to keep in touch. Though you may not take the journey together, you may be able to help one another as you travel down this road.

When some leaders begin to work with others on their development, they gravitate to weakness rather than strengths. Maybe that's because it's so easy to see other people's shortcomings, but if you start by putting your energies into correcting people's weaknesses, you will demoralize them and unintentionally sabotage the enlarging process. Instead of focusing on weaknesses, give your attention to people's strengths. Focus on sharpening skills that already exist. Compliment positive qualities. Bring out the gifts inherent in them. Weakness can wait, unless they are character flaws. Only after you have developed a strong rapport with the person and they have begun to grow and gain confidence should you address areas of weakness. Then those should be handled gently and one at a time.

Our influence has less to do with our position or title than it does with the life we live. It's not about position, but production. It is not the education we get, but the empowerment we give, that makes a difference to others. The key word is credibility. We gain credibility when our life matches our talk and when both add value to others. How are you doing when it comes to credibility? Are you the same person no matter who's with you? Do you make decisions based on how they benefit you or others? Are you quick to recognize others for their efforts when you succeed?

Many people avoid confrontation. Some fear being disliked and rejected. Others are afraid confrontation will make things worse by creating anger and resentment in the person they confront, but avoiding confrontation always worsens the situation. Confrontation can be a win-win situation, a change to help and develop your people, if you do it with respect and with the other person's best interests at heart. Positive confrontation is a sure sign that you care for a person and have their best interests at heart. Each time you build up your people and identify their problems, you give them an opportunity to grow.

As important as integrity is to your business success, it's even more critical if you want to become a person of influence. It is the foundation upon which many other qualities are built, such as respect, dignity and trust. If that foundation of integrity is weak or fundamentally flawed, then being a person of influence becomes impossible. That's why it's crucial to maintain integrity by taking care of the little things. Ethical principles are not flexible. Integrity commits itself to character over personal gain, to people over things, to service over power, to principle over convenience. Anytime you break a moral principle, you create a small crack in the foundation of your integrity. When times get tough, it becomes harder to act with integrity, not easier. Character isn't created in a crisis, it only comes to light. Everything you have done in the past, the things you have neglected to do, come to a head when you're under pressure.

Reactions of People

Some teams just don't bond and can't build because they never become a cohesive unit. Why do wounded Soldiers strive to rejoin their buddies on the battlefield? Because after you work and live with people, you soon realize that your survival depends on one another. For a team to be successful, the teammates have to know that they will look out for one another. When a team member cares about no one but himself, the whole team will suffer.

When somebody asks a question in a meeting, who do people look to for the answer? Who do they wait to hear from? The person they look to is the real leader. Identifying a real leader can be easy if you remember what you're looking for. Don't listen to the claims of the person professing to be the leader. Instead, watch the reactions of the people around him. The proof of leadership is found in the followers. People listen to what someone has to say not necessarily because of the message, but because of their respect for the messenger. How do people react when you communicate? When you speak, do people listen, really listen? Or do they wait to hear what someone else has to say before they act?

No one is excluded from being a leader or a follower. Realizing your potential as a leader is your responsibility. The prominent leader of any group is quite easy to discover. Just observe the people as they gather. If an issue is to be decided, who is the person whose opinion seems most valuable? Who is watched the most when the issue is being discussed?

Who is the one with who people quickly agree? Most importantly, who is the one the others follow? Answers to these questions will help you to identify who the real leader is in a particular group.

Far too often leaders drift. Once they get some experience under their belt and a track record of accomplishment, they often abandon the lifestyle that helped them reach the top. People do what people see. If they want to succeed, leaders must live the life they desire in their followers.

One of the biggest mistakes a coach can make is to believe that he must treat all of his players the same. Coaches are hired to win, not to make everyone happy or give everyone equal time, money or resources. Every player must be given support and encouragement, but to believe that everyone must receive the same treatment is not only unrealistic but destructive. Poor or mediocre performance should not be rewarded the same as the outstanding contributions. Great coaches give opportunities, resources, and playing time according to player's past performance. There will be times that you aren't sure about a players' performance level because you haven't had time to observe him, especially with a rookie player. Give that player frequent but small opportunities to determine his caliber of play and that will show you how to respond.

It takes a leader to create momentum. Followers catch it and managers are able to continue it once it has begun. Creating momentum requires someone who can motivate others, not one who needs to be motivated. Without momentum, even the simplest tasks can seem insurmountable, but with momentum on your side, nearly any kind of change is possible. No leader can ignore the impact of momentum. If you've got it, you and your people will be able to accomplish things you never thought possible. The choice to build momentum is yours.

The success of your marriage, job and personal relationships all depend greatly on communication. People will not follow you if they don't know what you want or where you are going. The key to effective communication is simplicity. Forget about impressing people with big words or complex sentences. If you want to connect with people, keep it simple. As you communicate with people, whether individuals or group, ask yourself these questions: Who is my audience? What are their questions? What needs to be accomplished? Believe in what you say. Then, live what you say. There is no greater credibility than conviction in action. As you communicate, never forget that the goal of all communication is action. Every time you speak to people, give them something to feel, something to remember, and something to do.

All leaders have vision, but all people who possess vision are not leaders. A compelling vision alone will not make someone a leader. Nor will a great vision automatically be fulfilled simply because it is compelling or valuable. Followers need to buy into the leader. Just because a person has vision and occupies a leadership position doesn't necessarily mean that the people will follow. Before they get on board, they have to buy in. That doesn't happen in an instant. Buy in is an ongoing process.

Connect with Individuals

One of the greatest gifts leaders can give to those around them is hope. Never underestimate its power. Winston Churchill was once asked by a reporter what his country's greatest weapon was against Hitler during World War II. Without pausing for a moment he said it was what England's greatest weapon has always been, hope. People will continue working, struggling, and trying if they have hope. Hope lifts people's morale. It improves their self-image. It re-energizes them. It raises their expectations. It is the leader's job to hold hope high, to instill it in the people he leads. We will have hope if we maintain the right attitude. Maintaining hope comes from seeing the potential in every situation and staying positive despite circumstances.

A leader can delegate anything except responsibility. Leaders simply cannot give it away. They can model it, they can teach it, and they can share it, but in the words of Harry Truman, the buck stops with the leader. The sign of great leaders is not what they accomplish on their own, but what they accomplish through others.

People are first influenced by what they see. If you have children, then you have probably observed this. No matter what you tell your children to do, their natural inclination is to follow what they see you doing. For most people, if they perceive that you are positive and trustworthy and have admirable qualities, then they will seek you as an influencer in their lives. When you meet people who don't know you, at first you have no influence with them at all. If someone they trust introduces you to them, then you can temporarily borrow some of their influence, but as soon as they have some time to observe you, you either build or destroy that influence by your actions.

It's not difficult to see the importance of having well trained, capable reserve players who sit on the bench in sports. In major league baseball, the teams who win championships do so because they have more then just a good pitching rotation and solid fielding. They posses a bench and a bullpen with strong players who can substitute or pinch hit. In the NBA, players and fans have long recognized the impact of the bench by talking about the all important sixth man, the person who makes a significant contribution to the team's success yet isn't one of the five starters on the basketball court. Football coaches express the need to have two skilled quarterbacks on their rosters. A great starter alone is simply not enough if a team wants to go to the highest level. Any team that wants to excel must have good substitutes as well as starters. That's true in any field, not just sports. You may be able to do some wonderful things with a handful of top people, but if you want your team to do well over the long haul, you've got to build your bench. A great team with no bench eventually collapses.

A leader can't connect with people only when he is communicating among groups, he must connect with individuals. The stronger the relationship and connection between individuals, the more likely the follower will help the leader. Successful leaders always initiate. They take the first step and make the effort to continue building relationships. Connecting with people isn't complicated, but it takes effort.

A person with integrity does not have divided loyalties, nor is he merely pretending. People with integrity are whole people and they can be identified by their single mindedness. People with integrity have nothing to hide and nothing to fear. Their lives are open books. A person of integrity is one who has established a system of values against which all of life is judged. Integrity is not what we do, so much as who we are. And who we are, in turn, determines what we do. We are all faced with conflicting desires. No one, no matter how spiritual, can avoid this battle. Integrity is the factor that determines which desire will prevail. We struggle daily with situations that demand decisions between what we want to do and what we ought to do. Integrity establishes the ground rules for resolving these tensions. It allows us to predetermine what we will be regardless of circumstances or persons involved. It frees us to be whole persons no matter what comes our way.

Care About Each Other

To discover the proper course concerning a poor performer, a leader needs to ask – should this person be trained, transferred or terminated? The answer will determine the appropriate course of action. If low performance is due to skills that are poor or under developed, it calls for training. Sometimes an employee is a low performer because be is being expected to perform a job that does not match his gifts and abilities. If the employee has a good attitude and a desire to succeed, he can be transferred to a position matching his gifts. By far the most difficult of the tough decisions a leader faces concerns terminating an employee, but terminating a poor performer benefits the organization and everyone in it.

As people who care about each other grow together and work toward a common goal, they get to know each other better. They begin to recognize and appreciate each member's unique qualities. That leads to the development of a team fit. A good team fit requires an attitude of partnership. Every team member must respect the other players. They must desire to contribute to the team, and they must come to expect a contribution from every other person. Above all, they must learn to trust each other. Trust makes it possible for people to rely on one another. It allows them to make up for each other's weaknesses instead of tying to exploit them. It enables one team member to say to the other, you go ahead and do this task because you are better at it than I am, without shame or manipulation. Trust allows the people on the team to begin working as a single unit, to begin accomplishing the things that they together recognize as important.

Rare are the people who begin their careers as stars. Those who do sometimes find that their success is like that of some child actors. After a brief flash in the pan, they are never able to recapture the attention they got early on. Most successful people go through an apprenticeship or period of seasoning. Look at quarterback Joe Montana, who was inducted into the NFL Hall of Fame in 2000. He spent two years on the bench as a backup before being named the San Francisco 49ers starter. He was breaking records and leading his team to Super Bowls. The person who sat on the bench as a backup to him was Steve Young, another great quarterback. Some talented team members are recognized early for their great potential and are groomed to succeed. Others labor in obscurity for years, learning, growing, and gaining experience. Then after a decade of hard work, they become overnight successes. Given the right encouragement, training, and opportunities, nearly anyone with desire has the potential to emerge as an impact player.

If a team doesn't reach its potential, ability is seldom the issue. It's rarely a matter of resources. It's almost always a payment issue. The team fails to reach its potential when if fails to pay the price. If you lead a team, then one of the difficult things you must do is convince your teammates to make sacrifices for the good of the group. The more talented the team members, the more difficult it may be to convince them to put the team first. Once you have modeled a willingness to pay your own price for the potential of the team, you have the credibility to ask others to do the same. Then when you recognize sacrifices that teammates must make for the team, show them why and how to do it. Then praise their sacrifices greatly to their teammates.

Just about everyone has experienced being on a team where people had to take on roles that didn't suit them. What happens to a team when members constantly play out of position? First, morale erodes because the team isn't playing up to its capability. Then people become resentful. The people working in an area of weakness resent that their best is untapped. Other people on the team who know that they could better fill a mismatched position on the team resent that their skills are being overlooked. Before long, people become unwilling to work as a team. When people aren't where they do things well, things don't turn out well.

Positions of Power

People tend to think of leadership only in terms of action, but leadership is so much more than just that. Leadership is not just something you do, it's something you are. That's one of the reasons good leaders have such strong magnetism. People are attracted to who they are. All leaders desire results, but being must precede doing. To achieve higher goals, you must be a more effective leader. To attract better people, you must be a better person yourself. To achieve greater results, you must be a person of great character. A common problem occurs when a leader's real identity and the desired results don't match up, but when leaders display consistency of character, competence, and purpose, it makes a powerful statement to the people around them and it draws those people to them. If you desire to do great things with your life, then seek to become a better person and a better leader. Nothing great can be achieved alone. Any task worth doing requires the help of others. If you want to attract good people, you've got to become a better person yourself.

Some leaders step into positions of power out of love and a sense of mission. Others seek leadership merely to gain power over others and to revel in a smug feeling of superiority. Normally it doesn't take long to determine which sort of leader you've got. Leaders are not given authority to better themselves, to enlarge their income or social status, or to improve their standard of living. They are first and always servants of others.

Champions don't become champions in the ring, they are merely recognized there. Boxing is a good analogy for leadership development because it is all about daily preparation. Even if a person has natural talent, he has to prepare and train to become successful. It is not the critic who counts, not the man who points out how the strong man stumbled, or where the doer of deeds could have done them better. The credit belongs to the man who is actually in the arena, whose face is marred by blood and sweat, who strived valiantly, who knows the great enthusiasms, the great devotions, and spends himself in a worthy cause.

Sharing with Others

Status quo is Latin for "the mess we're in". Leaders see what is, but they also have a vision for what could be. They are never content with things as they are. To be leading, by definition, is to be in front, breaking new ground, conquering new worlds, moving away from the status quo. Dissatisfaction with the status quo does not mean having a negative attitude or grumbling. It has to do with a willingness to be different and to take risks. A person who refuses to risk change fails to grow. A leader who loves the status quo soon becomes a follower. Taking the safe road, doing your job, and not making any waves may not get you fired, but it sure won't do much for your career or your company over the long haul. We're not dumb. We know that administrators are easy to find and cheap to keep. Leaders, risk takers, are in very short supply and ones with vision are pure gold. Risk seems dangerous to many people because they are more comfortable with the old problems versus what it takes to come up with new solutions. The difference is attitude. When you seek out potential leaders, seek people who seek solutions.

Any dream worth living is worth sharing with others. The person who shares his dream gets to watch it grow. The synergy of shared ideas often takes it to a whole new level. The dream becomes greater than the person launching it ever imagined it could be. Those who participate in it often adopt it as their own dream. As you give others an opportunity to share your dream, paint a broad landscape for them so that they can catch your vision. When you are willing to share the dream by including others, there's almost no limit to what you can accomplish. The impossible comes within reach.

Never work alone. I know that sounds too simple, but it is truly the secret to developing others. Whenever you do anything that you want to pass along to others, take someone along with you. This isn't necessarily a natural practice for many of us. The most common learning model in the United States is when a leader asks questions or lectures while the follower listens and tries to comprehend the instructor's ideas, but craftsmen use a different model for developing others. They take apprentices who work along side them until they master their craft and are able to pass it along to others. I have never found a better way to develop others.

Nothing in life can take the place of knowing your purpose. If you don't try to discover your purpose, you're likely to spend your life doing the wrong things. Everyone has his own specific vocation or mission in life. Everyone must carry out a concrete assignment that demands fulfillment. We can't be replaced, nor can our life be repeated. Thus everyone's task is as unique as his specific opportunity to implement it. Each of us has a purpose for which we live for. Our responsibility is to identify it. Your thoughts determine your character and the first person you lead is you.

Leaders need to respond to individuals based on their needs rather than their faults. Good leaders do this well. They don't lead out of a predetermined package of behaviors, but size up every situation to see what must happen to reach the desired goal. Like a quarterback who reads the defense, then calls an audible from the line of scrimmage, good leaders remain flexible and may change their response, based not on what a person deserves, but on what they need to succeed.

A point to drive home again. Many leaders commit the error of separating leadership from relationships. This happens when people step into leadership positions and assume that everyone will follow them because of their position. Some leaders wrongly believe that their knowledge alone qualifies them to lead others. People don't care how much you know until they know how much you care. We cannot separate leadership from relationships. Leaders help themselves by developing good relational skills.

Empowering People

Again, this point is very important to drive home. People don't follow others by accident. They follow individuals whose leadership they respect. The more leadership ability a person has, the more quickly he recognizes leadership or its lack in others. When people get together for the first time as a group, take a look at what happens. As they start interacting, the leaders in the group immediately take charge. They think in terms of the direction they desire to go and who they want to take with them. At first, people may make tentative moves in several different directions, but after the people get to know one another, it doesn't take long for them to recognize the strongest leaders and to follow them. In time, people in the group get on board and follow the strongest leaders. Either that or they leave the group and pursue their own agendas.

Remember this paragraph. The place to start empowering people is by evaluating them. With inexperienced people, if you give them too much authority too soon, you can be setting them up to fail. With people who have lots of experience, if you move too slowly you can frustrate and demoralize them. Sometimes when leaders misjudge the capabilities of others the results can be comical. For example, Albert Einstein applied for admittance to the Munich Technical Institute and was rejected because he would never amount to much. As a result, instead of going to school, he worked as an inspector at the Swiss Patent Office and with his extra time he refined his theory of relativity. Remember that everyone has the potential to succeed. Your job is to see that potential, find out what he lacks, and equip him with what he needs.

People rise or fall to meet our level of expectations for them. If you express skepticism and doubt in others, they'll return your lack of confidence with mediocrity, but if you believe in them and expect them to do well, they'll wear themselves out trying to do their best. In the process, both of you benefit. If you've never been one to trust people and put your faith in them, change your way of thinking and begin believing in others. Your life will quickly begin to improve. When you have faith in another person, you give him an incredible gift, maybe the best gift you can give another person. Give others money and it's soon spent. Give resources and they may not be used to the greatest advantage. Give help and they'll often find themselves back where they started in a short period of time, but give them your faith, and they become confident, energized, and self reliant. They become motivated to acquire what they need to succeed on their own. Then later if you do share money, resources and help, they're better able to use them to build a better future. Become a believer in people. Even the most tentative and inexperienced people can bloom.

People will not follow a leader who does not have confidence in himself. In fact, people are naturally attracted to people who convey confidence. Confidence is a characteristic of a positive attitude. The greatest achievers and leaders remain confident regardless of circumstances. Strong, confident leaders recognize and appreciate confidence in others. Confidence is not simply for show. Confidence empowers. Good leaders have the ability to instill confidence within their people.

One of the most common mistakes people make is trying to lead others before developing relationships with them. It happens all the time. A new manager starts with a company and expects the people working there to respond to his authority without question. A coach asks his players to trust him when they don't even know each other. A divorced father who hasn't see his children in years reinitiates contact and expects them to respond to him automatically. In each of these instances, the leader expects to make an impact before building the relationship. It's possible that the followers will comply with what the leader's position requires, but they'll never go beyond that. As you prepare to develop other people, take time to get to know each other. Ask them to share their stories with you, their journeys so far. Find out what makes them tick, their strengths and weakness, their temperaments and so forth.

Moving in the Right Direction

A person's ability to make things happen in and through others depends entirely on their ability to lead them. Without leadership, there is no teamwork and people go their own way. If your dream is big and will require the teamwork of a lot of people, then any potential leaders you select to go with you on the journey will need to be people of influence. After all, that's what leadership is, influence. When you think about it, all leaders have two things in common. They're going somewhere and they're able to persuade others to go with them. To be a good judge of potential leaders, don't just see the person; see all the people who that person influences. The greater the influence is, the greater the leadership potential and the ability to get others to work with you to accomplish your dream.

Nearly everyone has emotional filters that prevent them from hearing certain things that other people say. Your experiences, both positive and negative, color the way you look at life and shape your expectations. If you've never worked through all your strong emotional experiences, you might be filtering what others say through those experiences. If you're preoccupied with certain topics and if a particular subject makes you defensive, you may frequently project your own point of view onto others. You may need to spend some time working through some of your issues before you can become an effective listener. Freud stated that a man with a toothache cannot be in love; meaning that the toothache doesn't allow him to notice anything other than his pain.

Do you remember what it was like when you first got your driver's license? Just going for a drive was probably a thrill. It didn't really matter where you went. But as you got older, having a destination became more important. The same is true with a team. Getting the team together and moving it are accomplishments, but where you're going does matter. You've got to begin doing the difficult things that help the team to improve and develop high morale. The toughest stages in the life of a team are when you are trying to create movement in a team that's going nowhere and when the team needs change to make the team better. Those are the times when leadership is most needed. Times of failure not only reveal a leader's true character, but also present opportunities for significant leadership lessons. Many leaders attempt to hide failures and blame others.

Leadership is like head start for the team. Leaders see farther than their teammates. They see things more quickly than their teammates. They know what's going to happen and can anticipate it. As a result, they get the team moving in the right direction ahead of time and for that reason, the team is in a position to win. The greater the challenge, the greater the need for the many advantages that leadership provides. If you want to win and keep winning for a long time, then train players on the team to become better leaders. The power of leadership carries over into every field. Look behind the scenes of any great undertaking, and you will always find a strong leader. That's why the difference between two equally talented teams is leadership.

There's a difference between interest and commitment. When you are interested in doing something, you do it only when it's convenient. When you are committed to something, you accept no excuses. Don't equip people that are merely interested, equip the ones who are committed. Commitment is the one quality above all others that enables a potential leader to become a successful leader. Without commitment, there can be no success. To determine whether your people are committed, first you must make sure they know what it will cost them to become a leader. That means that you must be sure not to undersell the job. Let them know what it's going to take to do it. Only then will they know what they are committing to. If they won't commit, don't go any further in the equipping process. Don't waste your time. People never become more committed than their leader.

Belonging is one of the most basic needs that every person has. Positive influencers understand this need for a sense of belonging and do things that make people feel included. Parents make sure their children feel like important members of the family. Bosses let their employees know that they are valued members of the team. Great leaders are particularly talented at making their followers feel like they belong. Napoleon Bonaparte made people feel important and included. He was known for wandering through his camp, greeting every officer by name and making small talk. The interest and time he took with his followers made them feel a great sense of camaraderie and belonging. It's no wonder that his men were devoted to him. If you desire to become a better leader, begin looking for ways to include others.

We cannot lead anyone else farther than we have been ourselves. Too many times we are so concerned about the product we try to shortcut the process. There are no shortcuts when integrity is involved. Eventually truth will always be exposed. You play like you practice or you fight the way you train. When we fail to follow this principle, we fail to reach our personal potential. When leaders fail to follow this principle, eventually they lose their credibility.

When you're looking for potential leaders, if someone you're considering lacks loyalty, he's disqualified. Don't even consider taking him on the journey with you because in the end, he'll hurt you more than help you. When people combine loyalty with other talents and abilities, they can be some of your greatest assets. If you find people like that, take good care of them.

Charm and Inspire

War is increasingly shown not to be a particularly effective way of settling anything. Nuclear weapons are so devastating that no rational person would ever use them; that's not to say that in a still irrational world they will not be used. There are conventional forces in order to settle a dispute between them or to gain territory. Again, rationality does not always prevail. Qualities that make such a difference are the charismatic leader, who is rational under fire, unafraid to improvise or lead his men into battle against the odds and the confidence of victory. No matter how well intentioned, force does not resolve the most intractable problems. A country can be occupied for a while, but it will eventually oust the occupier. The cost benefit analysis does not justify war, except in deterring aggression.

Great military leaders have often shown an almost political ability to charm and inspire their men rather than rely merely on handling down orders. Great political leaders have often shown an almost militarist style of command, in place of the usual verbiage, particularly in times of crisis and conflict. Great business leaders have sometimes shown military style discipline or political persuasiveness. Perhaps the key to leadership, to genius in any of these three spheres, is the ability to transcend the norms of their professions. To think outside the box by winning the hearts of their people rather than their fear, may go a long ways.

Absolute victory is never attainable; war is limited by political objectives. The best strategy is clearly to be very strong and concentrating one's forces at the right time and place to secure your overall victory. Superiority of numbers is a most important factor in deciding victory, plus the element of surprise. There are no hard and fast rules of military strategy. An approach that may be right at a particular moment may also be entirely wrong at another. The art of war does not require complicated movement, the simplest are the best and common sense is fundamental. The lesson may be that in different circumstances, entirely different strategies and tactics apply. Sometimes it is right to attack, sometimes to flank, sometimes to retreat, sometimes to advance, sometimes to concentrate forces, sometimes to disperse, sometimes to divide the enemy and even sometimes to launch a full frontal attack.

An army is a most sensitive instrument and can easily become damaged. Its basic ingredient is people. To handle an army well, it is essential to understand human nature. Bottled up in people are great emotional forces which have to be given an outlet in a way which is positive and constructive, which warms the heart and excites the imagination. If the approach to the human factor is cold and impersonal, then you achieve nothing, but if you can gain the confident and trust of your people, they feel their best interests are safe in your hands. Then you have in your possession a priceless asset and the greatest achievements become possible. However, today superior technology and firepower is perhaps considered the defining reason why a war is won or lost.

— 3 —
Great Leaders

I would like to discuss great icons within the history of mankind with very different leadership styles. Their leadership worked for their given situation. Hannibal rose to the ranks of legend within his own lifetime, becoming the most feared man in the Mediterranean. Hannibal possessed an amazing knack for commanding diverse people and their tactical systems. Julius Caesar packed more into his life than most of history's great men and he shaped Rome for generations. Caesar was a complex man, both hero and villain. Napoleon, his principal genius lay in his military acumen and ability to inspire his troops. Educated at military schools, his talents were on display early and he made the rank of brigadier general before he turned twenty-five. He was handed a starving, demoralized army, which he turned into a dynamic fighting machine. He went on a winning streak in the field not dissimilar to Alexander's, meantime consolidating his power as head of the French government. Patton moved faster and farther, killed or captured more of the enemy, liberated more cities, towns, and villages than any other army in WWII, quite possibly in the history of warfare. Wars have been won or lost by the personality and leadership of an individual commander and we'll review a few in this chapter. Ulysses S. Grant was perhaps the most famous person in America during his lifetime. Yet today his military reputation is overshadowed by that of Robert E. Lee and his presidency is at the bottom in historical rankings. Plus, a quick look at some people which changed the world.

Hannibal Barca

One of the greatest Generals in our history was the great Carthaginian Hannibal Barca; nearly always fighting at a disadvantage in manpower and resources. Hannibal rose to the ranks of legend within his own lifetime, becoming the most feared man in the Mediterranean. It is even said his reputation was so fierce that Roman parents merely had to utter "Hannibal is at the gate" when their children misbehaved. What was at stake was more than the lives of the tens of thousands of men gathered on the battlefield, but the course of western civilization itself.

Prayers were offered to harsh Gods who demanded dramatic and severe forms of sacrifices, including child sacrifice. Though the addition of foreign Gods had a moderating effect on Carthaginian religious practices, human and child sacrifice continued in times of national crisis. The Gods were viewed as disembodied spirits or powers which could be won over by the right prayers and sacrifices, and whose will was revealed in the flight of birds and in thunder. This superstitious belief was so strong that it could determine if or when a battle took place. The story of Hannibal is more than how men maneuvered on a battlefield.

Like great commanders of any age, Hannibal was known for his personal courage in battle which endeared him to his troops. He demanded absolute obedience, sometimes disciplining his troops with beatings and death sentences by crucifixion. Hannibal was twenty-six years old when he took command of the Carthaginian forces in Spain. Hannibal possessed an amazing knack for commanding diverse people and their tactical systems. He understood how to manipulate the motivations of each of the nationalities in his army and exploit their military strengths on the battlefield, leading to spectacular victories against difficult odds. Like Alexander the Great before him and Julius Caesar after, he also shared in the personal dangers of combat and physical demands of his Soldiers on the battlefield.

Hannibal had confidence in his ability to beat the armies of Rome on the battlefield; burning, pillaging, and looting as they went. He demanded absolute obedience, beheading its leaders and enslaving its inhabitants as a warning to other potential defectors. Hannibal rode his horse in front of the troops to raise their spirits and organize their battles. He seemed to posses a certain confidence and charm which allowed him to get along with people from other cultures. Hannibal's orders were to exterminate every form of life they encountered, sparing none, but not to start pillaging until the word was given to do so. This practice was adopted to inspire terror, and so you may often see not only the corpses of human being but dogs cut in half and the dismembered limbs of other animals. The carnage was especially frightful.

Hannibal would ask if there was any way they could resolve their differences without fighting. Hannibal used diplomacy to soften his enemy and then boldly attacked his enemy with a standard of fighting. Hannibal placed war elephants in front of the entire formation to screen his forming troops and act against enemy cavalry attacks. Hannibal addressed his troops, rode up and down their front ranks, reminding them of the battles they fought in the past and to bear themselves like brave men who are worthy of their reputation and county. So when they meet the enemy, there are only two objects to keep in mind, to conquer or to die. He ordered his mercenary officers to address their men in their own languages, telling them to inform the men what would happen to their wives and children should the Romans be victorious. Hannibal went on to emphasize the inferiority of the Roman troops, both in numbers and experience. He would attempt a direct assault into the Roman infantry, sending first war elephants, then his less reliable allied infantry, holding his veteran troops in reserve until precisely the right moment.

Hannibal's basic strategy was brilliant in its simplicity, strike the Roman front and hope to win the day. Hannibal understood that although he possessed more infantry than his Roman counterpart, perhaps two-thirds of his infantry were not as well trained or as disciplined as the veterans. Hannibal's only real chance of victory was to break the Roman front with wave after wave of attack, beginning with a war elephant charge to break up the Roman first line, followed by several waves of infantry to punch through the Roman ranks.

Hannibal was a master tactician, who understood both the combat capabilities and motivations of his multinational troops. Infantry, in Hannibal's art of war, was used defensively and in support of his more mobile and more highly skilled cavalry. Hannibal understood the limitations of his forces and created a winning strategy to fit these limitations. His army was made up of people from many nations, a fact which presented numerous problems in battlefield command, control and communication.

Hannibal was sixty-four years old when he took his life with poison. He reportedly said right before his suicide, "let us free the Roman people from their long standing anxiety, seeing that they find it tedious to wait for an old man's death", his death denied his old enemies the triumph they had so desperately wanted. No longer would the Roman people fear "Hannibal at the Gates".

Julius Caesar

Julius Caesar packed more into his life than most of history's great men and he shaped Rome for generations. Caesar was a complex man, both hero and villain. He was a spokesman for the ordinary people of Rome, who rallied around him time and again, but he profited enormously from his conquests. Caesar invented the basic calendar we still use today. Following Roman custom, Caesar was given the same name as his father. Religion would be an important part of Caesar's life. The favor of the Gods could be gained by a libation of wine or the sacrifice of an animal. In return, the Gods would grant a respectful Roman his due rewards.

Caesar's personal bravery in the face of imminent danger became a hallmark of his fighting style that would serve him on battlefields from Britain to Egypt. He never hesitated to join his men on the front line and he was a strong believer of punishment. Crucifixion was among the cruelest punishments ever devised. Crucifixion was strictly a punishment for criminals and slaves, designed for as much torture and terror as killing. A condemned man would first be flogged to humiliate and weaken him, then forced to pick up his heavy wooden beam. When he had reached the prison yard or an out of the way spot on the edge of town, the prisoner was stripped naked and fastened to the beam with nails and cords. He was then hauled by ropes to the top of a sturdy pole driven deep in the ground. Many ambitious men like Caesar hoped, planned and schemed to rise through the ranks from army service to the highest executive power of the Republic.

Caesar had a very kind nature and was not easily angered. Caesar struggled with poor health, regularly suffered headaches and bouts of epilepsy. He never allowed his health to slow him down, but instead used the life of a Soldier as therapy. He marched endlessly, ate simple food, slept outside, and endured every hardship. In this way, he strengthened his body against illness. Everyone acknowledged that Caesar had a mild and forgiving nature, but he could also be pushed too far. When he was, he could strike out in fearful and ingenious ways against his foes.

The most powerful force in Rome was generals with professional armies behind them. Warfare in Caesar's time was a bloody, face to face affair in which men hacked, stabbed and killed their opponents. It was also a normal and natural part of life. No matter how well equipped the individual Roman Soldier, it was discipline on the battlefield that won or lost a fight. Caesar was determined to win by any means necessary. He was often merciful to a vanquished enemy, but only after the battle. It is to Caesar's credit that he never hesitated to reveal the many mistakes he made during his campaigns. He was a military genius, but even the best generals can be confounded by the fog of war.

Here is an example of his leadership. His men were marching through endless woods so thick the trees blocked out the sun for days at a time. Soon a cold panic began to spread through the army. Those few who had seen Germans before whispered around campfires that these barbarians were giants, ferocious in battle, with eyes so piercing you couldn't look them in the face. The common Soldiers were soon overcome by the same fear and began to make out their wills. Even older experienced Soldiers who had fought in battles throughout the Mediterranean started to feel panic creeping up their bones. Murmurings even arose among some who declared they would not move a step closer to the Germans no matter what Caesar ordered.

But like most challenges, Caesar approached this crisis boldly in an unexpected fashion. He immediately called together not his officers, but the dozens of veteran who were the true backbone of his army. These sergeants of the Roman legions were all seasoned Soldiers who directed life in the camp and on the march and most importantly, who stood by their men on the line in the heat of battle. Caesar knew if he could persuade them, the rest of the army would follow. Instead of negotiating or promising them rewards as other generals might have, he struck with a furious passion. "Who do you think you are", he demanded, "to question where I am leading you". You are Roman Soldiers, part of the greatest army the world has ever seen. Your job is to obey the orders of your commander and lead your men into whatever battle I deem fit.

You won't follow me? Fine, we're packing up and marching tonight. If you don't know the meaning of Roman duty and honor, if you are cowards, then stay here. I'll march alone with brave lads who have always stood by me and we'll conquer the Germans on our own while you crawl home in disgrace. They were so ashamed by his words that they immediately declared their willingness to follow him anywhere. Officers then fell all over themselves explaining that their hesitancy had all been a misunderstanding and that their loyalty to Caesar was unwavering. Caesar graciously accepted their explanations and considered the matter closed. When they struck camp that night, not a single man stayed behind.

Caesar had triumphed in two great wars against both Gauls and Germans, the two most feared enemies of Rome. It was a remarkable achievement in Roman military history, but it was only the beginning of Caesar's plans. Caesar displayed a genius for picking the right ground for a fight. No Roman general ever pressed his troops harder than Caesar, but no army ever followed its leader more willingly. Caesar didn't care what kind of background his men came from, whether they were Roman by birth or not. All that mattered to him was how they conducted themselves in war. During the season when they were not on campaign, he indulged his men shamelessly, turning a blind eye to minor violations of camp rules and regulations. But when his army was on the march, no one was stricter than Caesar. Punishment for shirking duty was severe and deserters were promptly executed.

Caesar's rule was that if an enemy opened their gates to him before the start of battle, they would be allowed to surrender peacefully and maintain their way of life. If, however, they forced him to seize their city by force, they were subject to the cruel laws of war. It was better to quickly intimidate a town into surrender and spare his men the risk of a battle.

Human nature everywhere yearns for freedom and hates submitting to domination by another. The Romans never pretended that they were bringing freedom or a better way of life to the people they conquered. They frankly admitted that they were only interested in increasing their own power, wealth and security through conquest. Caesar was learning a lesson that Roman generals had been taught many times in previous centuries, new foes often have unexpected weapons and techniques that must be overcome through ingenuity and adaptation. One lesson Caesar learned from Roman military history was that the best commanders knew how to recover from disaster. Caesar was not a man to hold a grudge. He believed in keeping his friends close and his enemies even closer.

It was Caesar's army, made up of no-nonsense, dependable and absolutely loyal men he raised from the farms and small towns that would determine his future. Caesar would tell his men, "All I want is for every man to follow his own conscience". But Caesar reviewed human nature as such that we become either too confident or too fearful when circumstances change. Armies, he declared, cannot exist without discipline. Caesar was always at his best when faced with impossible odds.

"I came. I saw. I conquered." Caesar landed near the town and jumped out of his ship, but in his haste he stumbled and fell on his face. The sight of their commander crashing to the ground with his first step on enemy soil sent a gasp through the superstitious troops. But Caesar was nothing if not quick witted. He quickly grabbed a handful of sand and turned the omen to his favor shouting – "I hold you now, Africa!"

Caesar used his office as chief priest to fix the problem of days and seasons by converting Rome to a solar calendar. Relying on an Alexandrian astronomer for expert advice, he added extra days to 46 B.C., so that by the end of December the year was 445 days long. This was a one time adjustment to synchronize the days and seasons, but to make sure the calendar functioned properly in the future he lengthened the months to yield a total of 365 days. Since the actual solar year is 365 ¼ days long, he also invented leap year by adding an extra day every fourth February to make up the difference. The revolutionary transformation of the calendar was such an obvious improvement over previous practice that even traditionalists had to concede its advantages. Caesar's system worked so well that it survives largely unchanged to this day.

It was at war that Caesar felt most in control of his world. While in his mid-fifties, Caesar still dreamed of conquering new worlds. Caesar had no legitimate Roman son, so he chose his great-nephew Octavius as his chief heir. This exceptionally bright young man was barely eighteen years old, but he greatly impressed Caesar. Octavius was to receive three-quarters of Caesar's immense wealth. But before filing his will, Caesar added one last line, adopting Octavius as his son upon his death. The choice of Octavius as his next of kin marked the teenager as his intended political heir as well. Even at leisure, Caesar was always a frenetic worker.

Caesar said that the best kind of death was one that was sudden and unexpected. One morning, Caesar awoke to find his wife, Calpurnia, in a panic beside him. She had been visited that night with horrible dreams that she was holding Caesar's lifeless body in her arms. Her dream came true that day. During a meeting with the Senators, one rushed at Caesar with his dagger drawn and stabbed him in the neck. The other conspirators joined in and began stabbing Caesar with knives as he fought them off furiously. From the front, side, and back they struck him over twenty times until the pain and loss of blood made him falter. With that, Caesar wrapped his toga about his face and died.

The battle for Caesar's legacy began with his assassination on the Ides of March. The Senators assumed that the Roman people would welcome the death of Caesar and that the Republic would rise again. They failed to realize that the army had become the deciding factor in Roman politics and that whoever could control the most troops controlled the empire.

Octavius emerged as sole ruler of Rome. As Caesar's heir, he lauded his great-uncle as a visionary leader and downplayed any hint of tyranny. After the fall of Rome, the courts of medieval Europe held Caesar up as the model of the ideal king. The Germans even borrowed his name for the title Kaiser, as did the Russians with Czar. The greatest man who ever lived was perhaps Julius Caesar.

Napoleon Bonaparte

Napoleon Bonaparte was not just the ultimate warlord, a man who would have been nothing without war and conquest, but he was never capable of setting the same limits on himself as the rulers and statesmen who had waged the conflict of the eighteenth century. No military figure in history has been quite as polarizing as Napoleon Bonaparte.

Napoleon is not just one of the most written about personalities in history, but he is also reputed to be the one that, after Jesus Christ, has been the most portrayed on film. Napoleon stated that "I have never really been my own master; I have always been governed by circumstances".

As in the case with many great men, the details that we have of Napoleon's life are not entirely reliable. Napoleon, the future emperor of France was born in the Corsican capital of Ajaccio to a family of the petty nobility in 1769. Napoleon was the second of eight brothers and sisters, not to mention five more died as infants or at a very early age. Napoleon seems to have been starved of love by his parents. His father was often absent on official business and his mother treated her children with considerable harshness. Desperate for the approval and attention for which he had to compete with his numerous siblings, Napoleon expressed his frustration by turning to violence. This same desire for recognition led to an ambition and hunger for success that was remarked on by all who met him. Frequent beatings reinforced this obsession with power and at the same time encouraged him to become a habitual liar. From an early age, he was fascinated by history. There seems little doubt that Napoleon was a loner who often retired for long periods to his room to indulge his love of reading and at the same time indulge himself with dreams of escape and heroism.

In 1778 he left his native island for the first time and sailed to France; where after four months of learning French, he entered the military academy. Relatively poor, he was only at the academy because his father had used his contacts. Desperately homesick and barely able to speak French, Napoleon was a classic outsider. Few of his teachers took much interest in him as a scholar and he was forever being teased. Napoleon was not liked and this marked an important period in his life. Dazzled by the concept of absolute power, he is recorded as having regarded the murderers of Julius Caesar as traitors. He also became obsessed by the concept of patriotism. Nor did it help that there was little improvement in either his looks or his stature. He looked so ridiculous that his nickname was "puss-in-boots", which was a mixture of frustration, arrogance, pride and ambition. He was an ungracious little fellow with an unpleasant face who had his nose stuck in a book the whole time.

There is no reason to doubt that Napoleon's failure at this point in his life came as a very severe blow to his ego and caused him real sadness. At the same time he was now a Frenchman and it was simply because he had nowhere else to go. Napoleon had made his name through his actions. He desired and systematically sought to get to the top of the ladder by any means possible. Engrossed entirely with his own interest, it became clear that all Napoleon cared about was glory. Even in love, he was unsuccessful. A bid to make the daughter of a wealthy local nobleman his wife was firmly rejected on the grounds of lack of prospects. Napoleon was a bitterly frustrated man.

By all accounts it was a miserable time. The cost of living was very high and Napoleon was forced to live very frugally in the most miserable of lodging. There is only one thing to do in this world, and that is to keep acquiring money and more money, power and more power; all the rest is meaningless. As a matter of fact he only acted on his own initiative, concerning himself with everything, making every decision himself and only acting as he himself thought best. Napoleon was convinced that he had a great destiny and was determined to rise to the top. Napoleon had become much more than a simple General. Very early on in the campaign, success in battle, the devotion on his troops, and a growing sense of his own power, convinced him that he was a man of destiny.

Napoleon was deeply irreligious and yet flirted with Islam and proclaimed his intention of governing in accordance with the Koran in the vain hope that this would win the cooperation of the local elite. In the same way, he pretended that he was a friend of the Catholic Church in Italy. According to Napoleon all he wanted was to govern all men as they wished to be governed and to treat all religions with equal respect. For Napoleon all that really mattered was the pursuit of power and his own glorification.

Napoleon's own stamina allowed him to concentrate on matters of detail for hour after hour. Given Napoleon's prestige, as far as educated opinion was concerned, he was the only man who could save France. Only military glory had brought him to supreme power. That same glory was all that associated him with hope and enthusiasm. It would be that same glory that sustained him to the end. Napoleon came to power as a peacemaker.

Though he was not actually insane, everything we know about his personality suggests that he was suffering from what has been described as an obsessive compulsive personality disorder. For such people, everything must be orderly and they themselves must be in total control. Napoleon wanted peace and it was peace through victory, rather than peace through compromise. Napoleon stated that next to Alexander the Great, Hannibal was the greatest hero of the ancient world.

From the moment that Napoleon acquired ideas, good or bad, he no longer consulted anyone with any intention of embracing their advice. He constantly followed his own ideas. His opinion was his only rule of conduct and he mocked all those who uttered ideas that were different from his own. Seeking ways to ridicule, he would often strike his head and say "this instrument is more use to me than the counsels of men of supposed instruction and experience". After enduring a sharp learning curve, one habit of Napoleon was initially to argue a course of action opposite to the one that he actually intended to follow to flush out his opponents and give the impression that he was yielding to argument.

With every day that passed, Napoleon was being confirmed in his belief in his own infallibility. At the same time, the state that he was ruling was becoming ever more powerful as a vehicle of his ambition. Napoleon grew bored quickly, wanted immediate results, would not recognize the word impossible, and was a poor loser to whom winning was always more important than playing the game. Napoleon may not have been a driven man in psychological terms, but as a ruler he depended above all on glory. In political terms, military success was also necessary to him, while his reorganization of France stimulated his sense of superiority and created the conditions in which war might bring fresh rewards. He could not accept that there were limits, whether military, political, diplomatic or moral, to what he could do.

To the end Napoleon claimed he was fighting for France and that he could not accept a peace that was dishonorable for France. Victory belongs to the most persevering. How many things apparently impossible have nevertheless been performed by resolute men who had no alternative but death? Impossible is a word to be found only in the dictionary of fools. "The word impossible is not in my dictionary" said Napoleon. In short, just as Napoleon had not understood the realities of strength in victory, in defeat he did not understand the realities of weakness.

So what finally brought down Napoleon? The answer, of course, is in part to be found in Napoleon himself. Tired, far from healthy, and increasingly living in a world of fantasy, he threw away his only hope of victory in Russia. Then he proceeded to repeatedly reject peace offers that would have left him ruler of a country larger than it had been when the war began in 1792.

George S. Patton Jr.

George S. Patton Jr. moved faster and farther, killed or captured more of the enemy, liberated more cities, towns, and villages than any other army in WWII, quite possibly in the history of warfare. Patton himself was convinced that greatness in battle was his destiny, his birthright, for he believed himself to be only the latest reincarnation of a line of warriors stretching back through Napoleonic times to ancient Rome and probably beyond.

Patton had a reputation for fearlessness, but he never claimed to be unafraid. In fact, he often remarked that he took chances with his own life in the front lines mainly to reassure himself that he was not a coward. Patton continually placed himself in danger, always subjecting himself to tests aimed at finding out if he possessed the kind of courage his father had told him about, the courage to face death from weapons with a smile. You are not beaten until you surrender.

A lifelong sufferer from what today would be diagnosed as dyslexia, Patton had great difficulty reading from a script. He therefore spoke from a mixture of memory and the inspiration of the moment. Patton's absorption in military history is nearly legendary, going hand in hand with his celebrated belief that he was the reincarnation of warriors stretching back to the Crucifixion and earlier. For Patton, looking backwards was a means of ensuring that he could always move ahead.

As a cavalryman, Patton believed that a man's time was best spend on the back of a horse, preferable risking his neck in competitions, like in polo because it was played the way war is fought. In many ways, Patton was a great warrior, who immersed himself in military history stretching back to the beginning of recorded warfare. He sincerely believed himself to have fought in past lives, as a Roman legionnaire and as a Solider in Napoleon's army.

Patton was always more inclined to think tactically than strategically. The combat doctrine of Napoleon and Ulysses Grant, that the aim of battle was not to capture territory but to destroy the enemy's army. Violence drove Patton, but his genius lay in knowing how to use violence to save lives. Tactically, his goal was to erase the distinction between offense and defense. Offensive tactics were the most effective defensive tactics. Attack was the best protection. Like a balanced equation, offense and defense were completely interchangeable, provided that you were fighting the right way. The right offensive tactics provided the best defense and the best defensives tactics were tactics of attack. Patton stated that he didn't want to hold any position. We're not holding anything, let the Hun do that. We are advancing constantly and we're not interested in holding on to anything except the enemy.

George Patton told his officers that he was not interest in holding on to anything except the enemy. We're going to hold him by the nose and we're going to kick him in the ass. It meant that he was all for advancing aggressively and quickly. When a major engagement came, he favored using infantry to pin the enemy down, hold it by the nose, while armor swung around like a boxer delivering a roundhouse punch to the side of the head. Of course Patton's own image was far more colorful. While infantry held the enemy by the nose, armor which had all the speed, would take the long way around to envelop the enemy, kicking him in the ass. Patton told his officers, we're going to kick the hell out of him all the time and we're going to go through him like crap through a goose.

Patton always conceived operations in terms of space and time, and time always trumped space and everything else. Patton was never content to make plans and let others execute them. To him, it was just as important to personally ensure the speed and accuracy of execution. Patton believed that a general had to make frequent trips to the front to assess for himself the situation on the ground and to encourage the troops. He believed that a general should be seen by the frontline Soldiers, who had to know that a general could get shot at just as readily as a private. He talked with the men who were on foot, attempting to lift their morale. Patton did a lot of talking to officers and men, but he knew that no communication was more powerful than action. War was ultimately a matter of will.

Patton was widely regarded as a showboat and just as widely resented for it. For his part, Patton never denied his hunger for glory, but he sought always to justify it in the context of his military effectiveness. Wearing his beautifully tailored uniforms, shiny cavalry boots, and shinier helmet even in combat zones was not an example to vainglory, but his attempt to emulate the greatest of history's commanders. It was an inspiring display of fearlessness in the face of the enemy and a demonstration of the top commander's willingness to share every danger to which his men were exposed. Patton repeatedly dared and defied death and he went out of his way to be seen doing so.

Did he have a death wish? Maybe. Did he always look for opportunities to prove to himself that he was no coward? By his own admission, yes. But whatever the psychological drivers of his compulsive defiance of death, there was a practical, tactical motive as well. He said an army is like spaghetti. You can't push a piece of spaghetti, you've got to pull it. The only way to pull something is to get in front of it. If you want an army to fight and risk death, you've got to get up there and lead it. For it was not only a general's verbal and written orders that were disseminated through his command, his very attitude also trickled down. A war is won as soon as the enemy army surrenders or is killed. It's not won as a result of taking this or that city.

It is often said that the history of any war is written by the winners. George S. Patton Jr. died on 21 December 1945 as a result of injuries sustained in an automobile accident. Patton liked victory, which he thought was very good for the morale of an army, but he also understood that it could easily breed complacency. Patton knew fear. He experienced it perhaps even more keenly than most other men. Whereas most tried to ignore, deny, or run away from fear, Patton embraced it. Victory is the only real rule in war.

Patton toured throughout the Third Army area, assembling units for morale lifting speeches and talking one-on-one with small informal groups of Soldiers. To unit commanders, he preached the critical necessity of maintaining morale. Patton drove his Soldiers hard, doing so in the belief that only maximum effort brings victory and that American troops are at their best when they are pushed beyond the limit. As Patton understood war, the object was to kill the enemy, not defend territory. Once the enemy armies were killed or captured, the territory would return to its rightful owners because the war would be over and won.

A good plan violently executed now is better than a perfect plan next week. War is a very simple thing and the determining characteristics are self confidence, speed and audacity. None of these things can even be perfect but they can be good. Patton would drive to every division headquarters to explain to his commanders as much as he could in person, to feel them out, to answer their questions, to build their morale and fire them up.

There were three ways that men get what they want; by planning, by working and by praying. Any great military operations takes careful planning or thinking as well as well trained troops to carry it all out. Nevertheless, between the plan and the operation there is always an unknown. That unknown spells defeat or victory, success or failure. Patton countered that war was precisely about driving men beyond their endurance. He believed that the collective emotion produced by a sustained maximum effort, in which rest would come only after absolute victory had been achieved, compelled men to victory and thus make their own relief possible. Patton felt that he was of a breed apart from virtually everyone else. He stated that I have it, but I'll be damned if I can define it. Patton could come up with no word more descriptive then "it" to describe his own nature.

Patton said that all good things must come to an end. The best thing that has ever happened to me is the honor and privilege of having commanded the Third Army. Patton could not help but speak his mind. Many outranked him, but Patton became and remains the most famous general of World War II. The single disappointment in Patton's young life was the great difficulty he had learning to read and write. His modern biographers have diagnosed dyslexia. It's true that idiosyncratic spelling characterized all of Patton's writings and that he always either improvised speeches or delivered them from memory rather than attempting to read from a prepared script.

Throughout his life, Patton would speak of his destiny as a Soldier. He became notorious for his candid and repeated admissions of his belief in reincarnation, which included descriptions of his own past lives. At various times, he expressed the belief that he had marched with

Napoleon and that he had been a Roman legionnaire. Patton believed that a Soldier should always do their best, not matter what.

Patton graduated from West Point in 1909, ranked 46 out of 103. It was the last time in his military career that he would ever allow himself to fall in the middle of the pack. In the end, Patton's desire was not so much to be a Soldier as it was to go to war. That was the purpose of achieving at least a measure of immortality. Patton having graduated dead in the middle of his West Point class, knew that he had to make himself stand out. He was praised for his incredible energy and his swordsmanship as calm, unusual and calculated. Most noteworthy was his skill in exploiting his opponent's every weakness.

Patton's expressly stated motive, not to perform well or to do his duty or to serve his country, but to become notorious. A great leader had the ability to convey his concern for his men even as he handed them a do or die ultimatum. For Patton there was no such thing as logistics troops versus combat troops. As he would explain repeatedly to subordinates, every Soldier is a rifleman. Patton always considered himself a fortunate warrior. You must remember that when we enter the army we do so with the full knowledge that our first duty is toward our government, entirely regardless of our own views under any given circumstances. Patton never wavered in his conviction that victory begins with training and the acquisition of discipline.

Patton had quick judgment and was willing to take chances. He instilled in his troops the almighty importance of looking like a Soldier. That meant creating a level of discipline enabling instant, cheerful and unhesitating obedience to orders. Patton was unremitting in his demands. At the same time, he ensure that his Soldiers had the most comfortable quarters and best food to be gotten anywhere. If you are going to demand the best from your Soldiers, he reasoned you had better treat them like the best.

Patton walked the walk. During a battle, he withdrew to a hilltop observation post he had prepared. Through his field glasses he saw a number of tanks sink down into the watery trenches. Determined to get them moving again, Patton descended from the hill and walked through live fire to personally supervise. After getting the stuck tanks moving again, Patton decided against returning to his hilltop observation post. Instead, in company with some of his staff officers, he walked among his troops directing them personally and individually in their advance. The tankers had at least a quarter inch of armor to protect themselves. All Patton had was his swagger stick and a holstered Colt revolver. Patton believed his role was to lead his troops in battle. He once again put action in place of words. Whether they liked him or not, all who served with Patton remarked on his extraordinary command presence. Patton would be notorious for profanity and impulsive behavior, both of which would repeatedly put his command in jeopardy.

Ulysses S. Grant

Ulysses S. Grant was perhaps the most famous person in America during his lifetime. Yet today his military reputation is overshadowed by that of Robert E. Lee and his presidency is at the bottom in historical rankings. One of his superstitions had always been when he started to go any where, or do anything, not to turn back, or stop until the thing intended was accomplished. Striking blow after blow, intent on his purpose to beat his way through. Grant stood firm in his faith in a future beyond the terrible bloody battlefields of war.

An undistinguished student in the West Point class of 1843, Grant gathered honors in the Mexican War but later resigned from the regular army in 1854 under questionable circumstances. He took up farming in Missouri, failing to achieve success in that occupation and then in a number of others as well. When Lincoln asked for volunteers in 1861, Grant was clerking in his father's leather goods store in Illinois. He responded eagerly to his country's call and rapidly won fame, scoring decisive and morale victories. Promoted to Lieutenant General in early 1864, Grant assumed direction of the entire Union military effort in the last year and a half of the war.

Grant became the first four star general in U.S. history, remaining as head of the army until 1868, when he was elected to the first of two terms as president on the republican ticket. His generalship was a major reason why the North won the Civil War. Grant believed that to maintain peace in the future it is necessary to be prepared for war, yet he was not a warmonger. He stated that although a Solider by education and profession, I have never felt any sort of fondness for war and I have never advocated it except as a means of peace. Grant's bottom line was that the Civil War had to be fought and won by the United States.

Grant was a quiet man, nothing heroic, the simple Solider and yet the greatest hero. Along the way, the shy youth from Ohio acquired strengths and developed talents that overcame his weaknesses of character and life challenges, setting the stage for his accomplishments. Grant's life is, in some ways, the most remarkable one in America history. His career, before the war was a complete failure. He was never baptized and felt no pressure to become a church member. Grant learned to handle a gun, winning praise for his marksmanship but refusing to kill animals for sport or food.

Grant stated that he didn't know if he felt any feelings on the field of battle. War seems much less horrible to persons engaged in it than to those who read of the battles. Grant rarely provided details of his own battlefield actions, but he remained cool and composed under fire. This ability enabled him to think and act decisively while others around him were rendered incapable of movement.

Grant did the best he could with the means given him. He had no organic, artistic or intellectual gifts. He did have limited though by no means inconsequential talents to apply to whatever truly engaged his attention. The only problem was that until he was nearly forty, no job he liked had come his way. So he became general and president because he could find nothing better to do. A much more analysis is that Grant's painful experience with financial and personal failure accounted for his unusually strong character displayed under stresses of wartime. A man was judged by the quality of his character in the nineteenth century. Grant's generalship was shaped as much by character as it was by intellect. Not Grant's intelligence but rater highlights qualities attributed to him by many contemporaries, such as tenacity, aggressiveness, modesty, integrity, simplicity, resoluteness and imperturbability. The sum of those qualities created the Grant symbolizing the endurance and power of the United States. The testing of those qualities under incredibly stressful conditions bore fruit in his Civil War career.

Grant is a story of a humble, patriotic Solider rising from obscurity to eminence as the relentless military commander who became the hero of the Union remains one of the most compelling in American history. The head of the greatest army in the world, acclaimed the most famous of living Soldiers, the hero of a nation ready to give him any honor within its power. What were the qualities that elevated him above his supposedly more intelligent, educated and successful peers? He simply was mediocre at best. But he won battles and campaigns, and he struck the blow that won the war. No general could do what he did because of accident or luck or preponderance of numbers and weapons. He was so complete that his countrymen have never been able to believe he was real.

Grant was a rare general willing to fight aggressively using the resources at hand. He had a calm, steadfast demeanor and purposeful leadership style. Grant knew that esprit de corps could be created in the ranks with strict training, battle experience, confident, dedicated leadership and a winning record. He stated that what I want, and what the people want, is generals who will fight battles and win victories.

Grant's surrender terms were generous. Men will always challenge the respect of an adversary. The Confederates were given paroles, pieces of paper signed by Soldiers that allowed them to go home if they promised not to take up arms again, thus sparing them from incarceration in a northern prison camp. Grant heard some criticism for his decision. He further elaborated the ideas behind his surrender policy. The men had behaved so well that he did not want to humiliate them. He believed that consideration for their feelings would make them less dangerous foes during the continuance of hostilities and better citizens after the war was over.

The fate of the Confederacy was sealed when Vicksburg fell. Today, Gettysburg, not Vicksburg, is designated the turning point of the Civil War. Vicksburg's most important outcome was Grant's elevation to the top rank of generals. When Lincoln heard of the fall of Vicksburg, he proclaimed momentously "Grant is my man, and I am his, the rest of the war".

Grant was a man of slim figure, slightly stooped, five feet eight inches in height, weighing only a hundred and thirty-five pounds. His eyes were dark gray and were the most expressive of his features. Like nearly all men who speak little, he was a good listener. But his face gave little indication of his thoughts and it was the expression of his eyes which furnished about the only response to the speaker who conversed with him. The beard was worn full, no part of the face being shaved, but like his hair, was always kept closely and neatly trimmed. He was civil to all who came in contact with him and never attempted to treat anybody with less consideration on account of his inferiority in rank.

Grant stood as the most successful Union general of the Civil War. The art of war is simple enough. Grant is reported to have said. "Find out where your enemy is, get him as soon as you can, strike him as hard as you can and keep moving on". Grant's style of command was practical, flexible, and above all decisive. He emerged as the leading Union general of the Civil War because he developed political skills that complimented his military abilities. He understood as did no other general on either side, that there was a relation between society and war. That sometimes in war generals had to act in response to popular or political considerations. Superior numbers and overwhelming industrial power did not translate into winning the war without the kind of military leadership that would bring decisive victory on the battlefield.

He was commander in chief during the Reconstruction phase of the continuing Civil War. For his part, Grant dreaded a life in politics. Why then, did he accept the party's nomination? If we believe his own explanation, he felt an overwhelming duty to say yes. The documentary record sustains the view that Grant did not seek the nomination, did nothing to enhance his candidacy and accepted the nomination as an obligation. Grant did not campaign actively, a wise decision given the fact that he was uncomfortable with public speaking. Remembering that the greatest good of the greatest number is the objective to be attained. This requires security of person, property, and for religious and political opinions in every part of our common country, without regard to local prejudice. Grant took office of the president with an impressive executive resume. As a commanding general, he strategize, organized and delegated. Taking the same attitude toward the government as toward army headquarters, Grant appointed men in whom he had trust and in whose loyalty he had confidence. His cabinet officers would be given wide latitude to run their own departments. While personally honest, seemed too trusting as supporters, friends and relations took advantage of him.

His deeply held conviction that the Union's cause was the just one because it came to stand for freedom as well as for preserving the Republic. Not only save the Union, but destroy slavery. Grant stated that we felt that it was a stain on the Union that men should be bought and sold like cattle. We were fighting an enemy with whom we could not make a peace. We had to destroy him. No convention, no treaty was possible, only destruction.

Grant was in the first rank of American heroes, alongside Washington and Lincoln. Today, it would be shocking to suggest that Grant (lowest rated president) and Lincoln (highest rated president) were of equal importance in American history. It did not seem so to many citizens in 1885 because they were not just judging Grant's presidency, but his overall importance to preserving and sustaining the Union. To them, Grant was every bit the equal of Washington and Lincoln. This linkage was made in countless newspapers articles and speeches just before and after Grant's death. Mankind shall hear of the deeds of Washington, Lincoln and Grant; they will stand as the three great characters of American history. Washington, who was the father of his country; Lincoln, who guided the ship of state through the late storm of civil strife; and Grant, the Great General, who saved the nation from over throw. Americans honored Washington the Father, Lincoln the Martyr, and Grant the Savior.

The services of General Grant cannot be estimated by any standard of value. He was the foremost General in the greatest war that ever moved the destinies of the world. His life will be through all history an incentive to every citizen of the United States. It is a Solider that he will be remembered. It is on his military services that his fame will rest. After Lincoln's death Grant was decidedly the most popular man in the United States. We may never appreciate fully General Grant's greatest. That will remain for the future. He did more for his country than any man since Washington, not even Lincoln, who could have done little without Grant. His only mistake of civil career was in trying to do too much for his friends. There was no other America that was as famous and as well loved by so many as Grant, both at home and abroad.

Grant was baptized on his death bed. At the request of the women in the family, they baptized a barely conscious Grant. "I baptize thee Ulysses Simpson Grant, in the name of the Father, in the name of the Son, and of the Holy Ghost". Grant did not care how much praying was done around him if it made his wife feel better. That Grant lacked devotion was of small consequence to the country. He clearly honored and respected, and tried to live by the Bible. Grant believed that whoever lived by the Scriptures will be benefited. He attended church to please his wife Julia. The politician Grant knew well that churchgoers voted in great numbers.

The war between the States was a very bloody and a very costly war. Grant's idealized individual characteristics with the traits that every America might posses; simplicity, honesty and a devotion to democracy. There is general agreement that all historical memory is as much about the present as it is about the past. The war was fought between brave Soldiers who, on both sides, believed in their respective causes. Grant himself did not abandon his deepest beliefs about what the Union Cause represented. Indeed, he never backed down either in public or private on his firmly held belief that slavery was the cause of the war. Aspects of Grant's life, career and character were truth, courage, modesty, generosity and loyalty.

Grant embodied simplicity. Rated a modest man, a simple man, a man believing in the honesty of his fellow man, true to is friends, faithful to traditions, and of great personal honor. Grant instinctively knew how tightly his part in the war bound him to veterans and vice versa. Our country could not be saved or ruined by the efforts of any one man. There are many men who would have done far better than I did under the circumstances in which I found myself during the war. If I had never held command, if I had fallen, if all our generals had fallen, there were ten thousand behind us who would have done our work just as well. We did our work as well as we could and so did hundreds of thousands of others. What saved the Union was the coming forward of the young men of the nation. They came from their homes and fields, as they did in the time of the Revolution, giving everything to the country. To their devotion we owe the salvation of the Union.

Grant was an ordinary, humble man who became a democratic hero. Perhaps a butcher general who sacrificed the lives of too many for a cause not worth the blood shed and the treasure lost. In his own era there was many who did not see Grant in a positive light. Some might flinch at honoring a man they viewed as one of the most dangerous and incompetent presidents ever elected. A majority of his contemporaries knew in their hearts that Grant, more than anyone besides Lincoln, made sure that the United States defeated the rebellion and prevailed in 1865, preserving the country for a greater glory. But Grant's legacy disappeared from popular memory. The $50 bill with Grant's portrait was issued in 1929, the year of the stock market crash. While Ulysses S. Grant's military reputation languished, Robert E. Lee's popularity rose even higher than it had been during the war. Lee's admirers outnumbered Grant's in the publishing world as well. Butcher Grant waged, as contrasted with the gentlemen warfare of Lee. However, Grant will never be entirely erased from the United States historical memory, he's just too important for that to happen.

Changing the World

Some people are world leaders in their fields. The world's best at what they did during their lifetime. Making a real claim to lasting change that will live on in their lifetime and beyond. Looking at the big picture and trying to understand human progress. These are some of the most influential individuals of all time that has changed our world.

Osama Bin Laden, not since Hitler had America's rage and hatred been so intently focused on one man. He was and perhaps still is, if he is still alive, a charismatic leader of a network of radical Islamist cells pledged to rid their holy land of infidels. Bin Laden declared jihad, a holy war, against the United States from his Afghan redoubt. To kill Americas and their allies, civilians and military, is an individual duty for every Muslim who can do it. He changed the world everywhere on 11 September 2001 or 9/11.

Charles Darwin changed the world and we have the term Darwinism. This refers to the monumentally important theory of evolution Darwin propounded, based upon his explorations, observations and investigations. Darwin had conceptualized his great theory, which included the crucial element of natural selection. But he spent a long time carefully marshaling his evidence as he suspected his conclusions would cause a furor. It did when he published "On the Origin of Species by Means of Natural Selection". Darwin changed the worldview of life itself. Advances in biology and anthropology after Darwin were manifold. Philosophical, religious and ethical debates in light of his findings continue today. Where does mankind fit within the Darwinian concept of "survival of the fittest"? Where does God fit into this concept?

Adolf Hitler is viewed by many as the personification of evil. Hitler was right there, before our modern eyes, a madman hell bent of dominating the world or annihilating any who would oppose him. Exploiting German poverty, blaming all ills on Jewish capitalism, Hitler and his Nazi Party rose quickly. Anti-Semitism became law, concentration camps were built to deal with enemies of the Third Reich. Nazism rolled over Europe until only England and Russia stood between Hitler and Continental domination. Hitler personally took control of the Russian front, with disastrous results. The end to his tyranny came by his own hand, with the Red Army closing in, he committed suicide in his Berlin bunker.

When you think of the computer age and who truly change the world, you must think of Steve Jobs and Bill Gates. Bill Gates with software and Steve Jobs with hardware. Leading to the breakthrough was the first Mac in 1984. Jobs knew what product was required by the masses and how to sell it. He did not carry the debate based solely upon the computers themselves, but with his charisma and intuition. Certainty style mattered just as much as mechanics did, he spun it all forward. Today, people talk to one another via the internet through their laptops, many households have no landline telephone at all, with each member possessing a personal cell that is a necessary appendage, which connects its user constantly to the world. Texting has replaced an actual conversation for many, there is little doubt that many of us already read in a new and electronic way.

Nelson Mandela stands today as the father of his country as much as George Washington stands as the father of the United States, he was South Africa's true president. The segregated way of life in South Africa that kept the imperial whites in power and the native blacks all but slaves. He felt he had to do something. Mandela was jailed which lasted nearly unbroken from 1962 to 1990, are not as important as what he once declared when hauled before the court. "During my lifetime I have dedicated myself to the struggle of the African people. I have fought against both white and black domination. I have cherished the ideals of a democratic and free society in which all persons live in harmony with equal opportunities. It's an ideal which I hope to live for and to achieve. But, if needed, it's an ideal for which I'm prepared to die." His may be the greatest story of individual resistance ever told.

Louis Pasteur made his crucial breakthroughs while experimenting with bacteria. After Pasteur, massive progress could be made in preventing and curing diseases. He discovered that many illnesses and infections have their roots in microorganisms. Once this was proved, sterilization came into play and physicians began to treat their equipment before treating a patient. He also developed a cure for rabies and came up with a vaccination technique against anthrax. Pasteur was the most important scientist the field of medicine has ever known.

A nation is prosperous or not. The people within it are prosperous or not, fairly treated or not. Their lives, liberty and ability to pursue happiness are in large part determined by the economic situation they find themselves in. No one has been more important to the formation of modern economic theory that Adam Smith, a university professor of moral philosophy and logic. Smith argued for the significance of labor when assessing the wealth of nations, and criticized government regulations that stifled industry. He encouraged free trade but admitted that certain restrictions on trade might be necessary.

Alexander the Great, already a veteran of the military and of Aristotle's tutoring, was thrust into a position of power at a young age. He lived to be thirty-three years old. What he would accomplish in that short time, in terms of world domination is truly astonishing. Alexander swept into Persia, defeated much larger armies time and again. He was, by all accounts, a brilliant, brave, inspiring general. He went forth beyond Persia into Afghanistan and India. After eleven years undefeated in battle, he pulled back to Persia and began to reorganize his empire into a kind of utopian melding of East and West. Perhaps the greatest warrior in world history.

Thomas Edison, the man who eventually registered more than a thousand U.S. patents during this long career. His inventions were useful to both the master of industry and the man on the street alike. His earliest contraptions included a transmitter and receiver for automatic telegraphing, stock-ticker system, phonograph and incandescent lamp. He developed the first central electric-light power plant in the world. He established a distribution unit to carry electricity into places of business and individual houses, not only juicing sales of his light bulbs but encouraging American industry to plug in. He would jump start the electronics industry, an early motion picture exhibition device, he synchronized moving images and sound. He produced a superior storage battery and built an experimental electric railroad. Edison changed the way the world saw and heard things, and the way it made things go.

Most modern forms of communism and socialism are drawn from Marx's arguments for societal change. Karl Marx predicted that the eventual outcome of the struggles would be the rise of the working class to a position of power. Such a vision, whether correct or not, has proved useful to many a political leader in preaching to the masses. Visionaries and political leaders alike have attracted support in invoking Marxist principles.

Civil rights in the United States was an issue that had hardly been settled by Abraham Lincoln's Emancipation Proclamation. Inequality was everywhere apparent and racism rampant in many sectors of society when a young preacher from Atlanta help launch the movement. In 1955 Martin Luther King Jr. assumed leadership of this movement in Montgomery, Alabama. A bus boycott that was organized in response to the treatment of Rosa Parks. He was one of the greatest in America history and could stir the masses with his biblical voice. In march after march, he led, where he declared his dream, "that my four little children will one day live in a nation where they will not be judged by the color of their skin, but by the content of their character." His followers kept their dignity and poise as they were being assaulted by dogs and fire hoses. All Americans saw this on the nightly news and public opinion turned. The stature of all minorities in the United States changed because of this one man. There is still prejudice and inequity today. But the Reverend Martin Luther King Jr. effected tangible change before he was assassinated in Memphis in 1968.

Alexander Graham Bell, with his master patent for his phone, changed the way humanity would communicate forever. With the recent explosion of computer and digital technology, this formerly straightforward device has changed by leaps and bounds on an almost annual basis. First there were cell phones replacing landlines, then camera phones, music playing phones, Black-Berries, it goes on and on. Millions of phones sold each year are now "smart", some of them seem smarter than we are.

He was born in India to wealth and power as Prince Siddhartha Gautama. His name became Buddha. The King, his father, wanted him to follow in his footsteps. He confined the prince to the palace and a life of luxury and ease, wanting for nothing. Yet thirsting for knowledge of the world around him, he eventually sneaked out of the palace and saw for the first time sick and dieing people. This encounter with human misery shook him to the bone. He abandoned palace life and determined to find an end to suffering. He began to examine his own mind through the practice of meditation. He attained enlightenment and became a Buddha, finding within himself an ever present basis of compassion. Proclaiming the existence of inherent wisdom and compassion in every human being and teaching the technique of mindfulness mediation as a means to awaken this potential. Many of the Buddha's discoveries about the inner workings of the mind are being confirmed and is now used by hospitals, schools, prisons, sports teams, by promoting healing and enhancing performance and creativity.

Sigmund Freud stimulated thought and debate throughout the 20th century and still today. The human id, ego and superego, our capacity to throw up defense mechanisms. Freudian theory has no doubt changed criminal investigation, wartime strategy, interviewing of a job, even football playmaking over the years.

President Ronald Reagan demanded in Berlin during 1987, "Mr. Gorbachev, tear down this wall!" The wall was in fact torn down and it was principally the work of Mikhail Gorbachev. Then came perestroika. Encouraged creativity and self-criticism in society, the latter allowed certain liberties, including greater freedom of speech. Before you knew it, the bloc collapsed and then do did the USSR. Gorbachev was awarded the Nobel Peace Prize for his efforts.

Charlie Chaplin, no moviemaker in history has meant more. Chaplin was and remains the one person in film history to have controlled every aspect of filmmaking, from casting to cutting, from writing and scoring his movies to producing and directing them. His "little fellow" more often called "the tramp" became by far the most famous screen icon in the world. Chaplin achieved something great and transformed entertainment while delighting audiences around the globe.

Confucius stated care for one's fellow man, honor your ancestors, don't do to others what you wouldn't want done to yourself. The sayings and writings of Confucius was written five centuries before Jesus was born. His way of thinking spread over time throughout Asia. Today, much of what is considered Asian custom can be traced to Confucius.

When you say the name Henry Ford, you may think of the automobile. But it's not about the automobile, it's about the growth of American industry and mass production. In Ford Motor Company plants, car weren't built, they were assembled. Workers stayed at their stations as the automobiles-to-be came to them on an assembly line. Each worker added the interchangeable part he or she had been trained to add. Women was a large part of the workforce. Unskilled labor could be hired by Ford since many of the tasks were so straightforward. The car became ever more attractive as Ford refined his operation and continually dropped the sticker price. He freely shared his production techniques and soon other America industries were being modernized with assembly lines. Productivity in the U.S. zoomed and the country was on its way to becoming a world power.

Genghis Khan rose from the bottom to the absolute top. He proved so successful at domination, in showing it could be done, he inspired future tyrants to give it a try, even global conquests. Emerged as particularly skilled not only on the battlefield but as a leader and organizer. Mongol warlords anointed him Genghis Khan, the universal emperor, and pledged fealty. The Khan went to work expanding the confederacy's reach. He began his conquest of China, then conquered Turkistan, Afghanistan, and penetrated southeastern Europe. Under his leadership, the Mongols took over Russia and pushed further into Europe. The Mongols controlled more land than any empire that had come before or has come since.

We do not eat today like our parents or grandparent did in the 1950s. Ray Kroc, we all have this man to thank or blame for it. He was not a chef nor even a cook. He was a salesman, and therein lies an American tale of McDonald's hamburgers. The concept was walk-up, buy them and eat them on the way out, and fast food was born. This was fast food's E=mc2 and Kroc was its Einstein. With restaurants in some 120 countries and the million served neon signs, McDonald's is a part of history.

Albert Einstein was one of the preeminent intellects in recorded history, this goes almost without saying. If a person is called "an Einstein" today, he or she is said to be among the most brilliant of the brilliant.

He set forth his special theory of relativity. He asserted the equivalence of gravity within a half decade were he completed the mathematical formulation of his general theory of relativity. Einstein was awarded the 1921 Nobel Prize in Physics.

Perhaps no one else changed the world as we would come to know it as Nicolaus Copernicus. Before Copernicus, we pretty much saw ourselves as the center of the universe. Literally all of science, philosophy and religion extended from that starting point. Copernicus said that the earth and other planets might actually be orbiting around the sun in a solar system. For more than 20 years he probed the planets and the stars, applying mathematics to his observations, becoming more and more convinced. The Copernicus universe had the sun at its center with planets rotating around it. Plus earth spun on an axis and the moon was revolving around the planet earth. Mankind began to reconsider all and it changed our thinking.

Aristotle studied under Plato, who in turn had been mentored by Socrates. If Plato is rightly seen as the father of Western political and ethical thought, Aristotle, who disagreed with his professor on crucial points, was the philosopher who consolidated the new way of looking at the natural order. He divided nature into four elements; earth, air, fire and water. This wasn't exactly fact but pointed a way ahead. Aristotle encouraged his followers to think for themselves and taught them how to think outside of the box.

In the 20th century, only a few individuals in the world of popular music stands by one name along, that is Elvis. Elvis Presley, a young man who emerged from a poor Mississippi background, may have been the biggest of all. Not only provoked screams of delight from his female fans but encouraged a generation, worldwide, to change its tastes and style. Elvis was everywhere, everywhere his look and sound were imitated. For most teenage boys, he was cooler than cool. For the girls, one look was enough. For adults, however, his hair, hips and lips were an alien presence that rankled, incurring above the waist TV images and the wrath of teachers and clergy. Of course, Elvis won the day and was a monster success, measured by record sales during his lifetime and are still going strong after his death. Measured also by the fact that he changed youth culture forevermore.

Observing an apple fall from a tree at the same time that the moon was visible in the sky. Isaac Newton was led to the principle of gravity. His laws of motion, that every object moves in a straight line unless impacted by a force. The acceleration of an object is dependent on its mass and the forces acting upon it. That every action had an equal and opposite reaction, were crucial to man's understanding of the physical universe. He devised a reflecting telescope and came up with calculus. His Mathematical Principles of Natural Philosophy, first published in 1687 and now known as the Principia, is perhaps the most important book of natural science ever written.

Jesus was born to Mary and Joseph, the Christ, God's son made of flesh. Jesus' life presages the phenomenon that would come after his brief time on earth, which may have been as short as thirty-three years. He showed a precocity for philosophy and teaching, lecturing even his elders and senior clerics. If his message offended some, it was alluring to others. Jesus' thinking was radical at best. After he had been martyred, crucified by the authorities when his cult of personality grew disruptive, disciples carried forth his principles. After a converted Jew named Paul and the first pope, Peter, took the theology to Rome, it slowly rose to become the ruling faith of the empire and it remains a dominant force today.

George Washington commanded and influenced other men, and thereby wrote history. It has been said that he was the indispensable man of the American Revolution. Could the colonials in Massachusetts have prevailed on the course they set for themselves without General Washington? Doubtful. Could a democracy have been born without a leader who so embodied democratic principles? Impossible. It's a mistake to think of Washington as a general only and not a man of philosophy. He led his men against the British with nobility and uncommon courage. He was certainly a different kind of man. America instantly turned its eyes to its singular hero and made him, unanimously, its first President.

Muhammad said that he was merely the agent. The Koran was the word of Allah, offered to him by an angel. Muhammad was born nearly six centuries after another great philosopher, Jesus of Nazareth. Muslim tradition tells us the Muhammad's heart was infused in his youth with love and charity. He went regularly to a cave outside Mecca to contemplate, to question the beliefs and to pray. In the cave, an angel came to him and charged him to proclaim. In Medina he built his following and eventually challenged Mecca for the soul of Arabia. Muhammad gave the Arabs a religion and today it is the second largest in the world.

Mohandas Gandhi was seen as a transcendent man of deep thought and wisdom. His political philosophies were by Hindu teachings. Gandhi, shirtless and tranquil at his spinning wheel, seemed the embodiment of the philosophies. He had very different ideas. Gandhi ordered oftentimes extraordinarily courageous war of passive resistance and nonviolent disobedience, initiating boycotts and hunger strikes. Over time, his methods worked, India was given its freedom. His message and methods lived on in other movements. For instance, Martin Luther King's crusade for civil rights in the United States.

The fate of a nation was imperiled by civil war. That it did emerge is attributable to many people and many facts but to one man above all, Abraham Lincoln. He was largely a self-taught man and a skilled politician for his day. During the war, he was an extremely proactive commander in chief. It has been said that his complete control over all matters practically amounted to a dictatorship. Members of his strong willed and smart cabinet were often at odds with one another and with him, and his generals. During the war he was bold enough to sign the Homestead Act and issue the Emancipation Proclamation, and he delivered the great Gettysburg Address. Soon after the war, he was assassinated for all that he represented. But Abraham Lincoln had preserved America.

Billy Graham began preaching while still in college, began his radio ministry and found his calling as an evangelist when hired to be the traveling preacher for Youth for Christ International. He is the recognized leader of what continues to call itself American evangelical Protestantism, and his life and activities have sustained the self-respect of that vast entity. Billy Graham helped make the second half of the 20th century the greatest period of Christian evangelization.

Oprah Winfrey has been credited with changing millions of lives, mostly women, not only in America but globally. Her support of Barack Obama influenced votes in the U.S. presidential election. She can make a book a best seller or turn a personal inclination into a trend. She has done all of this from the platform of a talk show. The Oprah Winfrey

Show is syndicated in nearly 150 countries. Winfrey preaches personal empowerment. Magazines have called her the most powerful woman in entertainment and the world.

Vladimir Lenin was smart and philosophically engaged, eventually forsaking a legal career to devote himself to the study of Marxism, then to revolutionary activities in Russia. He denounced imperialism as the end stage of capitalism. Oppose what he saw as an imperialist war, propagating a worldwide battle against capitalism everywhere. Leninism, as a practical philosophy separate from Marxism, was anti-imperialist. He was thoroughly atheistic, opportunistic and dedicated to the principle that a strong Communist party was needed to lead the people.

Pope John Paul II, few individuals have had a greater impact, not just religiously but socially and morally on the modern world. Working behind the scents with other world leaders, he played a crucial role in the fall of communism. Traveling more miles than all the previous popes combined, he brought the worldwide population of Roman Catholics to more than a billion strong. He was a holy man and a political one. His presence was felt in several realms.

Prime Minister Winston Churchill said, I have, myself, full confidence that if all do their duty, if nothing is neglected, we shall prove ourselves once again able to defend our home, to ride out the storm of war, and to outlive the menace of tyranny, if necessary for years, if necessary alone. No other figure on the world stage stood up so steadfastly against Hitler and so inspired the Allies to fight back, to fight on, to fight until the fighting was finished. He became a flesh and blood symbol of Britain, freedom, and resistance to tyranny. He perhaps most changed world history by accepting the communist Soviet Union as an ally and by courting United States President Franklin D. Roosevelt and lobbying for him to enter the war.

The Beatles. A group of four men, Paul McCartney, John Lennon, George Harrison and Ringo Starr, made some of the most popular music the world has ever heard. But they made more than just rock n roll history. They altered, as Elis had, youth culture altogether, and they became political and philosophical leaders of a generation that was shaking the world. The Beatles invaded America in 1964 and conquered immediately, they repeated the phenomenon around the globe. They began to stretch the boundaries of music. The Beatles redefined what a pop song or album could be in terms of length and structure. Wherever they led, the young followed. Rarely if ever has an entertainment act enjoyed the kind of power the Beatles did.

— 4 —

Human Behavior

I would like to start this chapter with a quote from Charles R. Swindoll. "The longer I live, the more I realize the impact of attitude on life. Attitude, to me, is more important than facts. It is more important than the past, the education, the money, than circumstances, than failure, than successes, than what other people or say or do. It is more important than appearance or skill. It will make or break a company, church or home. The remarkable thing is we have a choice everyday regarding the attitude we will embrace for that day. We cannot change our past, we cannot change the fact that people will act in a certain way. We cannot change the inevitable. The only thing we can do is play the hand we have. I am convinced that life is ten percent what happens to me and ninety percent of how I react to it. So it is with you, we are in charge of our attitudes. We are all faced with a series of great opportunities brilliantly disguised as impossible situations."

Counseling

Counseling is a fundamental responsibility of every leader. Leaders at all levels have a responsibility to assist and develop subordinates. All leaders must be coaches, trainers and teachers. All leaders are responsible for developing and preparing subordinates to assume higher positions. Counseling is one means of developing subordinates. A good leader counsels subordinates to; praise and reward good performance, develop teamwork, inform people on how well or how poorly they are performing, assist people to reach required standards, cause people to set personal and professional goals and help people resolve personal problems.

Such actions demonstrate that a leader cares about the individual person. Firm and caring leadership helps create a climate in which people are motivated and are enthusiastic, and willing to perform their tasks. Most people have always responded well to a leader who listens to their concerns, provides advice and assistance and deals with them fairly and honestly, even though, at the same time, he insists on high standards. This positive climate is developed through sincere and continuous effort over time, not just through scheduled counseling to meet a requirement.

The leader's efforts to develop people should accomplish four objectives. Cause the person to recognize strengths or shortcomings and define any problems; this calls for patience, sincere interest and clear thinking. Have the person determine possible courses of action based on facts and then cause him to select one; this requires skill, knowledge, and restraint. Cause the person to actually take the appropriate action; this will depend on the person's commitment to his decision. Have the person assume full responsibility for his decisions and actions; this can be met only if the first three objectives are accomplished.

Counseling requires that a leader's actions demonstrate knowledge, understanding, judgment and ability. It involves learning and applying techniques for developing more effective counseling skills. Of a leader's traits or characteristics promoting effective counseling, a caring attitude is the most important. The leader must develop an attitude of sincere concern for the person. Moreover, the leader's conduct must be consistent with that attitude if he is to be an effective counselor. He must apply various techniques and develop skills which show an attitude of sincere concern. Leaders must not just say they are concerned; they must do things to show concern for their peoples' well being. To be effective counselors, leaders must set a proper example. They must be ethical in all personal and professional actions. They must know their own duties, their subordinates' job requirements and their peoples' capabilities and limitations. They must understand what methods of counseling they are most comfortable with. They must also know their limitations, referring people to agencies when the need is there. Above all, they must demonstrate the standards of personal conduct and duty performance expected of their people.

Approaches to Counseling

In developing proper attitude and behavior, the leader should be aware of the characteristic aspects of effective counseling. Flexibility is fitting the counseling style to the unique character of each person and to the relationship desired. Respect is respecting people as unique, complex individuals with their own sets of values, beliefs and attitudes. Communication is establishing open, two way communications with people, using spoken language and nonverbal actions, gestures, and body language are keys for success. Effective counselors listen more than they speak. Support, supporting and encouraging people through actions and interest while guiding them through their problems. Motivation is getting every person to actively participate in counseling and teaching subordinates the value of counseling. People will respond differently. Those who need and want counseling are more likely to profit from it, but the leader's concern must extend to those who need, but do not want counseling. The purpose is seeking to develop responsible and self-reliant people who can solve their own problems.

There are as many approaches to counseling as there are counselors. Effective leaders approach each person as an individual and probably never use exactly the same approach with other people. The approaches used in counseling are the directive approach at one extreme, the nondirective approach at the other and the combined approach in the middle. They differ in the techniques used, but they are similar in overall objectives. During counseling sessions, leaders must be flexible in selecting their approaches. The type of problem, personality of the person, physical surroundings and time available will influence the selection of approach to be used.

The directive approach to counseling is counselor centered. Directive counseling is a simple, quick approach to problem solving that provides short-term solutions. This approach assumes the leader has all the skills and knowledge to assess the situation and to offer courses of action. It uses clear thinking and reason and combines suggesting, persuading, confronting, and directing specific actions to obtain the results desired by the counselor. The leader does most of the talking. He states the problem, identifies the cause, offers explanations and lists the options available. He gives advice, offers solutions and tells the person what must be done.

There are three possible disadvantages with using this approach. First, such dominant influence may create resentment because the person may see the leader as questioning his ability or as having all the answers. He may just let the leader solve his problem. This attitude may cause the person to always depend on the counselor, rather than to learn to stand on his own feet. Second, the leader may be treating symptoms rather than causes. The real problem may go undetected and result in other difficulties later on. The leader's analysis and advice may not be on target for the person's long term needs. Third, the leader makes decisions, not by the person being counseled. The person is then free to blame the leader for any future failure because he has no ownership of the solution.

Sometimes, the directive approach is the only method that can be used; especially with unresponsive people or with people who will not make a connection between their behavior and its consequences. This approach may also be the best way to correct a simple problem. The final decision regarding a problem rests with the person. When the counselor has selected a course of action, rather than assisted the person to select one, the person's only decision is to accept or reject the solution.

The nondirective approach to counseling is person centered. The counselor causes the person to take responsibility for solving the problem. This approach is usually more relaxed and focuses on self-discovery, hence taking longer than the directive approach. The role of the counselor is to help the person to become self-reliant. In this approach, the person has the opportunity to work out solutions to the problem through personal insight, judgment and realization of facts. However, you must understand and fully accept two basic rules. First, defensive attitudes must not prevent discussing the problems openly and honestly. Second, people must understand they will be responsible for the problem solving process and for the decisions they will make.

This type of counseling session is partially structured by the counselor. It is necessary from the beginning that the person understands and accepts his responsibility for selecting the topic of discussion, defining the problem and making all decisions. Structuring includes informing the person about the counseling process and what is expected and allotting a certain amount of time for each session. The person must understand that this is his time. This helps to prevent him from being defensive or from feeling guilty about taking up the leader's time.

The nondirective approach provides sheltered situations which people can look inside themselves. They can realize a freedom to be what they want to be, feel as they want to feel and think as they want to think. The result is individuals who better understand themselves. This self-understanding usually comes gradually from their personal insight into problems and their attempts to solve these problems. For this reason, the nondirective counseling is far more time consuming and can involve many counseling sessions. It is best used with a mature and capable person who is confused about something and needs some assistance in figuring out what to do.

The leader communicates to the person that someone is interested in listening to his problems. The leader is not the decision maker or advice giver but rather a listener. He tries to clarify statements, cause the person to bring out important points, understand the situation and summarize what was said. The leader should avoid giving solutions or opinions. He may, however, provide certain facts when the person requests or needs them to continue.

In the combined approach to counseling, the leader uses parts of the directive and nondirective approaches. This allows the leader to adjust the technique to emphasize what is best for the person. There is no one best procedure for all situations. The combined approach, which blends the leader's ability and personality to fit the situation, is the most frequent choice.

The combined approach assumes that the person must eventually be responsible for planning and decision making. The person will take charge of solving the problem but may need some help along the way. This approach allows both the leader and the person being counseled to participate in defining, analyzing and solving the problem. Still, the purpose is to develop self-reliant people who can solve their own problems. The leader can be directive, however, when a person seems unable to make decisions or to solve a particular problem. In counseling an individual for poor performance, for example, the leader may begin with a directive approach. When further discussion shows that a personal problem is causing poor performance, it may be best to switch to a nondirective approach.

The techniques involved in the combined approach often follow the problem-solving process. While the person is talking, the counselor should listen for information to define the problem. Then he will have a basis for suggesting solutions. He may suggest all the possible courses of action or he may suggest just a few and then encourage the person to suggest others. The counselor helps analyze each possible solution to determine its good and bad points and its possible side effects. The counselor than helps the person decide which solution is best for him. The person is enabled and encouraged to assume as much of the selection responsibility as possible. The decision whether or not to implement a solution will be the person's.

The most difficult part of counseling is applying the proper techniques to specific situations. To be effective the technique must fit the situation, the leader's capability and the person's expectations. In some cases, a problem may call for giving only information or advice. An improvement may call for a brief word of praise. In other situations, structured counseling followed by definite action may be appropriate. A leader may learn one or two techniques but still may lack the skills necessary to be an effective counselor.

All leaders should seek to develop and improve their counseling skills. Leaders are trained to analyze a mission, identify the required tasks and take action. Some of these skills apply to counseling. While leaders must not try to psychoanalyze their people, they can use problem-solving and decision-making skills to guide their people in solving their own problems. Counseling skills are developed by studying human behavior, knowing the kinds of problems that affect people and becoming good at dealing with people. These skills, acquired through study and through the practical application of counseling techniques, vary with each session. They can generally be grouped as listening and watching skills, responding skills and guiding skills.

Listening

Listening and watching skills involve the counselor concentrating on what the person says and does. Thus the counselor can tell whether or not the person accepts what is said, understands what is important and understands what the counselor is trying to communicate. Spoken words by themselves are only part of the message. The way they are arranged and spoken has meaning. The leader must try to recognize the amount and type of emotion used by a person when describing his concerns or problems. This emotion provides a clue to determine whether the person is discussing a symptom or the problem itself. The tone of voice, the inflection, the pauses, the speed, the look on the person's face, are all parts of the total message.

One important skill is active listening. Part of active listening is concentrating on what the person is saying. Another part is letting a person know the counselor is concentrating, hearing and understanding what is said and is getting the message. Elements of active listening that the counselor should consider includes eye contact. Maintaining eye contact helps show a sincere interest in the person. This does not mean that the counselor should stare at the person. Occasional breaks of contact are normal and acceptable. Excessive breaks of contact, paper shuffling and clock watching indicate a lack of interest or concern. Posture, a relaxed and comfortable body posture helps put the person at ease. A too relaxed position or slouching may indicate a lack of interest. Being too formal or rigid makes the person feel uncomfortable. Head nod, an occasional nodding of the head shows that the counselor is attentive, and it encourages the person to continue. Facial expressions; remain natural and relaxed is best. A blank look or fixed expression is disturbing. Smiling too much or frowning may also discourage the person from continuing. Verbal behavior, the counselor should refrain from talking too much. Let the person do the talking, stay with the topic being discussed and avoid interrupting. Speaking only when necessary reinforces and stimulates the person. Silence can sometimes do this too. Occasional silences may indicate that the person is free to continue talking. A long silence can sometimes be distracting and make the person uncomfortable.

Active listening also means listening thoughtfully and deliberately to the way a person says things. While listening, be alert for common themes of discussion. A person's opening and closing statements, as well as recurring references may indicate the ranking of his priorities. Inconsistencies and gaps in the discussion may indicate that the person is not discussing the real problem or is trying to hide something. Often, a person who comes to the leader with a problem is not seeking help for that problem. Rather he is looking for a way to get help with another, more threatening problem. Confusion and uncertainty may indicate where questions need to be asked.

While listening, the counselor must also be aware of the person's gestures or nonverbal behavior. These actions are part of the total message that the person is sending. Many situations involve strong personal feelings. By watching the person's actions, the counselor can see the feelings behind the words. Not all actions are proof of a person's feelings, but they must be watched. It is important to note differences between what the person is saying and doing. Boredom may be displayed by drumming on the table, doodling, clicking a ballpoint pen or resting the head in the palm of the hand. Self-confidence could be displayed by standing tall, leaning back with the hand behind the head and maintaining steady eye contact. Hate and other negative emotions may be indicated by the person being counseled by pushing himself deeply into a chair, glaring at the counselor, and making sarcastic comments. Arms crossed or folded in front of the chest often show defensiveness. Rubbing the eyes, pulling on an ear, taking short breaths, wringing the hands or frequently changing total body position may express frustration. Moving toward the counselor while sitting may indicate interest, friendliness and openness. Sitting on the edge of the chair with arms uncrossed and hands open may indicate either openness or anxiety.

Counselors should use these indicators carefully. All people are not alike and people react differently to a given situation. Further, although each indicator may show something about the person, it's important not to assume that a particular behavior means something. More importantly, it's better to ask the person about the indicator so that he can understand his behavior and take responsibility for his actions. This reinforces individual responsibility for self, as well as providing credibility to the counselor.

Responding skills are a follow-up to listening and watching skills.

From time to time the counselor needs to check his understanding of what the person is saying. The counselor's response to the person should clarify what has been said. Responses should also encourage the person to continue. As part of active listening, responding skills allow a counselor to react to nonverbal clues that the person is giving. Responding can be done by questioning, summarizing, interpreting, and informing.

Questioning is key to the counseling process. The questions of what, when, who, where, and how fits most counseling situations. When used properly, well thought-out questions can actively involve the person in his own problem, but a counselor who asks a constant stream of questions is saying, I'll ask the questions, you give the information, then, I'll tell you what to do. Questions that ask for an answer in the person's own words are more effective than those causing a yes or no response. A person's answers to how do you feel about this issue? What do you think needs to be done next? Questions that begin with why tend to put people on the defensive. The person is likely to give some excuse rather than explain what the real problem is. The counselor can be misled by the quick and defensive answer to "why" questions.

Summarizing pulls together all the information that a person has given. It is also a way for the counselor to check his understanding of what the person has said. Summarizing is done by restating the message in the counselor's own words and watching the person's reaction. This prevents a person from rambling on once a topic has been thoroughly discussed. It clarifies what has been said and stimulates further discussion.

Interpreting is similar to summarizing except that the counselor gives the person a new frame of reference or way of looking at something. Its purpose is to develop a total picture of the problem so that the person can view the problem differently than before. The counselor may suggest how others may view the situation. It is hoped that the person will better understand the nature of the problem and be able to deal with it.

Informing is giving information that may help or change the person's views. The information may have come from what the person has just said. The person can also be confronted with information provided by the counselor. The information may be needed by the person to continue or may be an answer to something he has asked the counselor. Informing can also be used to show the person his behavior that may lead to further conflicts, trouble and confusion.

Problem Solving

Guiding skills can add structure and organization to counseling. A counselor uses problem-solving and decision-making skills to help the person reach a solution. It is relatively simple to use these skills when using the directive approach. It is not so simple to guide the person through the process of examining the situation, setting a goal and then figuring out how to reach it. The person should be led through the steps in such a way that he figures out what needs to be done.

There are seven basic steps of problem solving, decision-making and planning. The steps can sometimes help us to structure counseling. These steps are examples of guiding remarks that may fit each step, depending on the situation.

1- Identify the problem. What is the cause of this problem? What is the biggest source of trouble? Tell me about what's wrong. Why are these problems for you? How did this happen? I'd like to hear how you think things got this way. Let's list all your concerns; then we'll prioritize them.

2- Gather information. Let's get the facts. What's the background of this? Who is involved? What has been done? Tell me how this works? Describe some examples of that.

3- Develop courses of action. What do you want? How would you like things to be? What are some ways to do that? How could you get things to be the way you want? Let's figure out what can be done. What else might work?

4- Analyze and compare courses of action. I'd like to hear about that. What are some problems with doing that? What makes that better? How come you are concerned with that? What are the disadvantages? What does that have to do with the problem? Will this get you what you want? How will this affect our organization?

5- Make a decision and select a course of action. What solution will work best? Which one do you like? Can you describe the most likely answer? You need to pick a course of action. It's time for you to make a decision.

6- Make a plan. What are your next steps? How do you get that done? Now you need a plan. How are you going to do that? Who's got to do what? What else must happen? What could go wrong? How can you avoid that?

7- Implement the plan. If you don't have any other concerns, you're ready to go. Now it's time for you to act. Okay, get started. I think you've got things figured out; it's up to you now.

Motivation

Performance counseling informs people about their jobs and the expected performance standards and provides feedback on actual performance. The purpose of counseling may be to help a person maintain or improve a satisfactory level of performance or improve performance that is below standards. Good leaders issue clear guidance and then give honest feedback to let people know how they have performed.

Honest feedback is essential for motivating people and controlling an organization's performance. The leader first observes the person's performance, their ability to complete an assignment and their approach to accomplishing a mission. The leader then tells the person where they stand. Those things that have been done well or that show improvement must be praised. Feedback should also include ways to improve performance. Performance counseling needs to be done continuously as part of the leader's role as a teacher and as a coach. Regardless of how it is conducted, performance counseling must be a teaching process with continuous growth and development. Through personal growth, people realize their full potential. Growth and motivation are stimulated by the challenge of a person's job and by the guidance and encouragement of the organization leaders.

The opportunity for learning to take place results from conditions created by the leader. Motivation, in turn, results from learning and is greatly influenced by personal values. Those conditions under the leader's control that stimulate learning and motivation include the following: The accurate evaluation of performance is key; Rapport between leader and subordinate; Clear and understandable communication between leader and subordinate; Mutual agreement concerning performance areas where improvement is required; Specific actions for improving performance; Feedback on progress; and expectation of success.

Performance counseling begins with evaluating the person's performances or actions. It should be restricted to appraising and discussing observed actions and demonstrated behavior rather than diagnosing character or suspected attitudes. The emphasis is on exchanging information about performance, not emotion. The emphasis on talking about specific actions applies to improved and positive performance as well. Praise and recognition are important.

Methods or actions to improve performance need to be discussed. In many cases, people know when they have failed or have not done well, especially if they know the standards. Some people require that the counselor be directive and list item by item what must be done to improve. Other people, with some nondirective guidance, can figure out what to do. Determining ways to improve is based on the leader's first evaluation of the person's performance. Specific actions must be viewed to figure out why a person is below standards in a given area. It may be that the person does not know how or does not want to do something or that something prevents proper performance. For each reason, the steps needed to improve performance are different. If a person does not know how to do something, he needs to take steps to practice and learn. A person who does not want to do something may just need to understand the reasons. By discussing specific actions, the leader will be far more effective in helping people to improve their performance.

Personal Counseling

Personal counseling involves helping a person solve a personal problem. Problems may vary from financial matters to marital difficulties. The emphasis must be to help the person solve their own problems. A person may ask to talk to the leader about a problem or someone else may refer them for counseling. Sometimes a need for personal counseling may be indicated during a performance counseling session or by a change in the person's behavior. The goal remains the same, help the person develop initiative, recognize their problems and solve their own difficulties. In personal counseling, the counselor must always consider the person's point of view. What a leader views as simple or minor may look overwhelming to the person.

Successful personal counseling follows two basic guidelines. First, the leader must be committed to the principle that every person, regardless of position with the organization, has the right to be heard. The leader should use counseling techniques that help subordinates clarify their feelings and consider alternate courses of action in solving their problems. The leader must not look down on people because they have personal problems. With this attitude, the person is never treated as a person and is less important than the counselor. The leader, as counselor, becomes a helper whose authority, training and technical expertise permits better understanding and acceptance of the subordinate who asks for help.

Second, the leader should realize that relatively mature and healthy personnel can look at their personal problems intelligently and reach satisfactory solutions. While people may seek help thinking through a problem, they should be free to choose their own solutions. A person should not be pushed into solutions that were selected by a counselor in answer to the person's personal problem. The person will not learn to find solutions if they are always given. The person cannot take credit for the success of someone else's solution. The person can shift blame for failure to the counselor.

The person should be helped to think through their problem and how they feel about it and to understand their involvement and what they want to have happen. To do this they must feel at ease with the counselor. Talking openly to someone about a personal problem is seldom easy. The counselor must listen to and understand the problem and try to get the person to define just what the problem is and what must be done. Once personal problems are resolved, people can more effectively perform their duties.

Leaders will find they are limited as counselors. They cannot help everyone in every situation. Not even professional counselors with a counseling degree can provide all the help every person in trouble needs. Leaders must recognize their limitations and offer only that kind of help for which they are trained and qualified.

The leader's experience, maturity and attitude are vital in influencing people to remain in the organization. Leaders must not only know their subordinates well, they must also be well-informed on professional development requirements and educational goals. Certain professional development opportunities for additional schooling, special programs or future assignments will be viewed differently by different people. A concerned and knowledgeable leader can help a person to determine those areas where he can make the greatest contribution. The more leaders know about their subordinates and current programs, the better equipped they will be to provide worthwhile career guidance. Preparation is needed for career counseling. To conduct effective career counseling the leader must know and understand the person. Be aware of the person's attitudes, motivations and skills. Be completely familiar with the advantages and benefits within the organization. Know the options available to the person. Identify which options are in the best interest of the person.

Action

Understanding without action is a waste of time. Many people read how-to books, attend how-to seminars and do nothing other than read more books, attend more seminars, and engage in more wishful thinking. While these activities become forms of therapy for some individuals, they should lead to positive actions. Goals give a sense of direction and purpose, force us to plan ahead and give us a clear understanding of what is expected. Leaders commit, even when and especially when it doesn't feel good to stay in a commitment. That really is what commitment is all about, acting and leading even when it is painful.

People aren't working to make me more successful, they are working to make us more successful in every way. We are all in this together. People don't lead to the top alone. You can't be a leader if you have no followers. The more people you attract to your team, the more likely you will succeed. Beating people down only drives away the real winners and destroys those that could became winners.

You must show appreciation for a job well done and encouragement when things do not go according to plan. Leaders find a way to give their people what they need when they need it. People of character make a point of making sure they do not compromise the overall good or doing what is right in the process of seeking any particular goal. Self-disciplined people know how to set a goal, define the steps to accomplish the goal and take each step, even though each one might be more painful than the one before.

The first thing you have to evaluate is what you want. Define it. Once you do, you can start changing the circumstances to achieve it. Such planning refreshes your outlook and reinforces your determination to move forward. It allows you to recognize and examine your strengths and weaknesses and take advantage of the knowledge to move at a faster pace to achieve your goal. It adds a planning tool to your life and puts you in control.

List your goals in writing, on paper. You need to be able to see your goals if you want to obtain them. Your goals should be listed on one page of paper and broken down into three parts; short term, long term, and life's goals. The short term is two years, long term is ten years, and life's goals are just that.

Control

Hard work is not stress. It's fun to work hard on things you've got under control. What does cause stress is loss of control. When you raise your control level, you lower the element of stress. Setting goals for yourself and achieving them can help give you the control over your life that will help to reduce stress. You are happier in life if you know what your goals are. Find out what you really want out of life. What would make you happy? Map out a plan to make it happen.

Make a game plan for your dream. You'll be able to think with improved clarity after doing your game plan. You can't formulate a game plan without looking at what's going on in the real world. The dream world must wait a little longer. Have patience, you'll get there. At this point you should be thoroughly convinced that your dream is obtainable if you do what's needed.

If you learn to accept the things in life that you cannot change and the things you have no control over; then you start to relieve yourself of a major burden. Quit worrying about these things. On the other hand, if you can recognize the things you can change, the things you have some measure of control over and start doing something to change them, you have started to change your life. It won't give you a higher IQ, and it won't change your basic physical appearance, but it will change your outlook on life and start to give you the opportunity to plan and control a large part of your life. It will help you discover your natural resources and use them to their fullest. It will help you build the confidence in yourself that you need to pursue your dream. Hindsight is always better than foresight. Learn from your past, it's still your best reference material.

You've identified your dream or where you want to be, determined that you have the right stuff and identified your strengths and weaknesses. Now you can begin to map out your game plan. Keep your plan flexible enough so that you will not be thrown into a tailspin if a disaster hits or be unable to respond to a sudden opportunity if it arises. Keep your eyes on your dream, but also keep your eyes open to the outside world.

Where and when do you start? You have identified your dream. Treat it as a reality. Your game plan will be a map of how to get there. Now that you have clearly and realistically identified the things that must be done to make your dream come true, you must take action to make them start happening. An action plan identifies what you must do, where you must do it, when you must do it, how you must do it and how much it will cost in time as well as money.

Be realistic, and don't try to achieve them overnight. Work in some time for relaxation and exercise. Pace yourself. Getting started and staying with it becomes a long process. If you don't stay with it every day, like everything else, it will become something you think about or work on occasionally. You must try to work on your action plan as a daily routine, then after a while you will work on your plan constantly without conscious thought.

Your action plan should include everything necessary to achieve your dream. The components of the action plan become a series of short-range goals. Review your action plan until you are absolutely positive it is achievable in terms of time and costs involved. After it's completed to your satisfaction, start putting it to work. Decide on a start date and stop procrastinating. Your action plan is a map to lead the way. If you make a little detour occasionally, that's okay. At least you have a map to guide you back.

If you are not making the kind of progress you had planned on a year ago, review all aspects of your game plan and action plan to find where you haven't progressed. Isolate these items and make part of next year's plan a concentrated effort to correct them. You may even want to re-evaluate your dream goal. If you are happy with your progress, don't lay back and become lazy in the New Year. Make a new plan and use it to improve upon your strengths and progress. Consider this Chinese proverb: The journey of a thousand miles begins with a single step. Once you take that first step, you're well on your way. The first step is the hardest. Once you've taken it, celebrate. Be proud of yourself.

A leader must have good time management techniques and skills to set goals. There are basic techniques to good time management skills. Time is NOW. The challenge is to get a greater return on the same amount of time invested. Distinguish between self-imposed and other-imposed time. Log time occasionally to discover where time goes. Have an organization system that keeps you organized. Be aware of bandits and thieves of time, stress, performance; money is at stake. Time barriers, resolve them, prevent them, or cope with them to minimize their negative consequences. First things first, know the priorities. Make excellent use of Prime Time. Set deadlines and goals that's consistently reachable. Celebrate "on time" victories and enjoy the success of effective time management techniques.

Beliefs

It takes beliefs, values and norms to build character. As a leader, you are responsible for understanding and directly transmitting values to your people. Beliefs are assumptions or convictions you hold as true about something, concept or person. They can range from the very deep seated beliefs you hold concerning such things as religion and the fundamentals upon which this country was established to recent experiences which have affected your perception of a particular person, concept or thing.

As a person of character, we must lead our children by giving them a role model to follow. When our children have a clear role model, they know how to function when they assume the responsibility of marriage and parenting. Children are the hope of the next generation. They are the parents of tomorrow. They must know who they are and what they are to do. They must see their role model in action. Be a person of integrity. That means going all out in everything you do. When you say something, you can count on it, take it to the bank. If I say I'm going to do something, you can consider it done. The first time I violate that, my credibility is shot. Our reputation is only as good as our last performance.

You have beliefs about human nature, what makes people tick. We usually cannot prove our beliefs, but we think and feel that they are true. Some people believe that a car is simply a means of transportation. Others believe a car is a status symbol. There are leaders who believe that rewards and punishment are the only way to motivate people. In contrast, other leaders believe that rewards and punishment should be used only in exceptional cases. The important point to recognize is that people generally behave in accordance with their beliefs. The beliefs of a leader impact directly on the leadership climate, cohesion, discipline, training and effectiveness of the organization.

Values

Our lives are filled with everyday questions of fact and finance. But the really fundamental questions of our lives are questions of neither fact nor finance. The really fundamental questions are questions of value. These are the deep questions that apply to every aspect of our lives. What is it that gives something genuine value? What things are really worth striving for? What is it that makes life worth living? Are there values that transcend cultural differences? Can we have ethical values without religion? If the universe operates in terms of deterministic laws, how can there be real choice? Is all value subjective?

Values are attitudes about the worth or importance of people, concepts or things. Values influence your behavior because you use them to decide between alternatives. You may place value on such things as truth, money, friendships, justice, human rights or selflessness. Your values will influence your priorities. Strong values are what you put first, defend most and want least to give up. Individual values can and will conflict at times. If you incorrectly reported something to your leader, do you have the moral courage to correct the report even if you know your leader will never discover you sent the incorrect report? In this situation, your values on truth and self interest will collide. What you value the most will guide your actions. The proper course of action is obvious. There are times, however, when the right course of action is not so clear.

The following are four individual values that all true leaders are expected to possess: courage, candor, competence and commitment. These four values are considered essential for building the trust which must exist for an organization to operate at peak efficiency.

1- Courage is overcoming fears of bodily harm and doing your duty. Moral courage is overcoming fears other than bodily harm while doing what ought to be done. Moral courage is as important as physical courage. It is the courage to stand firm on your values, your moral principles and your convictions. You show moral courage when you do something based on one of your values or moral principles, knowing that the action may not be in your best interest. It takes special courage to support unpopular decisions and to make it difficult for others to do the wrong thing. Others may encourage you to embrace a slightly unethical solution as the easiest or most convenient method. Do not ease the way for others to do wrong, stand up for your beliefs and what you know is right. Do not compromise your professional ethic or your individual values and moral principles. If you believe you are right after sober and considered judgment, hold your position.

2- Candor is being frank, open, honest and sincere with yourself and the people around you. It is an expression of personal integrity. If handled properly, disagreeing with others and presenting your point of view are not wrong. Remember these three important points. Select the right time and place to offer your criticism or advice. Do not criticize a plan without giving a constructive alternative. Recognize that when your leader has made the final decision, you must end your discussion and support legal and proper orders, even if you do not personally agree with them. There is often not time to verify reports or to question the accuracy of information. Demand it from your subordinates and expect it from your peers and superiors. Candor expresses personal integrity.

3- Competence is proficiency in required professional knowledge, judgment and skills. Each leader must have it to train and to develop a cohesive, disciplined organization with all the required individual and collective skills to be successful in your organization. Competence builds confidence in one's self and one's organization. Both are crucial elements of morale, courage, and ultimately a very successful organization.

4- Commitment means the dedication to carry out all of the organization's missions and to serve the values of the organization. This is shown by doing your best to contribute to the organization and to help your people develop professionally and personally.

Norms

Norms are the rules or laws based upon beliefs and values that members of a group follow to live in harmony. Norms can fall into one of two categories. Formal norms are official standards or laws that govern behavior. Traffic signals, the Uniform Code of Military Justice and the Geneva Conventions are formal norms that direct the behavior of American Soldiers. They dictate what actions are required or forbidden. Informal norms are unwritten rules or standards that govern the behavior of group members.

Beliefs, values and norms guide the actions of individuals and groups. They are like a traffic control system; they are signals giving direction, meaning and purpose to our lives. Individual values, beliefs, and attitudes are shaped by past experiences involving such things as family, school, work and social relationships. Leaders must understand the importance of nurturing and shaping beliefs and values in their subordinates because they are fundamental motivating factors.

As a leader, you have the power to influence the beliefs and values of your people by setting the example. You influence by recognizing behavior that supports professional beliefs, values, and norms, and by planning, executing, and assessing both realistic individual and collective training.

Training conducted to standards will teach your people to do things as individuals and as a team that they did not believe possible. It will give your people confidence in themselves, in each other and in you. If properly explained, it will help each person understand the linkage and the importance of their ability to perform individual tasks properly in support of the organization's collective mission.

Character

As a leader, you must respect your people and must earn their respect if you are to influence their beliefs and values. Subordinates will always respect your position, but they will base their genuine respect on your demonstrated character, knowledge and professional skills. Once your people respect you and want your approval, you can guide them to demonstrate unselfish concern for the organization and for other people. They will become concerned with excellence in everything that relates to the organization if this is the value you demonstrate. If your people respect and admire you, they want to be like you and they naturally tend to adopt your professional beliefs and values as their own. You can reinforce this behavior with positive feedback and by praising them for things they do that supports the organization. Praise, however, can be cheapened, either by overuse or when it is not sincere. It's easy to have strong character when things are going right. However, you will see a person's true character when something goes wrong.

As a person of character, you must stand up for what you believe to be right. A person may go through many situations within one's lifetime, but there is only one question - what will you do when you are challenged? Character describes a person's inner strength and is the link between values and behaviors. A person of character does what he believes right, regardless of the danger or circumstances. A person's behavior shows his character. In tough situations, leadership takes self-discipline, determination, initiative, compassion and courage. There is no simple formula for success in all the situations you may face. The key is to remain flexible and attempt to gather as many facts as the circumstances will allow before you make a decision. When dealing with others, every situation has two sides, so listen to both. The way you handle problems depends on the interaction of the factors of leadership, the led, the leader, the situation, and communications.

Character can be strong or weak. A person with strong character recognizes what he wants and has the drive, energy, self-discipline, willpower and courage to get it. A person with weak character does not know what is needed and lacks purpose, willpower, self-discipline, and courage. A person who can admit when he is wrong is exhibiting strong character. Some believe that apologizing is a sign of weakness and causes a leader to lose power, quite the contrary, admitting when you have made a mistake takes humility and moral courage. We are all human and we all make mistakes. Although placing blame on someone or something else when a mistake is made may be tempting, it indicates weak character, which your people will readily recognize.

Your people assess your character as they watch your day to day actions. They know if you are open and honest with them. They see whether you are indecisive, lazy or selfish. They will quickly determine whether you know and enforce standards. Your people's perceptions of your actions combine to form a continuing assessment of your character. People want to be led by leaders who will provide strength, inspiration, and guidance and who will help them become winners. Whether or not they are willing to trust their lives to a leader depends on their assessment of that leader's courage, competence and commitment.

Building character demands the honesty to determine your own character weaknesses. Have you demonstrated the self-discipline and will on which strong and honorable character is based? How have you handled the tough situations? Sometimes you are the best judge of your strengths and weaknesses. Other times you may have blind spots that keep you from seeing your own weaknesses. You must be open to feedback and advice. However, you must take the responsibility for continually building and strengthening your character. Others can help, but they cannot do it for you. To build strong and honorable character, you should assess the present strength of your values and character. Determine what values you want to promote. Seek out missions and situations that support developing such character. Select a role model that demonstrates the values and character you are trying to develop.

You build strong and honorable character by hard work, study and challenging experiences. You must develop habits that force you to continually develop your mind and character. The better you understand yourself, the easier it is to exercise your will and self-discipline and the more you strengthen your character. The character you want to instill in your people, that you should attempt to exhibit in the daily example you set, should be consistent with the values of courage, candor, competence and commitment. As a leader, you must teach and demonstrate the right values and norms of working, training, and living.

You must understand human nature. There is good and bad in everyone. A leader must bring out the good in each person. You must be able to eliminate counterproductive beliefs, values and behaviors and help a person develop character if he wants to change. Many people want to improve, but they need discipline and organization, a good role model and a positive set of beliefs, values, and habits to pattern themselves after. You, as a leader, must both demonstrate by example and assist in establishing the conditions for that individual, which will encourage the change.

Gaining the respect of people is important. A respected leader influences people by teaching, coaching, counseling, training, disciplining and setting a good example. Respected and successful leaders create a leadership climate that causes most people to develop the right professional values and character. Leaders can often change people's motivation from self-interest to selfless service to their organization. You have another major responsibility in developing character. You give your people confidence that they can develop their character. Convince your people that you are on their side, helping them. Their belief that you sincerely care about them and want them to develop the correct values and behaviors helps give them confidence to become able people with strong and honorable character.

Right Ethical Choice

Ethics are principles or standards that guide professionals to do the moral or right thing, what ought to be done. As a leader, you have three general ethical responsibilities. First, you must be a good role model. Second, you must develop your subordinates ethically. Finally, you must lead in such a way that you avoid putting your subordinates into ethical dilemmas. Whether you like it or not, you are on display at all times. Your actions say much more than your words. Subordinates will watch you carefully and imitate your behavior. You must accept the obligation to be a worthy role model and you cannot ignore the effect your behavior has on others. You must be willing to do what you require of your people and share the dangers and hardships.

You must shape the values and beliefs of your people to support the values of the organization. You develop your subordinates by personal contact and by teaching them how to reason clearly about ethical matters. You need to be honest with them and talk through possible solutions to difficult problems. Share your thought process with your subordinates when you make a decision that has an ethical component, when time permits. They will respect you for caring enough to discuss your personal thoughts with them and they will learn from you. Being sensitive to the ethical elements is a large part of developing your people.

Your goal is to develop a shared ethical perspective so that your people will act properly in the confusion and uncertainty of any given situation. Unless they have learned how to think clearly through ethical situations, they may not have the moral strength to do what is right. As I attended the United States Army Sergeant Major Academy, I was required to write an ethics thought paper. Leaders must always set an ethical example and develop our Soldiers ethically. Do we question the values in our Armed Services and the American society today? Does the world question the values of our Commander-in-Chief? Has the values of the American people changed from our founding fathers over 200 years ago? If so, what would our founding fathers say about our values in today's society?

The Uniform Code of Military Justice (UCMJ) outlines the rules and regulations of the United States Army. Sometimes these rules and regulations are not clearly defined. Sometimes we will find ourselves in a situation where the right ethical choice is unclear. True ethical dilemmas exist when two or more deeply held values collide. Now what do we do? The Army provides us with an ethical decision making process. We must interpret the situation, decide what the ethical dilemma is, analyze all the factors and forces that relate to the dilemma, choose the course of action we believe will best serve the nation, and implement the course of action. The Army has clearly defined everything for us, right?

I don't think so. Leaders have three general ethical responsibilities. First, become strong role models. Second, we must develop our people ethically. Finally, we must lead in such a way that we avoid putting our people into ethical dilemmas.

Character describes a person's inner strength and is the link between values and behaviors. We may have strong or weak character. We will face many situations and there is not a simple formula for success. Some of us believe that apologizing is a sign of weakness and causes a leader to lose power. Some of us will say that admitting when we have made a mistake takes humility and moral courage. We are all human and we will make mistakes. People will normally emulate their leaders. Leaders must lead by example and reinforce honesty and fairness. We must teach and educate people each day, 24 hours a day, seven days a week, and 365 days a year. Leaders must practice ethical problem solving daily and not just set the example, but be the example. We must become role models and do the right thing. Leaders must train people in recognizing areas of ethical dilemmas. Again, we must be the example for our people daily, then our people will respond in a positive professional manner.

In 2000 the Army developed a vehicle to personalize the seven Army values. Soldiers will carry the Army Soldier's card with the Armed Forces Identification Card and wear the tag in the same manner as their identification tags. The cards and tags will serve as tools for leaders to help the Army to focus on its core values. The Army's seven core values are: loyalty, duty, respect, selfless-service, honor, integrity and personal courage. Loyalty: Bear true faith and allegiance to the United States Constitution, the Army, your unit, and other Soldiers. Duty: Fulfill your obligations. Respect: Treat people as they should be treated. Selfless-Service: Put the welfare of the nation, the Army and your Soldiers before your own. Honor: Live up to all the Army values. Integrity: Do what's right, legally and morally. Personal Courage: Face fear, danger or adversity (physical or moral). Therefore, we have a nice term "LDRSHIP" for the seven core values. But has anything changed?

With all of the above, we will surely follow the Army's management philosophy. Do the right things, the right way, for the right reasons, and constantly strive for improvement. Somehow, I still don't think so. At the United States Army Sergeants Major Academy, much emphasis is placed on physical fitness, weight control, diet and nutrition, stress management, leadership styles, Army writing, and ethical fitness as leaders, but what about our spiritual fitness? Spiritual fitness is perhaps the most important of all. We must train ourselves and our people to always do the right thing. As George C. Marshall stated on spiritual activities, "The Soldier's heart, the Soldier's spirit, the Soldier's soul are everything. Unless a Soldier's soul sustains him, he cannot be relied on and will fail himself, his commander, and his country in the end." But perhaps you can have spiritual fitness without believing in God; by believing in yourself and the people around you.

Our ethical dilemmas can and will challenge the best of us. As leaders, will we always do the right things? Sometimes we will and sometimes we won't. I believe the things that we do are based upon our character and the way we view life in general. Our character at times is strong and at other times it may be weak. As leaders, it's easy to always do the right thing when we have everybody watching us, but what happens when nobody is watching? When we have our ethical dilemmas, perhaps we should ask ourselves a simple question. What would you do if your children, spouse, parents or someone you didn't want to let down was watching?

My son is very important in my life. As a Father, it's important that I'm a good role model for him because I know that he will do whatever I do, right or wrong. My wife and I have been married for many years and I love this woman so much. We are almost like one person as we grow old together. She has given me my one and only son. My parents are my role models and they are the ones that bought me into this world. My parents have been married for over 50 years and they have always been there for me, no matter what. I would never want to do anything that would hurt my son, wife or parents. My role model growing up in high school was my basketball coach. Because of him, I kept my grades up, did not drink or smoke and stayed out of trouble. One of the reasons that I made Sergeant Major is because of this man. I would not want to do anything that would disappoint my basketball coach.

As leaders, we are responsible for understanding and directly transmitting values to the people around us. True leaders have ethical responsibilities such as beliefs, values, norms, character, and an ethical decision making process. Whether we like it or not, we are on display at all times. Our actions say much more than our words. People will watch us carefully and imitate our behavior. We must accept the obligation to become a worthy role model and we cannot ignore the effect our behavior has on others. We must be willing to do what we require of our people and share the dangers and hardships. As true leaders, no matter what, always do the right thing. Regardless of the source of pressure, we know in our heart the right thing to do. The real question is whether we have the character to live by sound professional values when under pressure. We may also want to ask ourselves, what would our founding fathers say about our values today?

Since your people will want to please you, do not ask them to do things that will cause them to behave unethically to please you. Here are some examples that can get you into trouble; I don't care how you get it done - just do it, there is no excuse for failure, can do, zero defects, covering up errors to look good, telling superiors what they want to hear, making reports say what your leader wants to see, setting goals that are impossible to reach and loyalty up, not down. These examples may seem as though they would never be a problem for you. Do not assume this is true for others. Learn to give orders and lead without creating these kinds of dilemmas for your subordinates.

I would like to focus on this point again. Regardless of the source of pressure to act unethically, you know in your heart the right thing to do. The real question is whether you have the character to live by sound professional values when under pressure. If you have the right beliefs and values, the thing to do in most situations will be clear and you will do it. Sometimes you will find yourself in complex situations where the right ethical choice is unclear. True ethical dilemmas exist when two or more deeply held values collide. In such situations, using a decision-making process can help you identify the course of action that will result in the greatest moral good. Following are the steps of an ethical decision-making process to help you think through ethical dilemmas: Interpret the situation; what is the ethical dilemma? Analyze all the factors and forces that relate to the dilemma. Choose the course of action you believe will best serve the organization. Implement the course of action you have chosen.

Your integrity is one of the best friends that you will ever have. When the people around you know that you're a person of integrity, they know that you want to influence them because of the opportunity to add value to their lives. They don't have to worry about your motives. A person of integrity influences others because he wants to bring something to the table that will benefit them. If you're a basketball fan, you probably remember Red Auerback, president and general manager of the Boston Celtics from 1967 to 1987. He truly understood how integrity adds value to others, especially when people are working together on a team. His method of recruiting was different from that of most NBA team leaders. When reviewing a prospective player for the Celtics, his primary concern was the young man's character. He figured that the way to win was to find players who would give their best and work for the benefit of the team.

I believe that laws and ethical principles must come from human reason and compassion. Therefore, I have my own view on the ten commandments:

1- Seek the best in yourself and in others, and believe in your own ability to make a positive difference in the world.

2- Pursue truth and honesty in all you do. Be wary of allowing power, status, or possessions to substitute for moral courage, dignity, and goodness.

3- Be positive and constructive rather than negative and disrespectful.

4- To be healthy, you must balance work, play and rest.

5- All members of the family should respect each other.

6- Do not commit murder.

7- Do not be unfaithful to your spouse.

8- Do not seal.

9- Do not lie or speak badly about others.

10- When you see nice things owned by others, let them be your inspiration, rather than a source of bad feelings. If there are things that you want, work hard to get them.

— 5 —

Philosophical Point of View

Perhaps more than any other discipline, philosophy is best understood as a great conversation held across hundreds of years. All philosophers, and we are all philosophers or their followers, have the same eternal questions. Philosophy is all about arguing. Everything can be questioned and everything is up for debate. Some questions might not have answers. Suffering does exist on planet Earth. If God can do anything, he must not want to prevent suffering. But if God does not want to prevent suffering, he can not be perfectly good. Therefore, there is no all powerful and perfectly good being. Religious belief is not necessary for anyone to be a good person. The objectivity of moral value is simply independent of God's existence. We must do what is right simply because it is right.

The goal is to figure out what is true about the universe. Whether or not it had a beginning and if it did, how it begun. How the universe operates and how planet Earth developed into what it is today. Can Christians maintain their faith without defending the historical reality of Christ walking on Earth? Religion tells us how to live. It instructs us on how to treat each other and how to treat the planet we live on. Religious faith is a war with rationality. There is indeed mystery in life. There are a lot of unanswered questions of vital importance on planet Earth. What is it all about? It's commonplace that many parents attempt to realize themselves through their children's lives. They come up short by the fact that their children are independent people with projects and lives of their own.

The Bible

The Bible is perhaps the most important book on this planet. What do we really know about the Bible? Have you read the complete Bible? What about the Old Testament or the New Testament? Is everything in the Bible completely true? Do you understand the language, which language, has the language been translated correctly, the true meaning, the intent of the words in the Bible? Is the Bible complete or incomplete? Are you a believer or a non-believer? These are all interesting questions in the world that we live in today. I would like to apply some basic common reason to some issues in both the Old and New Testaments.

Are we a part of God's working life? We soon realize that we are included in the conversation. The Bible is not only written about us, but to us, perhaps to teach and guide us in this world that we live in. What is going on in this world in which we find ourselves? First, it's important to just read, leisurely and thoughtfully. As we read and the longer we read, we begin to get it or understand it to some degree. We are in conversation with God. Bible reading does not introduce us to a nice world. For most of us it takes years and years to exchange our dream world for this real world. This is not an escape from reality, but a true look into more reality. God does not force any of this on us. We are given space and freedom to enter into the conversation. We read in order to live our true selves, not just to get information to raise our standard of living. Bible reading is listening to God.

How do we fit into things? God is presented to us not in ideas and arguments, but in events and actions that involves each of us personally. But who are we? We make a lot of mistakes during our lives. Growing up in God takes a very long time. Maybe this is just part of the process. We try to reduce God to a size that conveniently fits our plans and interests. God can not fit into our plans; we must fit into his plans. The Bible is a kind of instruction, preparation for living holy in a culture that does not have an idea what holy is. God is actually present with us and every detail of our lives is affected by the presence of God. Embracing what God does for you is the best thing you can do for him. You'll be changed from the inside out. God brings the best out of you.

Life is not simple and we need help. We need help growing up. We learn how to deal with sin in oneself and others. Is God up in heaven, looking down on Earth, thinking all is well? Nobody suggests that life is simple; we all need a lot of help. We sin everyday, you name it and we do it. Impersonal forces and egos compete for the last word in power. Human beings, no matter how well intentioned or gifted, don't seem to be able to represent God's rule anywhere close to satisfactory. The rule is work from within, much of the time invisible and unnoticed.

There is always more than one way to tell a story. Gods' people are in danger of losing touch with what made them Gods' people in the first place. There is no true storytelling without names. Therefore, the Bible is filled with names. We are never out of danger in this lifetime. Listening and following God's words are the primary ways in which we keep obedient to the living presence of God among us. Work, by its very nature, is holy. All jobs are important to mankind; from the grass cutter to the medical doctor. Neither job is more or less important than the other.

It seems odd that the awareness of God, or even of the people of God, brings out the worst in some people. There is hardly a culture or century that doesn't eventually find a human determined to rid the world of evidence and reminders of God. When we do wrong, we get punished. Why me? We suffer in the vital areas of family, personal health and material things. There is no real correlation between the amount of wrong we commit and the amount of pain we experience. We do right and get knocked down. Sometimes we may believe that we are doing everything right when suddenly everything goes wrong. We should refuse to accept the role of a defeated victim. If you get knocked down nine times; you get back up the tenth time.

Suffering is a mystery that we learn to respect with time. Perhaps the greatest mystery in suffering is how it can bring a person into the presence of God in a state of worship. We take the good days from God, why not the bad days? Real faith can't be reduced to spiritual success stories. It is refined in the fires and the storms of pain. When we rush in to fix suffering, we need to keep a few things in mind. We don't really understand the full nature of our friends' problems. We need to quit feeling sorry for people who suffer and instead look up to them and learn from them.

Help people and give them thanks. What can you do? Do whatever you can do to help and give thanks. Helping them to give voice to the entire experience of being human, do it honestly and thoroughly. I'm not good enough for this. I'll wait until I clean up my act and prove that I'm a decent person. We tend to think that prayer is what good people do when they are doing their best. It is not. It is the means by which our language becomes honest, true and personal in response to God. They are not the prayers of nice people. I am what I am, both good and evil, doing the best that I can.

Heaven should not be the primary concern. Focus on wisdom. Focus on living everyday on earth as it is in heaven. A college degree is no certification of wisdom. Wisdom has to do with becoming skillful in honoring our parents, raising our children, handling our money, conducting our lives, going to work, exercising leadership and using kind words towards others.

We like verification of credentials. Trouble does require attention; everything that could go wrong did go wrong. What happens when everything you believe in and live by is smashed to bits by circumstances? Most people become closer to God from their troubles, not their good times. Suffering is a huge, unavoidable element in the human condition.

We rarely know what's coming next and not many things turn out the way we anticipate. We are faced with God as he is, not as we imagine him to be. Many times God doesn't seem to make sense to us. We want God to give us an edge in the dog-eat-dog competition of daily life. Everything we do or think or feel has to do with God. Our consequence is Judgment Day. A place of worship is not a building. God doesn't live in a building. In times of crisis, everything, absolutely everything, is important and significant. God and our relationship with God are on the front page. We become preoccupied with ourselves.

Old Testament

As scripture or as the most inspirational piece of literature ever written, the Old Testament is a source of constant wonder, inspiration and intrigue. It has meant more to more people than any other book in history. The cultural influence of this single work is in evidence all around you, in religion, politics, law, philosophy, art and more. It is a narrative of divine action in history that is holy to Jews, Christians and Muslims alike.

The Old Testament was written thousands of years ago in ancient Israel by a variety of different authors. This inescapable fact means that modern readers are often intimidated by this venerable work. Lacking solid background information most of us are confused by the organization of the Old Testament. We do not fully understand the timeline of events and find it difficult to grasp the geography. We are puzzled by the massive cast of characters and the relationships between them.

If we try to do things without God, we will never get it right. Where do we come from and where are we going? We build on what is already there, so we start with Genesis. The stories show clearly that we are never outsiders to anything in heaven and earth. Salvation is the biggest word in the vocabulary of the people of God, especially men and women in trouble. I want to apply some common sense to a few areas within the Old Testament at this point. As I stated earlier, many times God doesn't seem to make sense to us.

Let us make human beings in our image. Focus on "our image". Is there more than one God? God said the man has become like one of us, capable of knowing everything, ranging from good to evil. The word "us" is used, therefore, is there more than one God? Is man God-like by knowing everything, ranging from good to evil?

Cain slept with his wife. Cain is the son of Adam and Eve which God created. Where did Cain's wife come from? Was she his sister? Did God create Adam and Eve, plus more humans that the Bible does not tell us?

God was sorry that he had made the human race in the first place; it broke his heart. "I'm sorry I made them." We are informed that God has this overall master plan for everything, knows everything and is perfect in everyway. Did God make a mistake by making mankind?

God told Noah to take on board seven pairs of every clean animal and one pair of every unclean animal. Why seven pairs of clean animals and only one pair of unclean animals? The flood got worse until all the highest mountains were covered. Everything died. Anything that moved was dead. What about the fish in the seas? What about Noah, his family and the animals in the ark?

God makes a covenant with all living things. Never again will floodwaters destroy all life. The covenant is the rainbow in the clouds. All life was not destroyed by the flood. Does the rainbow tell us that God makes mistakes too?

At one time, the whole Earth spoke the same language. Mankind started building a tower to reach the heavens. God said one people, one language; this is only a first step. No telling what they'll come up with next, they'll stop at nothing. We'll go down and garble their speech so they won't understand each other and scatter them all over the world. Why? What was God afraid of? Why does God not want us to be of one people? What about our spaceship today going into space – into the heavens?

Lot's wife looked back and turned into a pillar of salt. How is it possible for a person to turn into salt or stone? How could this happen?

Take your dear son Isaac whom you love and go to the land of Moriah. Sacrifice him there as a burnt offering on one of the mountains. Would you, as a Father, sacrifice your son? Could you kill your son, just because God told you to?

God said you may not see my face. No one can see me and live. Does this mean we can never see God's face? If we see God, will we die or be dead?

If you sin by not stepping up and offering yourself as a witness to something you have heard or seen in cases of wrongdoing, you will be held responsible. What does this mean? If we know something is wrong and don't step up, will God send us to hell?

Worse yet, we saw descendants of the giant Anak. Everybody we saw was high. They looked down on us as if we were grasshoppers. Did real giants once walk the planet Earth?

Moses reasons with God. If you kill this entire people in one stroke, all the nations that have heard what has been going on will say "Since God couldn't get these people into the land which he had promised to give them, he slaughtered them out in the wilderness. Therefore, is God a God that can be reasoned with? The Bible says that Moses reasoned with God at this point. Can we reason with God?

New Testament

Whether you consider it a book of faith or a cultural artifact, the New Testament is among the most significant writings that the world has ever known. For over a billion Christians, this collection of books has had an incredible impact on history and culture. Yet, despite this importance, the New Testament is also among the most widely disputed and least clearly understood works in history.

In the New Testament God calls all the shots. The New Testament works in harmony with five stories, twenty-one letters and one poem; this is God's word. The first order of business is salvation; Jesus equals Salvation. Salvation is the main business of Jesus. The birth, life, death and resurrection of Jesus are all parts of our lives; work, family, friends, memories and dreams.

Is God on our side? Are we on the side of God? Most people in most centuries have believed in the existence of God or Gods. As common as the belief in God is, there is also an enormous amount of guesswork and gossip surrounding the subject. Does God truly want to save us?

Mary's pregnancy is Spirit-conceived. God's Holy Spirit made her pregnant. Using reason and logic, we know this can not happen. Therefore, how did Mary really become pregnant? Who is the real biological Father of Jesus?

Jesus was taken into the wild by the Spirit for the Test. Jesus prepared for the Test by fasting forty days and forty nights. What would be your state of mind without food for a 40 day period?

The supper for five thousand people consisted of five loaves of bread and two fish. Everyone ate their fill and then they gathered twelve baskets of leftovers. How could this have happened? Therefore, are we saying that all people and all crimes will be forgiven? Seven loaves of bread and a few fish were enough for over four thousand people. The crowd ate its fill and seven sacks of leftover were collected. Once again, how could this have happened? Listen to this carefully. There's nothing done or said that can't be forgiven. Therefore, are we saying that all people and all crimes will be forgiven?

After rising from the dead, Jesus appeared early on Sunday morning to Mary Magdalene. Why was Mary the first one to see Jesus after his rising? What was the relationship between Jesus and Mary? Plus, reason and logic tell us the rising after death just could not have happened.

Human beings have the capacity to generate moral value from within. Religion can actually increase one's psychic distress by populating the world with supernatural beings and powers. We should pursue our goals without illusions, to act morally without hope of reward. The Bible's apparent endorsement of slavery, genocide and collective punishment can be found in the scriptures.

Existence of God

A properly respectful atheist must take religious narratives at face value. The search for meaning, the struggle to overcome weakness, the need to mark ones way in life is the goal. If I genuinely believe that my religion is true and if my religion makes claims that yours rejects, how can I think it's reasonable for you to hold to yours? Plato stated thinking that the existence of God is neither necessary nor sufficient for morality.

If one relied on scriptural evidence, one would have to conclude that God is really evil. The story of Abraham and Isaac, that it's right to obey God even when he commands murder. Religious faith is at odds with ordinary norms of knowledge. There is no master story to tell about the origins or the ultimate future of the world. Human science has learned a great deal we think, but it's nothing of what is left to know. The question about the purpose of life is unanswered. We can have little confidence in the evidence of history being as it is, that truth will win out or that goodness will triumph in the end. Is there a fear of eternal punishment, but no hope of eternal reward? We want simply to explain what we believe and why we believe. In the end, that is the best we can do.

Stories of war, Holocaust, famine, earthquakes, and so on, are in both history and the daily news. Seems outright silly to praise or bless God when we have tragedies such as this all around us. Life is not fair and we all know that. So why should we believe that this universe was created by a being driven by principles of fairness? If the universe was created by a God being of some sort or other, why does this being deserve our worship? Free thinkers have been asking these questions for centuries. What is really important after getting kicked in the teeth by Mother Nature?

I'm most likely to be consistently pragmatic. What I can't calculate is very hard to accept. Sometimes lacking emotion and faith, one understands only cold, hard logic. No God would allow such tragedies to exist and that people can live meaningful, important, rewarding lives without a higher authority such as a God. Few of the most respected and influential scientists and philosophers today are deeply religious, but most philosophers and scientists are skeptical of religion.

Take the interaction between religion and science or philosophy; between faith and reason. They are at war with each other. The idea here is that religious faith is inherently irrational. One can attempt to reason one's way through to religion, which runs directly against one's personal will to the divine will. The directive is to obey, not to think first and then obey, if it seems reasonable to do so.

It certainly looks like the universe is much older than scripture says it is. Did God plant evidence in it that misleads the rational mind? If the creation story is literally true, then the world contains evidence that did mislead many rational minds in order to test our faith. Religious faith is irrational and that one should have faith nevertheless. The rational mind that comes standard with the human body is a gift that God has bestowed on us and we are supposed to use this gift to negotiate the world and to understand God's way. God would not ask anyone to believe something unreasonable. Passages in scripture that do not make sense are not to be understood literally. Every statement in them is true, but not every statement is to be understood literally.

The clash between faith and reason is exemplified in the biblical story of the sacrifice of Isaac. Even if we put the matter of morality aside, the commandment to sacrifice Isaac makes no sense. God had given Abraham and Sarah a son in their old age. At Isaac's birth, Abraham was 100 years old and Sarah was 90 years old. Abraham was explicitly promised that Isaac would have children. Abraham is commanded to give up his son as a sacrificial offering and Abraham tries to obey. God sends an angel to stop Abraham just before he kills Isaac. Abraham had passed this final test with flying colors. Apparently the test was to see if Abraham would obey this command, despite its irrationality and despite its immorality. Sometimes it is outright irrational to have faith and yet one should have this faith regardless. Maybe it takes an Abraham to get to that level of faith and the rest of us should stick to what is moral and rational. A seed of doubt and skepticism is healthy.

Nowadays, we read almost daily about people who kill innocent human beings, claiming that they are doing what God wants. We call them terrorists. Whatever else we may think of such people, I presume that we do not doubt the sincerity of their beliefs. They must be sincere since many of them deliberately kill themselves in the process. No God would want this, we tell ourselves. What's the difference between the near sacrifice of Isaac and contemporary religious terrorism? This is acting in an irrational manner, following ones faith. The focus is on the norm against the deliberate murder of an innocent human being.

The world was literally created in six days almost six thousand years ago and that the theory of evolution was mistaken. There is faith that God literally created the world from nothing in six days. The waters of the Red Sea were parted by God using Moses as his agent. God is above us in heaven watching over us. We are in a search for significance in one's life, lasting significance in particular. The belief in God can turn death from an ultimate end into merely another stage in one's journey.

The idea that there is a supernatural being that created our planet and watches over Earth takes faith and the chosen people are Jewish. I find that idea hard to buy into. I came to the conclusion that all people, even though there are certainly individual differences, are pretty much the same. There are conflicts with very basic moral principles concerning the value of every human life. I can no longer ignore how the ideology of special divine favor is being realized in practice. It can easily be seen as an expression of racial or ethnic superiority, the chosen people. I mostly define myself as an individual with my own projects and interests.

We must take responsibility of ourselves. While taking responsibility for our dark side, also take pride in our achievements. There's a comforting thought that however dark the world seems, the bright light of redemption may be just around the corner. With God gone, so is eternal life. We'll need to confront the reality of death in a new way. Welcome to life as it is rather than how it only seemed to be in your fantasy. Human innocence can no longer be sustained, now that we've eaten from the tree of knowledge. There's no guarantee good will triumph over evil. We must face our death without comfort of an afterlife. Religion is a fundamental fact of life for people. You can not ignore it and its effects. It penetrates intellectual life, social life, political life and daily life.

I don't pretend to have an argument against the existence of God. That seems no more possible to me than an argument for his existence. That is beyond the ability of reason to prove or to disprove. If there is a God, he is infinitely beyond our comprehension, being indivisible and without limits. We are incapable of knowing. Reason can not decide this question. Therefore, there is a fear about what will eventually become of us.

If God exists and you believe in him, then you win infinite happiness. If he exists and you don't believe in him, then you lose. If he doesn't exist, then it doesn't matter whether you believe in him or not. When you consider the probability that God actually exists, choose to believe that God exists. God will move your heart and genuine faith will come. A belief we hold simply because we want to live in a world in which God exists. Does this involve changing the way we look at the world?

The original sin, of course, was the one committed by Adam when he disobeyed God's command not to eat from the tree of knowledge of good and evil. This sin that Adam committed got passed down to the soul of every one of Adam's descendants. Why did God choose to make things so that you inherited your parent's guilt?

How could there be three persons in one God? The Father, the Son, and the Holy Ghost, are all inside of God. How can we believe in something we don't understand? Do we believe in Santa Claus with his flying reindeer? Curiosity is a marvelous thing. One must not take things for granted, one must always ask why. Follow your own conscience and instincts. What about the theory of evolution? If the evolutionary theory is correct, then biological differences are matters of degree. Apes just gradually become people. I think most people identify being religious with being good.

We will not all agree with each other, and given that, we can not all be right. Nothing about the world of experience can be demonstrated with complete certainty. Since no one can prove there is no God, then I'm not irrational if I believe in God. I can not prove that aliens have never visited Earth, but given all the considerations against it, I'd be irrational not to reject the idea. You are certainly entitled to believe whatever you like, if the matter affects you alone. God is to be thanked for the good things that happen but never blamed for the bad. God gets the credit if the outcome is good, but takes no responsibility if it's bad. Sounds like some of our politicians. We expect our politicians to behave like that, but God? Maybe we all should really believe in Santa Claus. If angels are real, then so are demons, and demons could take over your soul.

Why is this world not enough for some of us, and what does believing in God do to mitigate this sense of the world not being enough on its own? What are the alternatives? Heaven, after all, and its alternative, is forever. While this life is here and now, and how short it really is. The simplest answer is that this life is it and that we will not exist when our bodies fall apart. This is very hard to accept for many of us. So we invent another world and the soul will travel to that world when the body dies. This idea makes us feel better about the bodily mortality. God comes in on this way of thinking, which makes both this world and the other world possible.

Why would anyone feel they can't make meaningful life-altering decisions and live a truly meaningful life, if they no longer believe in God? That nothing can really matter if we live in a godless universe. We can not reasonably think there is no value without God. Would someone think this? Is this idea, perhaps, that something can have value only if God pronounces it valuable?

When I looked closely at the Bible, it's confused and arbitrary. I saw more and more inconsistencies. I could not see any reason to drown so many innocent children in Noah's flood. Why didn't God tell Noah to take same children along with the animals on his ark?

Maybe God is not all powerful or not all good. Maybe God is not a person but only an impersonal force or all of nature. Maybe religious language should be understood not as true claims, but merely as expressions of hope or fear. It might make some people feel good to talk about a higher level of existence or a guiding force, but there is no evidence for anything of the sort.

Many children have been born with horrible birth defects that caused them tremendous pain and early death. An all good God would prevent their harms if he could. There is no God who is both all good and all powerful. What does free will have to do with natural evils such as birth defects? Maybe God was teaching a lesson to the child's parents. Maybe mortals are too feeble and ignorant to see the justification for suffering. Maybe God is not subject to our human moral standards. Maybe we need some suffering to make us appreciate the good things in life. Why do we need so much? Why must it be distributed so unevenly? Perhaps we should adopt a more plausible position in which God does not exist. That we do not know whether or not God exists. No proof is possible in this area, but the evidence clearly led to atheism.

There are dangers with religions. Religion leads to wars around the world. It is hard to deny that many wars have been and continue to be fueled in large part by religious beliefs. It is no coincidence that terrorists are so often motivated by religion. It is harder to get non religious people to volunteer as suicide bombers. The dangers of religion are even more evident when abortion doctors are killed by openly religious groups. Scientists talked about the prospects for medical advances from stem-cell research and then some speakers replied that it was immoral on religious grounds.

We have been taught that it is somehow impolite or unconstitutional to criticize religion. Many atheists avoid religion because they find it boring. They don't want to spend their lives talking about God any more than they want to spend their lives talking about UFOs. The reason is that criticism of religious beliefs is often considered impolite or even unconstitutional. Atheists fear that their views will alienate friends and family, not to mention prospective clients and employers. Who would want a friend, hire someone, or vote for anyone with no morals? Most atheists see little to be gained by broadcasting their beliefs.

If God knows everything, he must have foreknowledge of the future, including mankind's ultimate destiny. So our belief that we might determine our destiny by the choices we have yet to make, choices that might go either way, must just be an illusion. If God can do anything he wants to do, then nothing can happen except by his will. If I wind up going to hell, God must have willed that I go to hell. This takes it out of my hands. If I am destined to go to hell, God will not only have known that from eternity, he will also have willed it from eternity.

We are all sinners, who require God's grace if we are to be saved. Once in your life you did something seriously wrong, no doubt all adults are sinners. I don't think many of us get very far in life without doing something that we are ashamed of, but it's absurd to claim that infants in their cribs are sinners. It's believed that infants come into this world tainted by the sin of Adam and Eve. This is the doctrine of original sin. We can not earn salvation by our works. If we are to achieve salvation, it must be by our faith in Jesus alone. It implies that those among us who lack faith in Jesus have not received grace and have not been forgiven. We will, if we continue in that state, go to hell. The idea that all who reject Christian doctrine must be damned, no matter how good they may be by ordinary standards. That these people could not be saved, no matter how good they might otherwise be, if they did not believe in Jesus.

Perhaps some people have sinned on such a grand scale that they deserve the most awful punishment we can imagine. Plausible candidates would be Hitler and Stalin, and others who have been responsible for the torture and murder of millions of people. Most people, whatever their shortcomings, had not sinned so extravagantly that they deserved eternal punishment. The punishment for an offense should be proportionate to its crime.

God tells us to always turn the other cheek. God must give us the opportunity to choose evil. You can't have the one opportunity without the other. If God does not exist, everything is permissible. God must exist if we are to make sense of morality. I was brought up believing that war against Germany was necessary and thought of military service as honor, not a violation of my duty to God. There is much joy in the world, but there is also much suffering. Much of it apparently is undeserved and there is sin. We call these things evil.

If you accept the theory of evolution, you will believe there were other animals on this planet long before humans appeared on the scene. Humans evolved from other species through a long and gradual process during which many of their ancestor species died out.

As God's creatures, our highest loyalty must be to God. This may require the sacrifice of our deepest human loyalties. God is our creator, our Lord and we owe him absolute obedience, no matter what he commands. He might command anything. If there is a God who could command anything, and then there is no act we can safely say is out of bounds. No act of a kind that simply must not be done, not even genocide, a crime I think most of us would shrink from committing, even if we believed God commanded it. If this God exists and we must obey him unconditionally, then anything might turn out to be permissible.

Salvation requires a special connection with God through faith in Christ. This causes conflict between our religious life and rational thought. One should endeavor to think clearly and honestly about things. The Bible has to be interpreted, just as you have to interpret your experiences, and interpreting passages in the Bible requires thinking about them. It is not necessarily the final word about historical or scientific matters. Christian faith is the only way to salvation, the only way to avoid going to hell, this is the idea of faith. So it is crucially important for the ultimate well-being of everyone.

Many people have lived and died without having Christian beliefs and this has happened through no obvious faults of their own. They were simply living their lives in situations where they never had a fair opportunity to become Christians. Would a fair and powerful God permit even those people to suffer in hell after death? The Old Testament's aggressive message of a vengeful God has been superseded by the New Testament's message of love.

We actually don't know. We do not know about Jesus, about his intentions and so forth. The past is irretrievably gone and there is much that we can never know about what happened concerning Jesus. We don't really know exactly what Jesus said, as opposed to what was added later by people who were excited by his life and teachings and who read things into his life story. The past is gone and many questions will simply remain unanswered.

It really could not matter to God whether or not one was a Christian or what one believed about Jesus. God must want us to think about things other than specifically religious beliefs, otherwise God certainly would have made it more obvious, in a general way assessable to everyone. Pay attention to this world. Don't be fixated on some other world. Incarnation can be seen as signifying that we should embrace our physical lives as well as the spiritual. We should dive into human life with all its complications, sorrows and joys. We should take life in one's stride, with all its duties and problems, its successes and failures, its experiences and helplessness. God doesn't really care what we believe about God. God couldn't possibly want me, or any of us, to spend our lives in this amazing world preoccupied with specific abstract religious issues. There is a great deal of suffering in the world, yet happiness is possible.

Even if the odds of God's existing seem very small, hell would be an infinitely horrible outcome compared with what one gives up to devote oneself to God in this life. One should strive to believe in God just to be safe. Is believe in God grounded in fear and pessimism? Things should make sense. This means that faith can not be of utmost importance in this life. One can avoid hell even without knowing about Christ at all in this life. It is only by living completely in this world that one learns to believe.

There is a general social custom of adopting a certain hands-off attitude toward religion, both as a matter of good manners and a principle of public policy. Jokes about specific religious are seen as 'in bad taste'. Conversations between you and your Chaplain are legally privileged. Churches are exempt from taxes. A citizen can be forgiven certain social obligations like military service when the obligations conflict with his religious principles. A way to keep peace in society, and as an acknowledgment of the importance of religion in many people's lives, we make this special allowance. Many people draw strength from their faith. Ideas like the existence of an afterlife where we can rejoin loved ones, or the existence of a God who, in this afterlife, rewards the just and punishes the unjust in accordance with their merits have an uncommon power. If religious faith can play such a role in someone's life, it's only decent to leave well enough alone, even if one takes it to be obvious that the relevant beliefs are false. If a grieving parent believes their child died a hero on the battlefield to whom Soldiers owed their lives and they find their belief in faith helpful, then this can't be a bad thing. This faith can give emotional support to people by providing the hope of a miracle.

There are no atheists in foxholes. There are atheists who have emerged from near death experiences to announce to the world that they have changed their minds. There are supportive themes to be found in every religion the idea that what really matters is in your heart. If you have good intentions, and are trying to do what is right, that is all anyone can ask. Not so in medicine if you are wrong. Your good intentions count for almost nothing. Most religious people will pray about everything. If they really wanted to do something useful, they could devote their prayer time and energy to some pressing project that they can do something about. Prayer simply doesn't work. But we prayed good and hard for the success. What more do you want? If you want to express your gratitude to goodness, you can plant a tree, feed an orphan, buy books for school kids or contribute in thousands of other ways for improvement of life on this planet now and in the near future. God has already redeemed the debt for all time, by sacrificing his own son. Thanking God is just symbolic. We should prefer real good to symbolic good.

A person pays attention to his surroundings and what he is doing. It should be obvious why most people believe in God. The various religious, moral, and life orienting actions that flow from that belief will lend value to one's life. Gods are by definition greater than us, beyond the realm of ordinary human experience. We learn at an early age the mere fact that if something is hidden from sight it does not imply that it's not there. To a large degree, we see what we are conditioned to see and what we expect to see. Perhaps we need to learn to see differently. In part by paying attention to aspects of what one sees that had been invisible and sees them as worthy of our attention. Learn to see our ordinary life and its ordinary surroundings as extraordinary. God is not the only invisible entity in our universe that is worthy of our attention.

I know many good people. I consider them to be good people because they respond with kindness, comfort and help when others are in distress or in need. They are warm, outgoing and compassionate, taking a genuine interest in others' lives. They are optimistic. They see the good in others and to see what's right with the world. They are resilient and are able to bounce back from setbacks, disappointments or personal tragedy. Because they are warm, cheerful, resilient and kind, others appreciate them and admire them.

There are great benefits to a religious life, a way of life inspired by religious values. Perhaps only God can provide the comfort we need when all seems lost. There are non-religious ways of life that are equally admirable and that contain these same great benefits. How kindness, and other admirable traits of character are not only possible, but also probable. Non-religious life that is admirable and worthwhile. We don't need religion to be good friends or good neighbors or to have moral strength.

What is the best life for a human being? Some people will think a happy life is focused on material and sensual gratification, that life of political power and status is the best life for a human being. It must be a life that we create and that is enduring and stable. Happiness is a human achievement. It does not come from God, our abilities to think and figure things out leads us to happiness. We look for reasons for acting or living one way rather than another. A well lived life is stable and enduring, that human happiness is an achievement that can not easily be taken away. Happiness is a human accomplishment. It's not given to us by a God or by faith or by chance.

All that is needed is ordinary reasoning ability and a solid general education. The courageous person is prepared to die for what he believes in. Some people have too little confidence in their own value. These people prefer to do what's easy. They find their pleasure in what others think of them. On the other hand, if people think too highly of themselves, they will act in ways that endanger the pleasures of friendship and social life. Have a strong sense of worth that is based on achievements as evidenced in the exercise of developed abilities.

These attitudes and behaviors emerge naturally, as a result of psychological tendencies we experience in the course of ordinary life. Ideas are important. We need ideals to guide us, both in our personal lives and in our political lives. One doesn't have to be a genius or even an intellectual. But one has to take some joy in the activity of figuring things out. I do live in a society that gives me many opportunities to work to make it better. So it strikes me that religious commitment can bring great benefits. It can provide a guide for how to live one's life, a guide for what is important, valuable and worth pursuing. It ties people together into relationships, friendship and can provide comfort in difficult times.

A commitment can develop a sense of our own value and can explain our willingness to perform acts of human decency to help others in distress and in need. Worth is based on our own achievements, concerned about the good of others and generous in dealings with them. Most people value themselves enough to have the strength and the determination to act on their vision of human good. As a result, people act generously, in good temper with care and concern for the good of others.

There is determination to go beyond acts of ordinary moral decency, to do what is right against great odds and in the face of great danger. People will be willing to risk their lives for what they take to be of the greatest value and worth. People are prepared to die for what they believe in. Sometimes things go badly in our personal lives and we are despondent and want to give up. We need personal courage, the courage to see ourselves through sadness or despair, the courage to pull ourselves up and keep going. In situations like these, we seek comfort from others who care about us and share our values.

God sees what we are going through and God cares about each of us. It will help to know that no matter what we do, God will always love us. For God is always there, right? Perhaps there is no God who loves and cares about human beings, but we have the comfort of family and friends. Friendship is a natural part of human life and without friends we can not live well. A flourishing human being is without question connected to other people, as family members, friends, colleagues, and political citizens. Each time we learn something, we feel that our life is more enjoyable, and that is precisely what we need to feel if we are going to conquer sadness and despair.

Many take comfort in the belief that there exists a God, who both loves humanity and who guarantees, through divine providence, that human history will ultimately culminate in an unqualifiedly good outcome. The long run of history may be a very long run indeed. We have known far more oppression than liberty, far more war than peace, far more famine than plenty. We ask not what we rationally ought to believe, but how, all things considered, we should rationally prefer to live. The answer can not be that we should always rationally prefer to live a life guided by beliefs that are rationally grounded in the evidence or even that we should always prefer that our beliefs be true rather than false.

Whatever else beliefs are, they are instruments for guiding and supporting our practical projects. If holding a belief would be instrumental to the success of a practical project, then that by itself may give us sufficient reason, in particular sufficient practical reason, for adopting that belief, even if that belief is false or unwarranted by the evidence.

Sometimes good evidence is simply not to be had. For creatures like ourselves, belief, or belief like commitment is often required to carry us all the way to action.

God has a plan for the universe. Assuming our freedom, we may either cooperate with that plan or fail to cooperate with it. If God foresees and prepares for all contingencies, then history will culminate in a state of what God wants, no matter our choices. Consequently, it is hard to see how it matters to God's plan what we do. Our freedom and our choices are entirely irrelevant to the outcome of history. If God is prepared for all contingencies, God evidently has no particular need that we perform any particular action. No particular need that we make one choice rather than another.

What matters to God is not the particular outcome. God himself guarantees the particular path that history must travel in order to reach that outcome. Perhaps that is why God rewards those who cooperate with his plan and condemns those who fail to do so. Why should God punish those who fail to cooperate with his plans is something of a mystery? Whatever path we choose, we can not possibly interfere with the ultimate fulfillment of God's divine plan. The universe will be as God wills it to be, no matter what we do. We choose freely at least our own destinies, whatever we will that to be.

Many believe that if God is dead, then everything is permitted, but if everything is permitted, then there really is no distinction at all between what is permitted and what is forbidden, no distinction between right and wrong. In the absence of God, we live in a universe utterly void of meaning, purpose, and value. Deny the existence of God, and resign ourselves to lives utterly devoid of meaning and value, in a universe governed by no moral law. If the universe contains nothing of objective value and no moral absolutes, then human life must, as a consequence, be utterly void of meaning and purpose. Whatever else the universe does or does not contain, we exist in it. We are creatures who value things. We create values. We do so simply by engaging in the merely human and entirely natural activity of taking things that matter to us. We may cry out with longing and despair to the cold uncaring universe to embrace our value, but we will hear only silence in return. The universe is mute to either affirm or deny the worth we place on either ourselves or on others. We do not matter to the universe. We matter to ourselves and sometimes to others, who sometimes matter to us in return.

What, if anything, shall we do, be or believe together as fellow rational beings? This happens when we confront each other with demands for respect and recognition that lies within. So what is the answer? How shall we orient ourselves in a world where nothing is guaranteed to us, where the pursuit of even our deepest most life affirming aspirations may lead us into moral darkness? What could be more exhilarating than to know that it falls entirely in our hands to make the world as we would have it be? If there is to be progress and moral harmony, only we humans can bring them about. Is humanity really capable of building an all encompassing moral order, in which all are valued and respected? Let us try it and see.

Science empowers us it gets us what we want. Science conquers superstitions and gives us a picture of the world, a theory of how the world works. The scientific picture of the world leaves out much that used to prevent us from doing what we want. It excludes from reality all sorts of imaginary beings, forces and powers that constrain us. Science must extend our ability to act, yet by draining meaning or purpose, science threatens to undermine this very capacity. Religious world views may not be true, but we may not be able to do without them unless we can find some other way of to obtain meaning.

Science tells us how to manipulate the world around us, how to bend it to our will. We figured out how living things evolve and replicate. We have conquered many of the major diseases that threaten mankind. One day we might be able to transform ourselves as we can now transform our bodies and the physical world around us. A superstitious belief in these forces might affect what happens in the physical world by influencing the way we behave in it, but the forces themselves have no impact whatsoever.

Science treats human beings as a part of the natural world. It tells us how we work. Once we know how we work, we can devise technologies of self-transformation, ways of making body and mind more pleasing to ourselves. Once our ignorance of the human body was dispelled, it fell under our control, we can cure disease, overcome handicap and remove physical deformities. Now that we are in control of the body, why should we limit ourselves to curing illness? Why shouldn't we improve the body and mold it at will?

The body is a machine that is there to serve our purpose. Once we know how this machine works, we can treat it just as we would our car or our house. Of course we may encounter technical difficulties in dealing with our bodies. The body may fail to do what we want because of disease or physical limitation, but in principle, all such technical obstacles can be overcome given the necessary knowledge and resources. The world puts no value on the life of a human being, only human beings do that.

Human beings don't just want to understand the world, they want to change it and scientists respond to this by giving us technology. To have a purpose is to have a certain combination of beliefs and desires. When we say that a person has a purpose, all we are saying is that they are in a state that will dispose them to behave in certain ways. There's nothing superstitious or mysterious about that. Normally, we act in an effort to satisfy our desires, but once we understand how behavior is caused, once we understand the physical basis of desire, for instance, we can exercise control over our behavior at an earlier stage, by manipulating its causes in the brain. Science tells us that human beings are bags of chemicals. Once we understand human behavior, we can predict and manipulate human behavior, our own included. If man is just a bag of chemicals, once we know what these chemical are, we can remix them at will. By remixing them at will, we can give ourselves whatever character we like. When learning the science of what we actually are, we also learn the science of what we might become.

Belief is a purely personal matter. It is said religions are just cults with armies, but they are also cults with a greater number of practitioners and louder voices, and those greater numbers exert more pressure on children and even adults to join in. What kinds of bodies, if any, will we find ourselves inhabiting after resurrection, or exactly what will happen to non-believers? Religion is not to be taken to describe other worlds, or even past and future events in this world, but only to orientate us toward this world. It is symbolic or expressive, orientating us toward each other or toward our place in this world. Perhaps God exists as an expression of love or delight and who wants to be put down love and delight?

People gradually realized that the classical arguments for the existence of God did not get you as far as you wanted. If your culture applauds vengeance, you find a vengeful God; if your culture applauds jealousy, you find a jealous God, and so on. Why bother with the theological journey in the first place? The value of religious sayings and doings becomes an emotional license. The fact simply serves to reinforce the stances of the culture.

Challenge the idea that religion itself occupies the entire territory of spirituality or the search for meaning in life. Our insignificance in this world is compensated only by assurance of significance in a wider scheme of things. There is hope in another world. If this is hard to believe, spiritual disciplines of contemplation and prayer are there to help us. Since the attitudes are possible only if we believe in a world beyond, there is sufficient meaning for human beings in the human world. The smile of a baby, the grace of a dancer, sound of music, activities and achievements, all give meaning to life. These things last only their short time, but that does not deny them meaning. There is nothing beyond the process of life. There is no such thing as the meaning of life, but there can be many meanings within a life. See pleasure in the everyday. Discover something precious in it, tranquility that requires no purpose beyond the objects of everyday life themselves. In moments of despair and desolation, the belief that this is all that there is may be hard to bear. Things do not gain meaning just by going on for a very long time, or even forever, indeed they lose it. Too much and they become boring, an infinity and they would be intolerable.

We should agree to disagree and conclude that reasonable people can disagree about the issues under discussion. Sometimes people respond by being intolerant of those with whom they disagree. The arguments about the existence of God may be philosophically interesting, but studying them did nothing to change things. Critical thinking, as I understand it, is the underlying idea that thinking clearly and carefully about any issue requires understanding and applying some fundamental concepts. These include the ideas of truth and rationality, the difference between good reasons and the fundamental concepts of logic. Arguments are tools for helping us figure out what it is most reasonable to believe.

Judgments about what social arrangements are best for our society are difficult to establish. Well intentioned people come to different conclusions. There's an idea that somehow a person could not be a decent person or a good leader if that person is not religious. Most people have their own view and will stick to it, since it is true for that person. When there is a disagreement, it is not possible for both sides to be right. If there is a God, then the atheists are mistaken no matter how sincere, well meaning and thoughtful they are. If there is no God, then theists are mistaken.

Another difference, that need not involve a genuine disagreement, involves the presence or absence of a spiritual attitude. There is a sense of wonder or awe that some people experience and this may play a role in religious belief. Of course, atheists sometimes express feelings of awe at the size, complexity and natural beauty of the world and may express this as a feeling of spirituality. It is obvious that theists and atheists do not merely differ in how they live their lives, they really do disagree about the truth of the proposition that God exists. Any attempt to turn religious disagreements into mere differences in lifestyles fails to do justice to the plain facts. There are obviously many things about which theists and atheists can agree.

If you think that God exists, then you must think that anyone who denies that God exists is mistaken. You must think that this person has a false belief. You must think that, with respect to the points about which you disagree with someone, you have it right and the other person has it wrong. Thinking someone else has a false belief is consistent with having any of a number of other favorable attitudes toward that person and that belief. It should be obvious that reasonable people can disagree, even when confronted with a single body of evidence. When a jury or a court is divided in a difficult case, the mere fact of disagreement does not mean that someone is being unreasonable. Paleontologists disagree about what killed the dinosaurs. People with vastly different experiences can justifiably believe very different things.

A belief is reasonable only when it has adequate evidential support. The issue I am raising about religious beliefs, and disagreements involving them, is not about whether religious belief is beneficial. It may in fact be beneficial to some people and not others. Perhaps there are some basic ways to looking at things that people typically just take for granted. Maybe acceptance of a scientific worldview is one such fundamental principle and a religious outlook in another. It requires us to admit that we really do not know what the truth is. One side simply is making a mistake and those on the other side are justified in sticking to their guns. The more I reflect on it, the more I realize that I am in no position to make any such judgment with any confidence at all. It may be that the search for the truth is most successful if people argue for the things that seem true to them.

Few people of religious faith object to atheism because they think the evidence for the existence of God is compelling to any rational inquirer. Most of the faithful haven't considered the evidence for the existence of God in a spirit of rational inquiry. That is with openness to the possibility that the evidence goes against their faith. I believe that people object to atheism because they think that without God, morality is impossible.

Why think that religion is necessary for morality? It might be thought that people wouldn't know the difference between right and wrong if God did not reveal it to them, but that can't be right. Every stable society punishes murder, theft, bearing false witness, and teaches children to honor their parents. People figured out these rules long before they were exposed to any of the major religions. This fact suggests that moral knowledge springs from people's experiences in living together, in which they have learned that they must adjust their conduct in light of others claims. The idea that religion is necessary for morality can't be right. People have many motives, such as love, a sense of honor and respect for others, that motivate moral behavior. Christianity beliefs Jesus is one's savior and the one thing that is necessary for salvation.

Are actions right because God commands them, or does God commend them because they are right? If the latter is true, then actions are right independent of whether God commands them and God is not needed to underwrite the authority of morality. But if the former is true, then God could make any action right simply by willing it or by ordering others to do it. By theism, I mean belief in the God of scripture. This is the God of the Old and New Testaments and the Koran, the God of Christianity and Islam. It is also the God of any other religion that accepts one or more of these texts as containing divine revelation. God, as represented in scripture, has plans for human beings and intervenes in history to realize those plans. God has a moral relationship to human beings and tells humans how to live.

Consider first God's moral character, as revealed in the Bible. He routinely punishes people for the sins of others. He punishes all mothers by condemning them to painful childbirth, for Eve's sin. He punishes all human beings by condemning them to labor, for Adam's sin. He regrets his creation and commits genocide by flooding the earth. He punishes the children, grandchildren, great-grandchildren, and great-great-grandchildren, and so on, of those who worship any other God. This is but a sample of the evils celebrated in the Bible.

Can all this cruelty and injustice be excused on the ground that God may do what humans may not? Look, then at what God commands humans to do. He commands us to put to death adulterers, homosexuals and people who work on the Sabbath. He commands us to cast into exile people who eat blood, who have skin diseases and who have sex with their wives while they are menstruating. That's just the tip of the iceberg. Therefore, there's no hope for any of the human race.

Consider also what the Bible permits. Slavery is allowed. Fathers may sell their daughters into slavery. Female captives from a foreign war may be raped or seized as wives. Disobedient children should be beaten with rods. In the Old Testament, men may take as many wives as they like because adultery for men consists only in having sex with a woman who is married or engaged to someone else. Prisoners of war may be tossed off a cliff. Children may be sacrificed to God in return for their aid in battle. Isn't the Old Testament God a stern and angry God, while Jesus of the New Testament is all loving?

Jesus tells us his mission is to make family members hate one another, so that they shall love him more then their kin. He promises salvation to those who abandon their wives and children for him. The rod is not enough for children who curse their parents, they must be killed. These are Jesus' family values. Peter and Paul add to these family values the rule of husbands over their silenced wives, who must obey their husbands as Gods.

At the second coming, any city that does not accept Jesus will be destroyed and the people will suffer even more than they did when God destroyed Sodom and Gomorrah. God will destroy the unbelievers. God sends Death to kill one quarter of the Earth by sword, famine and plague, and by the wild beasts. Apparently, it's not enough to only kill people. For we are also told that an angel will burn up one third of the Earth, another will poison a third of its water, four angels will kill another third of humanity by plagues of fire, smoke and sulfur. There will be assorted deaths by earthquakes. Death is not bad enough for unbelievers, they must be tortured first. Locusts will sting them like scorpions until they want to die, but they will be denied the relief of death. Seven angels will pour seven bowls of God's wrath, delivering plagues of painful sores, seas and rivers of blood, burns from solar flares, and darkness, but, for what reason? The New Testament is not consistent on this point. Salvation is granted as a gift from God, unaffected by any choice humans may make. This implies that the rest are cast into the eternal torments of Hell on God's whim.

Faith itself may be a gift of God, rather than a product of rational assessment under our control and for which we could be held responsible. Those who do not believe are blameless and cannot be justly punished, even if Jesus really did die for our sins. What are we to make of the thought that Jesus died for our sins? This core religious teaching of Christianity makes Jesus a scapegoat for humanity. The practice of scapegoat contradicts the whole moral principle of personal responsibility. It also contradicts any moral idea of God. If God is merciful and loving, why doesn't he forgive humanity for its sins straight-out? How could any loving father do that to his son? It's hard to resist the conclusion that the God of the Bible is cruel, unjust who commands and permits us to be cruel and unjust to others. Religious doctrine claim that it is all right to punish people for the wrongs of others and for blameless error, that license or even command murder, plunder, rape, torture, slavery, ethnic cleansing and genocide. We know such actions are wrong. Should we reject the doctrine that represents them as right? Christians and Jews have struggled with this difficulty for centuries.

One might hold that, while it is in principle perfectly all right to slaughter whoever God tells us to, in fact, God has stopped speaking to us. This argument runs into the difficulty that many people, even today, claim that God has spoken to them. Nevertheless, they insist that there is much worthy moral teaching that can be salvaged from the Bible. There are many admirable moral teachings in the Bible; rules against murder, stealing, lying, and the like that are acknowledged by all societies. Love your neighbor as yourself and provisions in the structure of property rights to liberate people from debts. Although the details of these provisions make little economic sense, canceling debts every seven years prevents people from taking out loans for a longer term. Their general idea, that property rights should be structured so as to enable everyone to avoid oppression, is sound. Such teachings were not only morally advanced for their day but would dramatically improve the world if practiced today. So, the Bible contains both good and evil teachings.

We have seen that the Bible is morally inconsistent. If we try to draw moral lessons from the contradictory source, we must pick and choose which ones to accept. This requires that we use our own independent moral judgment, founded on some source other than revelation or the supposed authority of God to decide which biblical passages to accept. Once we recognize the moral inconsistencies in the Bible, it's clear that the fundamentalists, who today preach hatred toward gay people and the subordination of women, and who at other times and places have, with biblical support, claimed God's authority for slavery and ethnic cleansing, have been picking and choosing all along. Some of the acts supposedly committed or commanded by God and reported in the Bible are just plain morally wrong.

But how do we know that the Bible accurately records God's revealed word? After all, the revelation has reached only through men and has been interpreted by men, even if it did appear to have come from God himself; like the command delivered to Abraham to slaughter his own son like a sheep. It is at least possible that in this instance a mistake has prevailed. We must further ask whether we should accept any part of the Bible as offering evidence about the existence and nature of God. Here we have a body of purported evidence for theism, consisting in what seems to be experiences of divine presence, revelation, miracles, prophecies and testimonies of the same.

Why do all religions appear to have access to the same sources of evidence? Why were the ancient biblical people as ready to ascribe evil as good deeds to God? Why did they think God was so angry that he chronically unleashed tides of brutal destruction on humanity? The answer is that they took it for granted that all events bearing on human well being are willed by some agent for the purpose of affecting humans for good or evil. If no human was observed to have caused the event or if the event was of a kind that no human would have the power to cause, then they assumed that some unseen, more powerful agent had to have willed it, precisely for its good or bad effects on humans. So, if the event was good for people, they assumed that God willed it out of love for them. If it was bad, they assumed that God willed it out of anger at them. This explanation is universally observed among people who lack scientific understanding of natural events. It appears to be a deeply rooted bias of humans to reject the thought of meaningless suffering. If we are suffering, someone must be responsible for it.

The spiritual world everywhere reflects the hopes and fears, loves and hatreds, aspirations and depravities of those who believe in it. The same bias that leads pagans to believe in witches and multiple Gods, leads theists to believe in God. Every faith points to its own holy texts and oral traditions, its spiritual experiences, miracles and prophets, its testimonies of wayward lives turned around by conversion, rebirth of faith or return to the church.

Is there one God or many? Was Jesus God, the son of God, God's prophet or just a man? Was the last prophet Jesus or Muhammad or Rev. Moon? It is on par with the evidence for Zeus, Baal, Thor and other long abandoned Gods, who are now considered ridiculous by nearly everyone. The sources of evidence for theism, revelations, miracles, religious experiences and prophecies, nearly all known only by testimony transmitted through uncertain chains of long lost original sources, systematically generate contradictory beliefs, many of which are known to be morally false. Of course, ordinary sources of evidence, such as eyewitness testimony of ordinary events, also often lead to conflicting beliefs.

For exactly the same certainty has been felt by those who think they've seen ghosts, been kidnapped by aliens or been possessed. Where independent tests exist, they either disconfirm or fail to confirm the extraordinary evidence. There is no geological evidence of a worldwide flood, no archaeological evidence that Pharaoh's army drowned in the Red Sea after Moses parted it to enable the Israelites to escape. The same types of evidence are the basis for belief in pagan Gods. The authority of moral rules lies not with God, but with each of us. We each have moral authority with respect to one another. No one has the authority to order anyone else to blind obedience.

If we take the core evidence for theism, which is the testimonies of revelations, miracles, religious experiences and prophecies found in scripture, then we are committed to the view that the most heinous acts are morally right; because scripture tells us that God performs or commands them. The only explanation that accounts for its tendency to commend heinous acts, as well as good acts, shows it to reflect either our own hopes and feelings, whether these be loving or hateful. Extraordinary evidence, in other words, is a projection of our own wishes, fears and fantasies. All religions claim the same sorts of extraordinary evidence on their behalf. The absence of any independent ordinary evidence that corroborates one system more than another strongly supports the view that such types of evidence are not credible at all.

What about the evils God fails to prevent, the pain and suffering of human beings and animals, and the sins people commit? Focus on evil that God fails to prevent. For God, if we are to believe an orthodox story, has prescribed eternal torment as a punishment for insubordination. Some say that the mere fact of not believing in him is enough to receive eternal torment. Others think that you must violate one of the commandments. The punishment is to go on forever. The torment is infinitely worse than all the suffering and sin that will have occurred during the history of life in the universe. God is supposed to torture the damned forever and to do so by vastly surpassing all the modes of torment about which we know.

Perhaps there are alternative ways of reading the idea of God's punishment or understanding torment. Perhaps you think judgment and punishment isn't to be taken literally. Maybe what happens in this life is that people make choices. Some choose salvation and others damnation. Then God does evil. He places people in a situation in which they must make a judgment that binds them for eternity. He knows that some will be so inadequately informed that they will opt for an eternity of torment. If God is genuinely worthy of our worship, then to be fully informed is to recognize the attributes that make this so.

Can Christians afford to deny divine evil? Christianity requires redemption. At its heart is the claim that Jesus was born to save us from something. The condition from which we have been redeemed must be truly horrible. What can be horrible enough except for eternal torment? The crucifixion serves to cleanse us from our state of sin and no punishment after death is needed. Based upon God, he has no wish to punish any of us. Christians think that the sufferings of Jesus give us all a second chance. But that some of us don't give ourselves the opportunity. But it doesn't provide instant salvation for all. That's why Christians emphasize the importance of faith. If everyone wins without regard to performance, not only do all these doctrines drop away, but so does the rationale of the earthly life. If even the most wicked of people can be immediately forgiven without punishment. One possible condition would be nonexistence. Those who take advantage of the sacrifice of Christ, the faithful, are called to salvation. The rest of us simple die.

Christians firmly believe that in the hereafter, their God will consign people they know, some of whom they love, to an eternity of unimaginable agony. Moved by this thought, they do whatever they can to urge others to join them in faith. They genuinely think that their God will commit those who do not accept him to eternal torment. They may prefer not to dwell on the point, but when they consider it, they accept his judgment. Of course, they don't see this as divine evil. Instead they talk of divine justice and the fitting damnation of sinners. The balance seems to tilt in the negative direction. The evil that God causes is infinitely greater than the entire sum of mundane suffering and sin. It is infinitely intense and it lasts forever. The magnitude of the torment isn't taken seriously. There must be some nice version of the story, one that won't literally end with billions of damned souls in eternal agony.

With the learning of science and after a little reflection it seemed to me pretty obvious that most of the claims about God, although still attractive, is wishful thinking. This has led me to wonder whether people really do believe them. Clearly lots of people claim to and seem to live and sometimes die for their religious views. People often claim to believe things that they merely want or are in some way committed to believing, even though at some level they know the belief is false. Simple examples are the standard one of people ignoring the symptoms when they have some disease, or the obvious evidence of the infidelities of a spouse. My hunch about what passes as religious belief is that it frequently involves self deception. Despite appearances, many adults who've been exposed to standard science and sincerely claim to believe in God are self deceived at some level. They believe the claim is false. Religious claims are so intensely familiar that we tend not to hear how truly bizarre and unbelievable they are without really attending to what they literally mean.

God is a supernatural, psychological being, that is, a being not subject to ordinary physical limitations, but is capable of some or other mental state. There is some such being that knows about our lives, cares about the good, either created in the physical world or can intervene in it, and is in charge of a person's whereabouts in an afterlife. It doesn't seem even a remotely serious possibility that such a God exist. His nonexistence is far beyond a reasonable doubt. Arguments about the existence of ghosts, gremlins or evil spirits are simply not worth any serious philosophical consideration. The straightforward reason not to believe in these things is simply that there is no serious evidence for them. If someone thinks there is, then they need to produce the evidence. There's simply no reason to take them more seriously than claims about witches and ghosts.

If you poke around enough in the places where it would be reasonable to expect evidence of X and you don't find any, that's a pretty good reason to believe there is no X. This is surely why sensible people don't believe in elves, fairies or the bogeyman under the bed. It's true that we ordinarily take for granted the operations of a mind and so often rest content with an explanation of something that ends with some appeal to what someone wanted or intended. Thus, God's wanting to create the world can seem like an ultimately satisfying explanation of why it exists.

How does one know he is in the presence of the genuine creator of everything? Many of our ordinary beliefs based on memory and perception are not arrived at by reasoning, but by experience, involving little or no reasoning at all. Beliefs about ghosts by misty graveyards and decrepit old houses are caused by real ghosts. That's partly because there's no reason to think that ghosts or God exist. We have to rely on basic beliefs which for some people may include a belief in God. The question of how we manage to know anything about logic, mathematics or the external world is a terrifically hard one. Beliefs based on memory are confirmed by the evidence of sight, sound, touch and the testimony of others, which in turn receive confirmation from that of still others and so forth.

Consider yourself at communion with an actual piece of human body and a glass of real blood. Think of how most religious people react to hippies who sometimes emulate Jesus, who forsake their worldly goods to wander and proselytize among the poor or how they react to people who murder their children because God told them to. Remember the claims of the Koresh cult in Texas or those claims about the Hale-Bopp comet made by the Heaven's Gate cult and then remember that many religions were themselves once just such a cult.

How do you know which translation or interpretation of a text or authority to trust? Why believe one of them does and the other does not express the word of God? It is common knowledge that the familiar Bible we posses is at least in part the result of the efforts of a great many ordinary mortals, as susceptible to sin and error as anyone, working in very different languages, times and conditions. One would think it would behoove someone worried about which version genuinely reflected God's word to be constantly trying to sift through the intricate historical details, anxiously ascertaining which writers really did have a main line to God. Serious biblical scholarship has little effect on most people's actual religious practices. This all contrasts dramatically with science and common sense.

God designed or created the world and permits so much pointless suffering. People do tolerate plenty of mysteries about how the world works. Most people have only the dimmest idea about how things live and grow. People haven't the slightest reason to doubt that things grow, despite the mystery about how it occurs. By contrast, anyone aware of the basic ideas of contemporary science and lack of evidence of God has plenty of reason to doubt God's existence. Why should there be no normal evidence of God's existence? Why shouldn't it be possible to establish it in the same way as the existence of bacteria or the Big Bang? Many religious people readily recognize the failure of evidence but then go on to claim that religious beliefs are matters of faith, not evidence. On the other hand issues of faith do arise precisely in those cases in which a person is asked to manifest loyalty to a person or cause despite the evidence that might otherwise undermine it. A father has faith in his son's honesty despite what the police say.

People may simply have uncontrolled responses to overwhelming personal experiences, or to desperate situations, as when recovering alcoholics rely on a higher power or turn to religion in their lonely and miserable old age. One thing many people find satisfying is being a part of some emotionally fulfilling community or project they endorse that goes beyond their own individual lives. People pretty regularly find depressing the thought that their labors, especially their sufferings, are meaningless in that they don't contribute to some larger good. Someone might look for still further nesting of one's projects, wondering, perhaps what's so important about human welfare. It apparently can be gratifying to be told there is some still larger project in which humanity is an integral part. It may explain why many people think of a life without God as meaningless.

Death may not be as bad as people suppose, but it's hard to think of any story, least of all the glory of God, that would justify the sufferings of people slowly dying from a plague, cancer, AIDS or people wasting away with Alzheimer's or completely debilitating strokes. Most of life is a pretty local affair, seldom requiring attention to all one's concerns, least of all to the big questions. Thinking your effort is worthwhile for some larger project that you approve is probably necessary to get your heart into those efforts. It can successfully sustain the thought that what we're doing really matters, which sufficiently motivates us to engage in the efforts.

Traditional religion seems to be based on dangerously simplistic conceptions of human life and its troubles; leading people to see conflicts not in terms of the complex conflicting interests and situations of the different parties, but rather as a war between good and evil, good guys and bad guys. This is a serious historical hypothesis about the causes of all the world's wars and the like. For one thing, these wars are often fought by people willing to sacrifice themselves for a greater cause, like Hitler and Stalin. Present day conflicts in the Middle East play a role in the horrors of the world.

How do you explain the intellectual dimension of fanaticism, particularly as it leads to terrorism? Fanatics put forth arguments with which they try to persuade others to share their commitments. So convinced are the fanatics that their cause is just that they are willing to pursue actions, including terrorism, that shatter the most fundamental of ethical boundaries. Fanatical reasoning resides in a lack of self restraint, not just from how the fanatic acts but from how he reasons and how he maintains his beliefs. Yet the need for self restraint is a lesson we all learn. Supernatural religious faith promotes denial of these self restraints, the explanation that provides understanding of why faith is fertile ground for fanaticism.

Religious commands can readily justify overruling the restraints of your background beliefs and values, since the authority of those commands ultimately derives from an all knowing supernatural being. Religious commands demand obedience even when they violate basic ethical prohibitions and when their rationale reaches beyond the grasp of the faithful. The demand for obedience is often backed by a promise of an eternally blessed life for the faithful and its opposite for others. This is illustrated in God's order to Abraham to sacrifice his son Isaac. The faith demonstrated is in Abraham's willingness to perform an act normally unthinkable, murder. Within a supernatural setting there is a strong tendency to tune out a range of common sense questions and responses.

The attempt to immunize religious claims from everyday requests for validation is pervasive. When it is believed that turning wine into blood, the obvious question is whether we can corroborate this claim chemically. When eternal life is promised to the faithful, one asks for real details. How is this know, especially when so much else, like why God allows evil is mysterious? How often does prayer help the ill recover compared to crossing one's fingers or wishful thinking? What about Santa Claus to a young child? To understand fanaticism requires an inquiry into how it is possible to believe the unbelievable.

The Catholic Church appears more concerned on maintaining authority and followers then searching for truth. The faithful can't take seriously the challenges of whether or not a person can literally walk on water, a woman can have a virgin birth, and the dead can be alive. Respected historians are not to be relied on to determine the origins of religious texts and their stories. If you really believe that you should act a certain way, then when opportunity arises, you act without hesitation. Lives of extreme religious devotion direct a great deal of time and energy toward a singular focus, at the expense of human pursuits.

We must be open-minded to move opinion toward a point of view by reasonable argument, not by fear. The arguments of Gandhi or early civil rights workers drew heavily on the democratic and ethical principles of their respective governments and its citizens. Open-mindedness is advantageous because if one is wrong, one wants to discover it before one acts. If one is right, one expects corroboration, even if the occasional source is mistaken. Faith reflects a personal choice to believe, in the absence of proof or evidence, view of faith with standard readings of biblical passages.

Because what we believe is what we take to be true, belief is central to our lives. We care deeply about being correct, since our beliefs guide our actions. The failure of belief based on faith is shown by the impossibility of believing that there is a God or an afterlife or a heaven on the basis of faith. It is a wise strategy to believe in God, regardless of whether or not God exists. The argument for belief is that you lose little if there is no God, but you will be infinitely blessed if there is and infinitely damned otherwise. At least learn your inability to believe, since reason brings you to this, and yet you cannot believe. This provides no reason to actually believe there is a God, but this much self deception is normally impossible, since belief is so fundamental to the guidance of our lives. No one can deceive himself that he is Superman or Napoleon and proceed with his routine life, not without a mental breakdown.

This intellectual honesty is essential to common sense. We all recognize that our experience and learning, which helps constitute common sense, is severely limited. You want to know whether you are leading well, but realize that your own observations are bound to be biased. So you seek the observations of people under conditions favorable to objectivity. Assume the contrary to the evidence, that there is a supernatural realm, one not governed by natural laws like gravitation or rational motives for actions. Perhaps God is not subject to any laws. If biblical texts are treated as authoritative, God commands what is unjust, actively orders and commits atrocities.

Early Israelite religion grew out of earlier religions. Eventually grew into a more modern God of late Israelite religion; a single all powerful and all knowing God of Jews, Christians and Muslims. It would be a God of unprecedented influence, a God that in various centuries would dominate people who were dominant in the world. So today, when the faithful points to scripture as proof that their God is different from all other ancient Gods, their God is the one true God. But why would anyone place their faith in a book persistently at odds with historical reality?

Perhaps we should emphasize the power of facts on the ground. It seeks to explain how the conception of God has changed in response to events on earth. We've seen the divine, or a least the ideas about the divine, reshaped by the mundane. Facts on the ground, facts about power and money and other things, have often been the leading edge of change, with religious belief following along. Balance is the best way to explain the long road of evolution to God. At the risk of oversimplifying, politics and economics gave us the one true God. Seeing facts on the ground provides us with a new kind of evidence for higher purpose. In ancient times, when men of royal blood married foreign women, it wasn't usually on a romantic whim. It was part of foreign policy, a way to cement relations with another nation.

People who are profitably doing business with other people tend not to question their religious beliefs – live and let live. For that matter, the basic dynamic goes beyond the question of religious tolerance to the question of tolerance in general. People naturally, without really thinking about it, judge enemies and rival critically in various realms. If two men are pursuing the same woman, and you ask them what they think of each other's tastes – in politics, in clothes, in literature, whatever – you'll probably get some negative feedback, and it will be heartfelt. Darwinian Theory says that traits that spread through a population will tend to be traits that further survival and reproduction.

The problem of evil doesn't arise unless you believe in a single all powerful and good God. A God who governs the actions of the greatest know empire is a God who can govern history itself. Religion has always been interplay between thought and feeling. People can look at their holy texts and see what they want to see. See what meets their psychological, social, political needs. In all languages, words can have more than one meaning, so reading involves making choices. When the context of the original composition is very different from the reader's context from long ago and far away, choices made may steer the text away from the author's intent.

Capacity for growth is a good thing, but what the world really needs is a God that does grow. Today globalization has made the planet too small to peacefully accommodate large religions that are at odds. If the God of Jews, the God Christians and the God of Muslims don't foster tolerance, then we're all in trouble.

Does God exist in people's heads? There was no particular reason to believe that there was a God out there that matched this internal conception. What I'm really saying is that people's conception of God moves in a morally progressive direction. From the standpoint of a traditional believer, of course, this isn't an inspiring thought. The worldview I'm laying out amounts to a kind of good-news and bad-news viewpoint for traditionalist Christians, Muslims and Jews. The bad-news is that the God you thought was perfect is in fact imperfect. The good-news is that this imperfect God isn't really a God anyway, just a figment of the human imagination. Obviously, for the traditional believer, this is all bad-news.

Then again, traditional believers come into the conversation with high expectations, that an ancient theology which took shape millennia before science started revealing the nature of the world should survive modern critical reflections. These days there are people who could call themselves religiously inclined, or at least spiritually inclined. They are born into a scientific world that seems to offer no particular sustenance to spiritual inquiry, and they would settle for evidence that the inquiry isn't hopeless after all. An atheist would say no God and no immortality. There's absolute nothingness at death. However, I say that perhaps there is something. Anything is better than nothing.

Is there something? Is there anything? Is there any evidence of something? Any signs that there's more to life than the sum of its subatomic particles, some larger purpose, some deeper meaning, maybe even something that would qualify as divine in some sense of the word? If you approach the spiritual quest with hopes this modest, with the humble skepticism of modernity rather than the revealed certainty of the ancient world, then a rational appraisal of the situation may prove more uplifting. There may be some evidence of something. What might qualify as evidence of a larger purpose at work in the world? Maybe a moral direction in history is evidence. If history naturally carries human consciousness toward moral enlightenment, however slowly, that would be evidence that there's some point to it all. At least, it would be more evidence then the alternative, if history showed no direction or if history showed a downward direction. God tends to grow morally because humankind is growing morally.

It is easy enough to say that God defies human conception and is off in another realm, beyond the merely material, that he is ineffable and transcendent. But if that's the case, then what exactly is his connection to the world? How does he get credit for its everyday operations? What is his connection to us? How can we get consolation, spiritual sustenance and moral guidance from a God who has been sealed off? God himself is beyond the material universe, somewhat the way a video game designer is outside of the video game. Yet the video game itself is an extension of the designer, a reflection of the designer's mind. God may be outside the physical universe, but there is a presence and cooperation of divinity in the created world. The job of human beings is to cooperate with the divinity, a task we do best if we sense this presence and the purpose.

Is a kind of direct contact with God somehow possible? People talk about a union with the divine that falls short of communion with God himself. However direct the connection, the first step to making it is to try to understand God and God's will. What direction does God want us to move in? Maybe toward greater harmony with other people, cities, nations and countries and so the whole human race may advance to supreme happiness. So that's a start. Be nice to people, even people who aren't like you and don't think like you do. Perhaps the path to God lies in acting wisely. Jealousy and anger shortens life and worry ages a man prematurely, modern studies of emotions and physical health bears out this claim. A glad heart is good for the body. For people who live by the sword die by it.

If Jesus was the son of God, sent here to die, you would think he might accept his death with grace. After all, he would have known about the plan all along, and he knows that he'll be resurrected in the end anyway. Yet in Mark his last words are "My God, my God, why have you forsaken me?" as if the crucifixion was a terrible surprise and the end. Why Jesus, sent by God to convince people of the kingdom of God, convinced so few people? Those were around him along with the twelve asked him about the parables. He said to them, to you has been given the secret of the kingdom of God, but for those outside, everything comes in parables. In order that they may indeed look, but not perceive, and may indeed listen, but not understand, so that they may not turn again and be forgiven. Odd, the one sent from heaven to spread the divine word purposely encodes the word so that most people won't get it. Why a secret?

For many Christians, the word "Jesus" is virtually synonymous with the word "savior". God sent his son so that as the New Testament put it "all flesh shall see the salvation of God." But none of this is what Christians mean by "salvation". When they call Christ the savior, they're not talking about the salvation of the society or even the physical salvation of the individual, but rather the salvation of the individual's soul upon death. The heart of the Christian message is that God sent his only son to lay out the path to eternal life. Jesus is, in this view, a heavenly being who controls access to heaven. He is seated on the right hand of the Father and will judge the living and the dead.

Believing that heaven awaits you shortly after death makes death a less harrowing prospect. This belief can also make dying in a holy war a more attractive prospect, a fact that has shaped history and even today shapes headlines. Eternal life of a certain kind may well have been part of Jesus original message. But it may not have been, in any event the details of the story, the part about heaven, for example changed consequentially in the decades after the crucifixion. The way the now official story took shape is a case study in how God evolves to fill the psychological needs of his followers. The idea of followers of Jesus getting to join him in heaven upon dying probably didn't take shape until about a half century after he died.

Christians worship a loving God and many of them think this God is distinctively Christian. Whereas the God of the Old Testament is a vengeful God and the God of the New Testament is revealed as a kind and forgiving God. This view is too simple because a God who is kind and vengeful shows up repeatedly in the Bible. The Bible came from dozens of different authors working over a millennium, if not more. The guiding assumption is that people get their ideas about God from mundane sources such as other people, scriptures or from their own creative synthesis. In short, religions that reach great stature have a tendency to rewrite their history in the process. We see history through the eyes of the man that won the battle. They cast themselves as distinctive from the get-go.

When people feel like fighting, they are pretty good at coming up with reasons why the fighting is justified, reasons why God is on their side. None of this is to say that scripture doesn't matter. If you are recruiting suicide bombers, it matters that the Koran says martyrs who die in holy war go to heaven. Presumably if you spend much time reciting verses that embrace the torment of your enemies, you are more likely to embrace their torment, and perhaps even do the tormenting yourself. Certainly the Koran features many such verses.

If we could magically replace the Koran with a book of our choosing, or could magically replace the Bible with a book of our choosing, we could probably make Muslims, Jews and Christians better people. But we don't have that option. So we're lucky that scripture isn't as important in shaping behavior as the circumstances on the ground, circumstances that shape the interpretation of scripture. Circumstances can be stubborn, but at least they're not fixed in print. It was in Mecca that Muhammad had much in common with Jesus. He led a small band of devotees, warning that Judgment Day was coming. The Koran says more than once that not just Muslims but Jews and Christians are eligible for salvation so long as they believe in God and in Judgment Day and live a life worthy of favorable judgment.

Today the argument isn't over which God exist but over whether any God exist or even whether anything you could call a higher purpose exists. The kind of argument that has to be made if people are to be persuaded is an argument that evidence of divine purpose is embedded in the natural world. Organisms are like pocket watches, they're too complex to just happen by accident. So organisms must have a designer, namely God. Thanks to Darwin we can explain the complex functionality of organisms without a God. The explanation is natural selection.

Terrorist leaders have aims that are at odds with the welfare of westerners. The West's goal is to hurt their cause, to deprive them of new recruits and of political support. What's good for Muslims broadly is bad for radical Muslims. If Muslims get less happy with their place in the world, more resentful of their treatment by the West, support for radical Islam will grow, so things will get worse for the West. If on the other hand, more and more Muslims feel respected by the West and feel they benefit from involvement with it, that will cut support for radical Islam, and westerners will be more secure from terrorism. The basic idea is that terrorist leaders are the enemy and they thrive on the discontent of Muslims. If what makes your enemy happy is the discontent of Muslims broadly, then you should favor their contentment, if the West can win the hearts and minds of Muslims. Westerners view

Muslims with suspicion, and view relations between the West and the Muslim world as a clash of civilizations. Many Muslims view the West in similarly win-lose terms. Pure understanding, uncolored by judgment is hard to come by.

Are we under the illusion that we are special? We all base our daily lives on this premise, that our welfare is more important than the welfare of pretty much anyone else, with the possible exception of close kin. The premise is that our welfare is much more important that the welfare of others. We work hard so we can afford dessert while other people don't have dinner. We are all like this, all of us walking around under the impression that we're special.

If you step back from the differences we have with one another and with other religions, you'll see a bigger divide in modern thought. It's between people who think there is in some sense a divine source of meaning, a higher purpose in this universe and people who think there isn't. Perhaps there is no source of meaning or moral orientation. Perhaps there's not a moral order out there, it's something we impose. Scriptures illustrate that there is a moral order out there and it's imposed on us. This gives humankind a choice between progressing morally and paying a price for failing to. The fact that there's a moral order out there doesn't mean there's a God. The way history draws people toward moral truth is by rewarding them for moving toward it and punishing them for resisting.

Lots of people don't believe in an afterlife, an increasing number perhaps, and certainly an increasing number of well educated people. Fortunately, it turns out that everyone does seek salvation. The word salvation comes from a Latin word meaning to stay intact, to remain whole and to be in good health. Everyone is trying to stay in good health, to keep body and soul together.

There are the gods that have populated human history, rain gods, war gods, creator gods, all purpose gods, and so on. There might be a kind of god that is real. It's reasonable to suspect that humankind in some sense has a higher purpose or meaning in life. Maybe the source of this higher purpose, the source of the moral order is something that qualifies for the label god in at least some sense of the word. Some superhuman being with a mind remarkable like our minds except way, way bigger is out there. Of course, we can't rule out the possibility that some superhuman version of a human lies above and beyond the universe.

The good news is that the hopelessness of figuring out exactly what something is doesn't mean it doesn't exist. The believers believe there's something out there, in some sense of the word. Though the best we can do is conceive, even misleadingly, conceiving of it that way makes more sense than not conceiving of it at all. If you believe in God, even while acknowledging that you have no clear idea what God is and that you can't even really prove God per se exists, your belief has no foundation. A believer in God perceives patterns in the moral world. God is that unknown thing that is the source of the moral order, there is a moral dimension to life on Earth and a moral direction to time on Earth. God gave each of us a moral axis around which to organize our lives, should we choose to.

Do you really need God in order to sustain moral progress? It depends on who you are. Some people can lead morally exemplary lives without the idea of God. Others need God in their lives, to fear hell and long for heaven. They need to feel that if they're bad they'll be disappointing someone and if they're good they'll be pleasing someone. This one above all others, it is good to please and bad to disappoint. For many people, carrying these human relations to the superhuman level works well. They are better people, often happier people, thinking of a God who is aware of their daily struggle and offers reprimand. They can best stay aligned with the moral axis of the universe by thanking God, asking God to help them stay righteous, seeking forgiveness from God for their lapses.

How did religion built from the ground up? People naturally try to exert control over their environment and believing that they have such control naturally makes them feel good. Therefore, people's minds are open to ideas that promise to give them such control. If you pray for someone to recover from illness and they don't, then prayer would seem to have lost credibility. But religions usually have ways of explaining such failure. Maybe you or the sick person had done something horribly wrong and this is God's punishment. Or maybe God just works in mysterious ways.

According to the book of Genesis, God created man in his own image. According to Aristotle, men create the gods after their own image.

Roy K. Lintz

The more we learn about the character of human nature, the easier it is to explain the origin of religion without invoking such a thing. Elements of early religion, though themselves of mundane origin, could through subsequent cultural evolution come to acquire a deeply, validly spiritual character. This idea isn't implausible. But how far humanity has traveled along the path of spiritual evolution is another question altogether.

— 6 —

Religious Extreme Terrorism

An international terrorist kills in the name of God. Do you believe this? The world lacked the democratic courage, intellectual honesty and willingness to act to stop Hitler's war machine when he came to power. If they had stopped him then, over sixty million people would not have died. What will it take to jar the West from its comfortable complacency? We fight to bring peace to the streets of Iraq. The war was not only justified in the first place but also part of a much larger picture. Just a reminder, Hitler's war machine in the 1930s and 1940s; and Lebanon in the 1980s. If we don't learn from history, we will repeat history. We will pay more down the road if we don't find a strategy for victory in Iraq. If we pull out, get ready for another fight down the road and the fight could be in the United States. If we let the terrorists off now, they will be that much stronger the next time we face them.

Liberals

Are the liberals in America helping international terrorists to succeed? We are losing the support of the American people in the fight with Iraq. All that is required for evil to triumph is for good people to do nothing. The battle of good versus evil is being fought from within. At the heart of liberalism is a belief that evil really does not exist, people are basically good. Liberals believe that it's better to talk with people since we are basically reasonable and not bring criminals to justice or fighting to stop those committing crimes upon humanity. We should always talk with reasonable people, but everyone is not reasonable. Sometimes we must fight for justice in the name of humanity. The liberals want God and the Bible out of America. Was our Constitution made only for a religious and moral people? A Christian will tell you that when you turn your heart and your life over to Christ, when you accept Christ as your Savior, it changes your heart and your life. By accepting Jesus Christ as your Savior, you have God's promise of eternal life in heaven.

There is a conflict for our planet, both physical and spiritual. This conflict can not be won without dealing with the forces of evil. If you believe the Bible, you know that extraordinary things happen. If we ever forget that we are one nation under God, then we will be a nation without God. Are we guided by the truths of the Bible or even understand them? There is an inability to know who our friends are and who our enemies are. We must know our enemies and friends alike. Liberals focus on appeasement because they do not believe in evil and therefore refuse to confront it. We currently have a great opportunity in history to confront the sources of evil. Liberals reject absolute standards of good and evil or right and wrong. Evil is real and must be opposed. Is it simplistic to look to God and the Bible for guidance? Liberals make excuses for evil or deny evil's existence, refusing to confront it. Hitler's intent was to kill all Jews. The Nazi Party maintained plausible deniability about their injustices to the Jews, just following orders. If the devil does exit, as the Bible says he does, there is not better proof of it than those following his agenda to destroy Jews and then Christians. Has America lost courage to confront evil in the world? The West keeps advancing socially with the help of technological progress. Is the Western civilization on the dangerous trend of worshiping man and his material needs? Some of our intellectual elites believe that one who believes in God is not to be taken seriously.

Terrorists

We value life; the terrorists destroy life. We value education; the terrorists do not believe that women should be educated, have health care or leave their homes. The 9/11 Commission stated that the situation in Iraq is grave and deteriorating. America does not have the political will to win the war on terrorism. It is Iraqi's problem to clean up their internal security issues, not the United States.

Perhaps winning the war on terrorism means we must defeat the ideology of Islam. Stop and consider the cost of retreat. If we don't win the war in Iraq and end the terrorist threat there, we will certainly have the chance to do it again, maybe within the United States. Washington refuses to let the military on the ground fight the war without being micromanaged by congressional committees and commissions. Do politicians think they know better than military experts about how to win a war?

Defeating the terrorists and extremists is the challenge of our time and the calling of this generation. Pulling out now would guarantee a greater and more costly conflict down the road. Most politicians believe things are bad now and there is nothing we can really do to change them, so why not pull out and cut our losses. This is short sightedness. If we don't find the moral clarity to fight this evil until it is soundly defeated, all we will be doing is importing the war back to the United States. We will face a bloodier war down the road. Is that what we really want to do?

The planned invasion of Iraq had nothing to do with terror and everything to do with oil. Iran could see the handwriting on the wall and resistance to occupation is a legitimate right to American's warmongering and expansionist politicians. Iran is certain that a flood of terror would demoralize the United States military and the American people. Therefore, influence the Bush administration to bow to pressure from Congress to withdraw the troops as quickly as possible. Americans are good at quick response but have a very poor track record when it comes to defending prolonged occupations. Perfect examples can be found in Vietnam and Lebanon. Terrorist organizations are capable of humiliating and killing American troops at will.

Is the terrorism threat to the United States and Israel the beginning of World War III? It is the beginning of a new type of warfare, a new kind of warfare that the West is clearly at a disadvantage? United States is caught in the crosshairs of every terrorist organization in operation in Iran, Iraq, and Syria and can do little to stop the bloodshed. Fostering an Islamic revolution that is aimed at the bloodiest clash of religious ideologies the world has ever seen between Islam and Christianity. The United States invasion of Iraq is declared to be the best thing that had ever happened in inspiring the Islamist cause.

In the years since the fight in Lebanon in the 1980s, we have done little but encourage the use of terrorist tactics over and over again. We shake our fists, but in the end we withdraw before any real victory. Iran stands stronger for our lack of resolve and inability to truly curb its ambitions. Iran poses a serious threat because religious extremism is always more dangerous. Remember, Iranians are not Arabs but Persians. Theirs is not a racial war but a religious one. Iran wants nothing more than every knee on earth to bow to Allah and believes that there will be no peace in the world until the world is Muslim. Become Muslim and we shall all live in peace. "Aslim – Tuslim" Submit to Islam, thou shall then be at peace. If you do not submit, then we have to wage war. Become Muslim or die.

Iran poses a real nuclear threat, not only to the region but to the whole world. Iran sees America as the Great Satan and has become the unifying force that all love to hate. The American embassy in Tehran was overrun and Americans were held hostage for 444 days. There was a deadly blow to the marine compound in Lebanon that resulted in the United States packing its bags and going home. Today, Iran has focused on Iraq with every intention to drive coalition troops out of the country, just as they did in Lebanon. Create a unified Shiite state from the Persian Gulf to the borders of Syria and perhaps beyond. The fact is, while all eyes are focused on the battle in Iraq, the real danger is Iran. Iran, with the help of Russia and probably North Korea, is on the brink of becoming a nuclear power. Iran's dream is to wipe Israel off the map. The point of no return for Israel will come when Iran has within its grasp the ability to produce a nuclear weapon. Such an attack could set the stage of every nation in between Israel, Lebanon, Syria, Jordan, Saudi Arabia, Iraq, Kuwait and Iran to become the battleground for World War III. Just like France, Great Britain, Russia, and Germany were in World War II. While the United States and Europe might possibly delay too long, Israel will not.

No United States president in the history of our nation has faced such pressure in the international arena with troops in Iraq and Afghanistan, nuclear threats from Iran and North Korea. A war on terrorism is losing its focus in the eyes of the American people. Iran is the real center of gravity. Perhaps the only nation that can shut down Iran's nuclear program and neutralize their ability to retaliate is the United States. The decision to act to protect our nation and our families is ours to make.

The plan is ours to execute and the safety of future generations is in our hands. Do we have what is takes to win the war on terror regardless of what it takes?

I would like to make a case and point in this paragraph. You want to install a home security system. Go to a second-hand store and buy a pair of men's used size 14-16 work boots. Place them on your front porch, along with a copy of Guns & Ammo Magazine. Put a few giant dog dishes next to the boots and magazines. Leave a note on your door that reads: "Hey Bubba, Big Jim, Duke and Slim, I went for more ammunition. I'll be back in an hour or so. Don't mess with the pit bulls, they attacked the mailman this morning and messed him up real bad. I don't think Killer took part in it but it was hard to tell from all the blood. Anyway, I locked all four of 'em in the house. Better wait outside." A reasonable person would stay away from your home. Not the terrorists or extremists of Islam, the extremists will come into your home ready to die for Islam. Reminder, become Muslim and we shall all live in peace. Submit to Islam, thou shall then be at peace. If you do not submit, then we have to wage war. Become Muslim or die. Radical Islam is one who seeks a form of world domination and sees the United States as the Great Satan.

Some have the belief that every crisis can be resolved with diplomacy. Unfortunately there are times when evil must be openly confronted and defeated. Without a strong military backup with a proven track record of victories, diplomacy can be meaningless. Speak softly, carry a big stick and use it when needed. It is never advisable to sell one's soul to the devil in order to keep him at bay. Evil demands the supreme sacrifice. Not through compromise, but through terror and coercion. Israel has already given away land in failed attempts to achieve peace with its neighbors. Young Iranians are volunteering for suicide missions, even youngsters as early as twelve years old are to become living minesweepers. A winning Iran would result in its controlling the oil reserves of Iraq, as well as the Persian Gulf.

Nuclear Weapons

It appears likely that the United States, not Israel, will be the one to go it alone in order to stop the process of nuclear enrichment in Iran.

If all efforts to persuade Iran to drop its plans to produce nuclear weapons should fail, the US administration will authorize Israel to attack. President Harry S. Truman issued orders to drop two atomic bombs on Japan to end World War II more quickly – Hiroshima and Nagasaki.

Threats posed by biological and chemical weapons are real, but not as grave as nuclear weapons. Many people will die with a biological or chemical attack, but you still have the infrastructure to run the nation. A biological or chemical attack would not destroy the infrastructure that our country depends upon. With a biological or chemical attack we would still have our telephone lines, electricity, highways, railroads and computer networks. Both biological and chemical weapons do not destroy buildings or bridges or any other vital infrastructure or interfere seriously in the operation of the government. From a military perspective, using nuclear weapons just makes more sense.

A nuclear weapon changes the entire structure and balance of power. You can deter people who don't want to die, but many of Iran's leaders welcome death. They are a part of the culture of death and it's very hard to deter a culture that welcomes death. During the Cold War, Russia and the United States were armed to destroy the other several times over in the event of an attack. The outcome of such an event would bring about the near total destruction of both countries and the world. Both nations had sufficient incentive not to engage in a direct nuclear conflict. Iran thinks in a different way than you and I, and most of the Western world. An Islam regime is not a normal regime where you make cost benefit calculations and compromises. This regime does not negotiate in the same manner that the Western world would negotiate.

Islamic Fundamentalist

The people does not matter for an Islamic fundamentalist. People don't matter, just like Hitler. Another lesson of history is that while it may begin with Jews, it doesn't end with Jews. We learned that in World War II. People are only elements to establish a goal. With Islamic fundamentalism and Nazism, two things are very similar. The end justifies the means, and there is no respect for borders. Apparently in the fanatical Islam mind set, it's alright to kill Muslim brothers, for they

172

will attain heaven. Young Iranian students are literally brainwashed by textbooks found in their school. The youngsters are taught that to sacrifice themselves as martyrs for the cause is the ultimate goal.

Anybody who recognizes Israel will burn in fire of the Islamic fury. The radical Islamic psyche of human life has no value except for how the person dies, not even the lives of women and children. The belief is that anyone who dares disagree against the Islamic religion is wrong. They will stand against the whole world and will not cease until annihilation of all. Either we all become Islamic or we die. Either we shake one another's hands in joy at the victory of Islam in the world or all of us will turn to eternal life and martyrdom. In both cases, victory and success are ours. Every knee will bow to Islam and every Christian and Jew will be enslaved.

Islamic religious fanatics are convinced they will win. They see Americans as weak. They see Americans as having the weapons, but not the will, determination or resolve to carry out a prolonged war. The United States lacks the will and determination to challenge the Islamic revolution that is willing to fight for centuries if necessary to reach its goal. When push comes to shove, the United States and its Western allies would abandon Israel rather than go to a prolonged war on its behalf.

We have the hope of intercepting intercontinental ballistic missiles in flight through something like the Star Wars program of defense satellites. No country with nuclear weapons would dare attack America because they know immediate retaliatory annihilation would result. However, a terrorist organization with no physical address, no telephone number and no zip code would not fear such retaliation. The thought about a nuclear terrorist attack in the United States is very real. Only about 5 percent of the millions of cargo containers entering the United States each year are inspected. Our military minds are deeply concerned about a nuclear attack in America. It will happen; it's inevitable that it will happen, not if – but when.

In God We Trust

Most can remember the classic painting of Jesus standing outside a door waiting to be allowed entry. Prayer has been removed from our schools, suits have been filed to force Congress to remove "under God" from the Pledge of Allegiance. Displays of the Ten Commandments have been removed from public buildings. The motto "In God We Trust" is in danger of extinction. Teachers have been forbidden to carry a personal Bible in view of students and Christian literature has been removed from library shelves. Religious Christmas carols have been banned from school programs and spring break has replaced Easter vacation. We should ask ourselves, are we better off today? Are the schools safer for our children? Are fewer kids on drugs? Are there fewer crimes in our nation today?

The American courts support such movements as gay rights, abortion rights and even animal rights; take a look at the NFL superstar quarterback Michael Vick on animal rights. We are now pursuing the right to be godless. We have rejected the foundation of our culture that has traditionally held us together. Are things falling apart? We have separation of church and state, first Amendment rights are denied to those who would speak for God. When the first Continental Congress set out to write the document that would govern the United States, not one time did they adopt the words "separation of church and state". It's not there – read it. The writers of the Constitution would be amazed at the interpretation of the document over which they shed blood, sweat and tears. God has been replaced by science. We are at a crucial point in the history of this country. Be a participant; don't just sit on the sidelines while our basic freedoms are lost.

Are we trying to bring God down to our level? Take the Constitution, all men are created equal. We have applied it to religion and have declared that all religions are the same. We are all going to the same place; we're just taking different roads to get there. The cross of Christ has been reduced to costume jewelry and the blood of Christ has been counted as worthless. Babies die daily, aborted or sacrificed for self interest; it's all about me, me and me. Abortion has become a valid means of birth control for many women. Have a one night stand, get pregnant – no problem. Take a morning after pill or visit the local abortion clinic. After all, it's only tissue, not a real baby. But we now have AIDS, is God telling us something?

On 11 September 2001, America met evil head on when nineteen Islamic fanatics commandeered four American airliners and piloted them into the World Trade Towers and the Pentagon. It was our first taste of hate, as preached by the radical Islamic religion. Immediately following the attack, the politically correct were hard at work to avoid calling a terrorist a terrorist. Some objected to the use of the words Islamic or Muslim. One man's terrorist is another man's freedom fighter. America was declared guilty of aggression, having deserved the attacks due to some perceived ill against Islam and the American flag stands for intimidation, censorship and violence. President Bush stated that Americans should not expect one battle, but a lengthy campaign, unlike any other we have ever seen. Either you are with us or you are with the terrorists. Any nation that continues to harbor or support terrorism will be regarded by the United States as a hostile regime. America was labeled a terrorist state and President Bush was equated to Adolf Hitler.

The Great Satan

There has long been a fascination in the Islamic world with all things Hitler. The Arab states of Syria and Iraq were patterned after Hitler's concepts. Just as Hitler's vision was a world under the domination of his Nazi regime, so the vision of today's radical Islamic world is a world under the domination of Islam. The Islamic world calls America "The Great Satan" and our closest ally Israel "The Little Satan". Radical Islam has given birth to a weapon that truly cheapens human life, the suicide bomber. It is not a matter of land for peace; it is a matter of using any means possible to rid the Middle East of the Jewish population altogether.

Americans in general still attend church. Look at the success of the Left Behind series by Tim LaHaye and Jerry Jenkins. I have read the complete series and greatly enjoyed it. We also have the Mel Gibson's "The Passion of the Christ", which received much attention and it was a movie that made you think. The Bible is still an all time national best seller. Why has God been taken out of schools, while the distribution of condoms is allowed? Many churches, which once stood for everything good and right, have become just another club where people gather to socialize. Behavior stems from what we think and from our attitudes, beliefs, values and opinions. There is a lack of moral clarity in America's church today. The church is paying millions of dollars out to Americas due to sexual misconduct on behalf of men of God. Men of God and their sexual misconduct with our children is just wrong.

There are prisoners in Guantanamo Bay that have not been tried, have no legal representation and their families cannot see them. There is no international monitoring of their conditions and fate. No one knows whether they are prisoners, POW or criminals. Did we defend the rights of the underprivileged or ignore them? Did we defend the rights of all people around the world or impose wars on them? Are you pleased with the current condition of the world? If billions of dollars spent on security, military campaigns and troop movement were instead spent on investment and assistance for poor countries, promotion of health, combating different diseases, education and improvement, creation of employment opportunities and establishment of peace, where would the world be today? Just think about it. If Jesus Christ was with us today, how would he judge such behavior? Is there no better way to interact with the rest of the world?

Share a common responsibility to promote and protect freedom, human dignity and integrity. Embrace the promotion of human ideals, respect for the rights of human beings, defending the innocent and the weak against oppressors and bullies. We have common concerns, face similar challenge and are pained by the sufferings in the world that we live in. We can do better as a human race. The global position of the United States is in all probability weakened because we have continued to use force in supporting our interests. We all condemn terrorism because its victims are the innocent. Many victims of Hurricane Katrina continue to suffer and countless Americans continue to live in poverty and are homeless. Is it possible to sincerely serve and promote common human values with honesty and compassion? Injustice and transgression will eventually bring about decline and demise.

Iran believes that America is the "Great Satan", Europe is the "Middle Sized Satan" and Israel is the "Little Satan". They deny that the Holocaust, the murder of six million Jews took place. Iran is not the Soviet Union during the Cold War. Iran is not a rational force, anything but that. Whatever you could say about the Soviet Union, it acted fair on the world scene. Every time their ideology of world domination conflicted with their survival, they always backed off. They were rational in that regard, but you can't count on Iran, while armed with nuclear weapons, to be rational and back off like the Soviet Union. Have you ever heard of a communist suicide bomber? The militant Islam produces battalions of them. They smash into buildings in Manhattan, the Pentagon, US warships, schools, buses, you name it. Anything for their twisted ideology and to further their interests; this is the danger of this creed. It's not a choice for them; it is almost like an order from Allah. That's why these people are willing to commit suicide. Believing they will somehow inherit paradise while they cause hell for everybody else and for their people as well. Imagine a world in which Hitler had atomic bombs. It begins with Israel, just like the case with Nazis began with the Jews and then proceeds to everyone else.

The US administrations, from Jimmy Carter through George W. Bush, have treated terrorism as a law enforcement problem up until 911. Just go out and catch some of the terrorists and put them in jail; that would deter the others, but terrorists are not deterred by some of their numbers being arrested and imprisoned. They are not burglars or white collar criminals, they are fanatics. They have a belief of some divine religious mission. Their religious beliefs are at the heart of this fanaticism. Persians invented the game of chess, so deception is certainly something that is part of their repertoire. Moral clarity is very important in winning the war on terrorism. We shouldn't have self doubt about ourselves. These people hate us for who we are. They hate us for freedom of speech. They hate us for freedom of religion.

The Iranians have good reason to doubt our will. They seized our hostages in 1979 and we had an ineffective rescue operation. In 1983 they blew up our embassy and our marine barracks in Lebanon and we left. For various Iranian and terrorist attacks in the 1980s, we basically sent lawyers. We treated it as a matter of law enforcement. Then in 1991 we had half a million troops in Iraq. Both the Kurds and Shiites rebel against Saddam, succeeding in fifteen of Iraq's eighteen provinces. We stopped, stood aside and invited Saddam to move against them and watched while they were massacred. What did we do next? We left once again. In 1993 Saddam tries to kill former President Bush in Kuwait with a bomb. We launched some cruise missiles against an Iraqi intelligence building in the middle of the night so it would be empty. Also in 1993, we had Black Hawk Down in Mogadishu and once again we left. Up until 911 we basically ran this as a law enforcement operation, tried to catch a few terrorists and put them in prison. It's understandable that the Iranians think that we are paper tigers. The most dangerous thing to do in dealing with religious fanatics is to talk big and then not follow through. This is what we have done since the 1980s. We should think and act like Teddy Roosevelt, "speak softly and carry a big stick". Sometimes, we must use that big stick.

War of Ideas

We achieved initial victories in both Afghanistan and Iraq with a minimum of military force. Then we didn't plan in either case for the long haul. We're having difficulties in Afghanistan and big difficulties in Iraq because of that. Terrorism is a tactic, it's a terrible tactic, but it's a tactic. We have got much bigger problems than terrorism – Islamic Nazis. From Al Qaeda's point of view, they want to get the United States and all Western countries, including Israel, out of the Middle East. They want to govern the Arab world, then the Muslim world and then finally the whole world. That's the way things should go from their point of view. Afghanistan and Iraq are only the beginning of a very long war.

This is a war of ideas that we're in today. It requires an information war that is carried out in concert with our allies around the globe. We really need a more effective campaign to show the good things that are coming about as a result of not only America's efforts, but also our allies that are in this war with us. You find more liberal universities in America that would invite the president of Iran to come over and make speeches at their university. We must not be opposed to freedom of speech and opposing opinions, but we should be concerned about the support of terrorism that is coming out of Iran in almost every aspect. Look back at Bosnia and Kosovo. Look at the Khobar Towers and Afghanistan. Now look at Iraq. There are ties into Iran that cannot be denied. We have a military that is committed very heavily right now and seem to just turn the other way, and so they get away with it.

Fighting terrorism is more like fighting organized crime. You want to go after their economics, their base of support. You want to do everything politically and diplomatically that you can. Al Qaeda is a snake and you must chop the head off of the snake. The head of that snake is Osama Bin Laden. Unlike a military organization, they don't have tanks, airplanes, and infrastructure that you can attack and bomb. So you've got to go after individuals and in that regard it's more like fighting crime.

How do we stop Iran? It's in America's best interest to use the international community, not just America, to form a coalition. Use that coalition either to bring pressure against them to settle peacefully and accept a UN supervision of their nuclear development, or use them to go in and take it. Do whatever you need to do militarily that the international community feels is necessary. Stop Iran from obtaining nuclear weapons.

If we must go into Iran, go with an international force. It's extremely important because of the perception throughout the Middle East that America is there just for the oil. If we go into Iran, we want to do it as part of an international force. After all, they're defying the international community now with their nuclear program, not just America but the international community and the UN. Therefore, it should be the UN that makes that decision.

Needless to say, it's always easier to get in than it is to get out. We've learned that time and time again. But it's a lot easier to get out if you've got a good plan going in for transitioning into the nation building aspect. From that withdraw plan, pull all forces out or remain with a small contingent. A small contingent that stays as part of an international force until the new government is fully stood up and ready to maintain peace and security themselves.

The freedoms that we enjoy may be our greatest weakness in the eyes of Al Qaeda. It's not a matter of if we're attacked; it's a matter of when. Anyone that really puts their mind to it and has time on their side with resources can eventually get the stuff where they need it in the United States to carry out an attack. Our greatest defense could be our intelligence community and it has to be done on a worldwide basis. Look at Indonesia, the fourth largest nation in the world and the largest Muslim nation in the world. It's an ideal breeding ground for terrorism. It could be the next training ground for Al Qaeda.

The Cold War was considerably simpler. You had two superpowers, the United States and Russia. The Soviet Union and all of its partners in the Warsaw Pact countries; lined up against the United Nations and all of its partners. No one stepped out of line without checking with the leader; America being the leader of the free world and Russia being the leader of the Warsaw Pact. When the wall came down, all those nations broke away from Russian. It became a more complicated world because you no longer had just the two superpowers talking. You have independent actors now doing their own thing and no one kind of a reign in power.

When you look at America, our commitment of forces went up over 300 percent in the ten years following the wall coming down, than it had been in the previous twenty-five years. It is more complicated in today's world. Is the world safer today with the wall down? At the time, we really believed that the wall coming down was a great thing. But what will history show a hundred years from now? We have to build new coalitions with new partnerships for a safer world.

There's probably a lot of resistance to joining any kind of a coalition that might get them involved in something like we're involved in with Iraq. That's something we're going to have to overcome. We've got to stand for what's right and it may mean sacrifice, but in the end, it's doing what's right for peace and security throughout the world; not just worrying about own little piece of it. There's not any nation out there that wants to see Iran running around with nuclear weapons, particularly given the importance of the Middle East region to the rest of the world.

We have to recognize that this is a global war that we're facing. It is a war that we've got to win. We must build an international coalition and it doesn't have to be all Americas' resources that we can turn against the terrorist threat. You must ensure that you have definitive proof of terrorism. Once you get it, the group that does it to you and that kills your citizens has got to pay a price. Hit them, and hit them hard. It's going to be a lot worse than what they did to you.

When people think of the war, they think of Iraq or Afghanistan only. What they don't come to grips with is that those are battles in a real war. The real war is against Islamic Fascism. We see each individual battle as a war, the war in Afghanistan, the war in Iraq, but they're not. We should say the current battle is Afghanistan and the battle in Iraq.

Islamic Fascism is a belief that is driven by a twisted version of religion where you pick certain parts of a religion; a tremendously unbalanced view of religion. Take people who have grievances against their government or the situation in their country. Then you tell them that it's not really their fault that they live that way, its' really the fault of the Jews and the Americans. Your society will get better by killing all Jews and all Americans.

Many people think of a war as a war for land or war for wealth. The fact of the matter is these people do not want what we have; they just don't want us to have it. The option that they're presenting is to either do it their way or they kill us. So we have to want our way of life more than they want us to live under theirs. If we don't, we're in for a very long and painful journey.

The group running Al Qaeda, who are the Sunni Extremists, are politically aware of world events. They understand that the center of gravity in the war against them is the will of the American people to fight. They are trying to shake the will of the American people to sustain that effort. If we back away from Iraq and Afghanistan, there will be such a vacuum. Our grandchildren will be fighting this war for a very long time and the freedom of the free world is at risk.

The front of the Islamic revolution started in 1979 when they took our embassy down. They have been fighting us and have been at war with us ever since. We have yet to truly realize the magnitude of that and we've been denying it through several administrations. We are where we are and if we don't get serious about this soon, they're going to have nukes. When they have nuclear weapons, a lot of options that we have today are going to be gone. Bad news does not get better with time. We must front the Islamic revolution. There are some who believe that the Iranians already have nuclear weapons.

How are the terrorists being funded? It's being funded mostly through Iran and it's coming from the cost of oil. Iran is a major oil producer. They're taking that money and they're using it to subsidize their political activities. There are probably sleeper cells here in our country right now and they're going to keep coming. That's the thing we have to get in our heads. They are at war with us. They don't want to negotiate. They want to kill all of us.

Iranian ideology

Western minded people don't understand the Iranian ideology. They call it Nation of Islam. The Nation of Islam perceives the West as threat to their ideology, to their culture, and they believe that they'll be able to defeat the West from the cultural point of view. Their intent is to impose this new government by use of terrorism. Today the Iranian regime is determined to acquire military nuclear capability. We are facing different Islamic ideologies. The ideologies of Iranian and Al Qaeda are very different, but share the same agenda and strategy. This is the case of the Muslim Brotherhood coming from this different ideology, calling to impose the Nation of Islam all over the world. The Iranian ideology actually is to dominate the Islamic world and to dominate the world by imposing Islam. The ideology is to reach peace all over the world. All the people, all over the world, would be Muslims, this is the idea.

Today the Iranian regime is concentrating on dealing with the American interest in the region, like in Iraq, the Persian Gulf state and Israel. They see America as a spearhead of Western culture and religion, but the strategic goal is to defeat the United States, to defeat the Western culture, to defeat the Western values and impose the Nation of Islam. In order to win this kind of war, we need the awareness of Westerners. Then we need moral clarity and a clear strategy.

Iran is the big winner of the most recent crisis in the Middle East. They gained power, influence and have tried very hard to send a message to the United States and Israel that their nuclear facilities are invulnerable to attack. Iran hides behind their civilians. They build a nuclear facility and put a hospital on top of it. They build a nuclear facility and build a school on top of it. Iran says either kill our children, our weak and elderly and get condemned by the United Nations or leave us alone.

Our greatest generation in World War II killed hundreds of thousands of civilians in Germany. We are in a war that will go beyond our children and grandchildren's lives. Iran is a major threat to the United States. Iran, if not stopped, will get a nuclear bomb and will use that nuclear bomb to blackmail America and other countries. It changes the entire structure and balance of power. You can deter people who don't want to die, but many of Iran's leaders welcome death. They are part of the culture of death. It's very hard to deter a culture that welcomes death, so Iran would be a great threat to the United States.

Iran has figured out how to use terrorism. They have figured out how to hide behind civilians and make it difficult for people with high moral standards to get at the terrorists. Most Americans don't understand why Iran poses a great threat. If Iran got a nuclear weapon, the risk is simply too high that Iran would use that nuclear weapon.

The way to make terrorism stop is never to reward it and always to hold the terrorists responsible. Terrorism has to be dealt with the way piracy was dealt with in the eighteenth and nineteenth centuries. We were able to abolish piracy for the most part because pirates were regarded as international criminals that no country would give in to. We need to understand that this is a long term war, which will not be won in our lifetime, maybe even our children's lifetime. Change the rules of engagement and adapt then to the new threats that we have today.

The most important and fundamental right that a human being has is the right to live, the right to have children and the right to be free. Terrorism has been around almost as long as mankind, but we are in the beginning of a new type of warfare. One of the great dilemmas of the modern world is how do we find some way to prevent people from using innocent women and children as shields? Iran is the most radical, extremist, religious, religiously motivated group in the Middle East.

This is a religious extreme that we have never encountered. It is compounded by the fact that they do not have a culture of life; it's a culture of death. We have never been up against a group of people who believe that there is a higher calling by dying for their religion, not living for it. We have great challenges and interesting times ahead of us as a nation.

— 7 —

America's Economy

In the past century, our debt has ballooned, currently over 14 trillion dollars. Which means that every American citizen, every man, woman, and child in America has a debt of $50,000. What are we doing to our nation? When will our out of control spending stop?

In 2001, George W. Bush won perhaps the most bitterly contested presidential race of the past century over Al Gore. Almost immediately he sprung into action, trying to avoid the same fate that crippled his fathers political career almost ten years earlier, tax increases. Bush signed one of the largest tax breaks in history, close to 1 trillion dollars over eight years. Then, September 11, 2001 changed the face of Bush's presidency forever. The 9/11 terrorist attacks would define a generation, and in turn, indebt the next generation of Americans. George Bush launched the Afghanistan and Iraqi wars, while at the same time, imposing more and more tax breaks on Americans. This was an unprecedented act, no president had ever launched two wars while at the same time reducing taxes. Wars are very expensive.

So was the new Medicare bill passed by Bush. In 2002, the "Pay As You Go" bill that hampered Clinton's spending as president, and in turn developed some sort of fiscal responsibility back into the White House, expired. Bush Jr. was free to spend however he wanted, and used that to his advantage by passing a new Medicare in 2003 that required government to subsidize healthcare spending for seniors. The combined costs of Medicare, the Iraq and Afghan wars, and the widespread reduction in taxes (mostly for the wealthy Americans) led to a quadrupling of the American national debt, and destroyed any semblance of fiscal responsibility in America. The debt is expected to double, over $23 trillion, in the next ten years.

The United States remains the greatest country in the world but there is no doubt we are facing difficult economic times right now. We are in a serious recession and we must be willing to tackle it by putting aside partisan politics and sticking to the core principles of our founding fathers of a free market and limited government. Our problems can be traced back to the housing market and that is where our recovery must start. We must get to the root of the problem, rather than addressing only the symptoms. Jump-starting the demand for housing is essential to boosting our economy we must fix housing first. All homeowners should be eligible for refinancing opportunities to help homeowners in trouble. We should not punish responsible homeowners or deny them access to the proposed refinancing opportunities. Something must be done to assist the decline that our nation has seen in mortgage backed securities and real estate. This has caused tremendous problems for our nation's banks. These rules should be replaced with a mechanism to absorb assets over time. This would allow those assets to be more reflective of reality and less reflective of the dire straits that our nation is currently in today.

The Great Depression was a period of worldwide economic depression that lasted from 1929 until approximately 1939, 10 years. The starting point of the Great Depression is usually listed as October 29, 1929, commonly called Black Tuesday. This was the date when the stock market fell dramatically. This was after two previous stock market crashes on Black Tuesday (October 24), and Black Monday (October 28). The Dow Jones Industrial Average would eventually bottom out by July, 1932 with a loss of approximately 90% of its value. However, the actual causes are much more complicated than just the stock market crash. In fact, historians and economists do not always agree about the exact causes of the depression. Are we about to travel the same road once again? Throughout 1930, consumer spending continued to decline which meant businesses cut jobs thereby increasing unemployment. Further, a severe drought across America meant that agricultural jobs were reduced. Countries across the globe were affected and many protectionist polices were created thereby increasing the problems on a global scale.

The Great Depression, an immense tragedy that placed millions of Americans out of work, was the beginning of government involvement in the economy and in society as a whole. After nearly a decade of optimism and prosperity, the United States was thrown into despair on Black Tuesday, October 29, 1929, the day the stock market crashed and the official beginning of the Great Depression. As stock prices plummeted with no hope of recovery, panic struck. Masses and masses of people tried to sell their stock, but no one was buying. The stock market, which had appeared to be the surest way to become rich, quickly became the path to bankruptcy. The Stock Market Crash was just the beginning. Since many banks had also invested large portions of their clients' savings in the stock market, these banks were forced to close when the stock market crashed. Seeing a few banks close caused another panic across the country. Afraid they would lose their own savings, people rushed to banks that were still open to withdraw their money. This massive withdrawal of cash caused additional banks to close. Since there was no way for a bank's clients to recover any of their savings once the bank had closed, those who didn't reach the bank in time also became bankrupt.

Herbert Hoover was president at the beginning of the Great Depression. He tried to institute reforms to help stimulate the economy but they had little to no effect. By 1933, unemployment in the United States was at a staggering 25%. Franklin Roosevelt became president and immediately instituted the first New Deal. This was a comprehensive group of short-term recovery programs. It not only included economic aid and work assistance programs but also the end of the gold standard. Then followed by the Second New Deal programs which included more long term assistance such as the Federal Deposit Insurance Corporation (FDIC), the Social Security System, the Federal Housing Administration (FHA), Fannie Mae and the Security and Exchange Commission (SEC). However, there is still question today about the effectiveness of many of these programs as a recession occurred in 1937. During these years, unemployment rose again. Some blame the New Deal programs as being hostile towards businesses. Others state that the New Deal, while not ending the Great Depression, at least helped the economy by increasing regulation and preventing further decay. In 1940, unemployment was still at 14%. However, with America's entry into World War II and subsequent mobilization, unemployment rates dropped. While some argue that the war itself did not end the Great Depression, others point to the increase in government spending and increased job opportunities as reasons why it was a large part of the national economic recovery.

Businesses and industry were also affected. Having lost much of their own capital in either the Stock Market Crash or the bank closures, many businesses started cutting back their workers' hours or wages. In turn, consumers began to curb their spending, refraining from purchasing such things as luxury goods. This lack of consumer spending caused additional businesses to cut back wages or, more drastically, to lay off some of their workers. Some businesses couldn't stay open even with these cuts and soon closed their doors, leaving all their workers unemployed. To many at the time, President Franklin Roosevelt was a hero. They believed that he cared deeply for the common man and that he was doing his best to end the Great Depression. Looking back, however, it is uncertain as to how much Roosevelt's New Deal programs helped to end the Great Depression. By all accounts, the New Deal programs eased the hardships of the Great Depression; however, the U.S. economy was still extremely bad by the end of the 1930s. The major turn around for the U.S. economy occurred after the bombing of Pearl Harbor and the entrance of the United States into World War II. Once the U.S. was involved in the war, both people and industry became essential to the war effort. Weapons, artillery, ships, and airplanes were needed quickly. Men were trained to become soldiers and the women were kept on the home front to keep the factories going. Food needed to be grown for both the home front and to send overseas. It was ultimately the entrance of the U.S. into World War II that ended the Great Depression in the United States.

Poverty

Poverty in the United States is roughly 15% living below the federal poverty line at any given point in time, and roughly 40% falling below the poverty line at some point within a 10 year time span. The definition of the word poverty is the state of one who lacks a usual or socially acceptable amount of money or material possessions. The word poverty means poor. However, the government's definition of poverty is not tied to an absolute value of how much an individual or family can afford, but is tied to a relative level based on how much the average individual makes, around $23,000 annually or less. Around 60% of Americans will spend at least one year below the poverty line at some point between ages 25 and 75. There remains some controversy over whether the official poverty threshold over or understates poverty.

The most common measure of poverty in the United States is the poverty threshold set by the USD government. This measure recognizes poverty as a lack of those goods and services commonly taken for granted by members of mainstream society. The official threshold is adjusted for inflation using the consumer price index. Relative poverty describes how income relates to the median income, and does not imply that the person is lacking anything. In general the United States has some of the highest relative poverty rates among industrialized countries, reflecting both the high median income and high degree of inequality. In terms of pre-transfer absolute poverty rates, in 2000 the United States ranked tenth among sixteen developed countries, though 2000 was a 'trough' year and subsequently absolute poverty rates have increased. The US does worse in post-transfer absolute poverty rates. According to a 2008 report released by the Carsey Institute at the University of New Hampshire, on average, rates of poverty are persistently higher in rural and inner city parts of the country as compared to suburban areas.

The official number of poor in the United States as of this writing is about 39 million people, greater in number but not percentage than the officially poor in Indonesia, which has a far lower Human Development Index and the next largest population after the United States. Number of poor are hard to compare across countries. Absolute income may be used but does not reflect the actual number of poor, which depend on relative income and cost of living in each country. Among developed countries, each country then has its own definition and threshold of what it means to be poor, but this is not adjusted for cost of living and social benefits. For instance, despite the fact that France and US have about the same threshold in terms of dollars amount for poverty, cost of living and health benefits may differ (with universal health insurance coverage for poor people in France). Some countries like India where poverty is important have strong social family structure that makes poverty less unbearable.

Another way of looking at poverty is in relative terms. "Relative poverty" can be defined as having significantly less access to income and wealth than other members of society. Therefore, the relative poverty rate can directly be linked to income inequality. When the standard of living among those in more financially advantageous positions rises while that of those considered poor stagnates, the relative poverty rate will reflect such growing income inequality and increase. Conversely, the poverty rate can decrease, with low income people coming to have less wealth and income if wealthier people's wealth is reduced by a larger percentage than theirs. In 1960, a family at the poverty line had an income that was 42% of the median income. Thus, a poor family in 2000 had less income and therefore less purchasing power than wealthier members of society in 1960, therefore, "poverty" had increased. But, because this is a relative measure, this is not saying that a family in 2000 with the same amount of wealth and income as a family from 1960 had less purchasing power than the 1960 family.

Relying on income disparity to determine who is impoverished can be misleading. The Bureau of Labor Statistics data suggests that consumer spending varies much less than income. In 2008, the "poorest" one fifth of Americans households spent on average $12,900 per person for goods and services (other than taxes), the second quintile spent $14,100, the third $16,200, the fourth $19,7005, while the "richest" fifth spent $26,600. The disparity of expenditures is much less than the disparity of income.

The median household income is much higher in the US than in Europe due to the wealth of the middle classes in the US, from which the poverty line is derived. Although the paradigm of relative poverty is most valuable, this comparison of poverty lines show that the higher prevalence of relative poverty levels in the US are not an indicator of a more severe poverty problem but an indicator of larger inequalities between rich middle classes and the low-income households. It is therefore not correct to state that the US income distribution is characterized by a large proportion of households in poverty; it is characterized by relatively large income inequality but also high levels of prosperity of the middle classes.

There are numerous factors related to poverty in the United States. The relationship between tax rates and poverty is disputed. A study comparing high tax Scandinavian countries with the U. S. suggests high tax rates are inversely correlated with poverty rates. The poverty rate, however, is low in some low tax countries such as Switzerland. A comparison of poverty rates between states reveals that some low tax states have low poverty rates. For example, New Hampshire has the lowest poverty rate of any state in the U. S., and has very low taxes (46th among all states).

Income is directly related to educational levels. The median earnings of individuals with less than a 9th grade education is $16,000, while high school graduates earned $31,000, holders of bachelor's degree earned $57,000, and individuals with professional degrees earned $100,000. In many cases poverty is caused by job loss. The current poverty rate is around 21% for individuals who were unemployed, but only 2% for individuals who were employed full time. Around 8% of children in two-parent families were likely to live in poverty; 19% of children lived with father in single parent family; and 47% in single parent family headed by mother. Drug use and poverty are directly related. Over three quarters of drug users in treatment left school before 16 years of age while 70% of drug users are unemployed.

Income levels vary along racial/ethnic lines: 21% of all children in the United States live in poverty, about 46% of African American children and 40% of Latino children live in poverty. What is unclear is why so many minorities live in poverty. It is noted, however, that the poverty rate is 10% for black married couples. But only 30% of black children are born to married couples. Only 11% of black women aged 30–44 without a high school diploma had a working spouse. The poverty rate for native born and naturalized whites is 10%. On the other hand, the poverty rate for naturalized blacks is 12% compared to 25% for native born blacks suggesting race alone does not explain income disparity. Not all minorities have low incomes. Not only do Asian families have higher incomes than blacks and Hispanics, they have higher incomes than white families. For example, the current median income of Asian families is $68,900 compared to the median income of white families of $59,100. Asians, however, report that they face discrimination more frequently than blacks. Specifically, 31% of Asians reported employment discrimination compared to 26% of blacks.

The conservative speculates that illegal immigration increases job competition among low wage earners, both native and foreign born. Additionally many first generation immigrants, namely those without a high school diploma, are also living in poverty themselves. Much of the debate about poverty focuses on statistical measures of poverty and the clash between advocates and opponents of welfare programs and government regulation of the free market. Since measures can be either absolute or relative, it is possible that advocates for the different sides of this debate are basing their arguments on different ways of measuring poverty. It is often claimed that poverty is understated, yet there are some who also believe it is overstated; thus the accuracy of the current poverty threshold guidelines is subject to debate and considerable concern.

In recent years, there have been a number of concerns raised about the official U.S. poverty measure. The National Research Council's Committee on National Statistics convened a panel on measuring poverty. The findings of the panel were that "the official poverty measure in the United States is flawed and does not adequately inform policy-makers or the public about who is poor and who is not poor." The official U.S. poverty measure "has not kept pace with far-reaching changes in society and the economy." The panel proposed a model based on disposable income. According to the panel's recommended measure, income would include, in addition to money received, the value of non-cash benefits such as food stamps, school lunches and public housing that can be used to satisfy basic needs. The new measure also would subtract from gross income certain expenses that cannot be used for these basic needs, such as income taxes, child-support payments, medical costs, health-insurance premiums and work-related expenses, including child care.

Many sociologists and government officials have argued that poverty in the United States is understated, meaning that there are more households living in actual poverty than there are households below the poverty threshold. A recent report stated that as much as 30% of Americans have trouble making ends meet and other advocates have made supporting claims that the rate of actual poverty in the US is far higher than that calculated by using the poverty threshold. While the poverty threshold is updated for inflation every year, the basket of goods used to determine what constitutes being deprived of a socially acceptable minimum standard of living has not been updated since 1955, the year that I was born. As a result, the current poverty line only takes goods into account that were common more than 50 years ago, updating their cost using the Consumer Price Index. The official poverty line today is essentially what it takes in today's dollars, adjusted for inflation, to purchase the same poverty-line level of living that was appropriate to a half century ago, in 1955, for that year furnished the basic data for the formula for the very first poverty measure. Updated thereafter only for inflation, the poverty line lost all connection over time with current consumption patterns of the average family. Quite a few families then didn't have their own private telephone, or a car, or even a mixer in their kitchen. The official poverty line has thus been allowed to fall substantially below a socially decent minimum, even though its intention was to measure such a minimum.

When you hear that someone is "poor," it brings to mind images of a person who may be homeless and malnourished. Fortunately, however, that description is not reflective of the majority of individuals labeled as poor by the federal government. The 2000 Census indicates that 73% of U.S. poor own automobiles, 76% have air conditioning, 97% own refrigerators, 62% have cable or satellite TV, and 73% have microwaves. There are many homeless and malnourished individuals in the United States, but the poverty thresholds are high enough to include many individuals who live with some modern comforts. Instead of being homeless, almost half (46%) own their own homes with most of the rest renting their homes. On average a poor person in this country lives in a home with 1,200 square feet which they often own, and as noted the home is likely air conditioned, with a refrigerator, cable or satellite TV, a microwave not to mention many other comforts. A person could conclude that if the American poor formed a country of their own, they would be as well-off or even slightly better-off than the typical family in most European countries.

Non-cash income is ignored when measuring poverty rates. Welfare benefits provided in-kind such as food stamps and public housing are excluded. Even though such benefits may raise the standard of living for recipients, they, by definition, remain impoverished under federal guidelines. On the other hand, benefits provided in the form of cash, such as social security benefits, are included in income. This explains, in part, why the poverty rate for older Americans is lower than the poverty rate for younger Americans.

No one avoided the unnecessary expenditures, such as the occasional trip to the Dairy Queen, or a pair of stylish new sneakers for the son who might otherwise sell drugs to get them, or the Cable TV subscription for the kids home alone and you are afraid they will be out on the street if they are not watching TV. Poverty rates might be misleading because they merely measure the number of people living under the poverty line, but do not tell us how well-off the average people and people above the poverty line are, thereby potentially providing a distorted picture of people's well-being in that country. This means that a country with a higher rate of absolute poverty is not necessarily a country of average worse-off people, or even a country of some very poor and some very rich people. While there is about double as much poverty in the US compared to many European countries, average Americans might turn out to be much better-off than average Europeans. The average Americans are in fact rich by European standards. Most states of the US have a higher per capita which correlates with wages and salaries, and people in the US are much more likely to have dishwashers, microwaves, clothes dryers, VCRs, personal computers, TVs, and cars than people in any European country, while as likely to have other appliances except for cell phones.

There have been many governmental and nongovernmental efforts to reduce poverty and its effects. These range in scope from neighborhood efforts to campaigns with a national focus. They target specific groups affected by poverty such as children, people who are autistic, immigrants, or people who are homeless. Efforts to alleviate poverty use a disparate set of methods, such as advocacy, education, social work, legislation, direct service or charity, and community organizing. Recent debates have centered on the need for policies that focus on both "income poverty" and "asset poverty." Advocates for the approach argue that traditional governmental poverty policies focus solely on supplementing the income of the poor, through programs such as Food Stamps. These programs do little, if anything, to help the poor build assets and begin to lift themselves out of poverty. Some have proposed creating a government matched savings plan (similar to the private 401K) system to provide a savings incentive to poor and lower-income individuals and families.

Homeless Population

Homelessness in the United States increased significantly in the late 1970s and became an important political topic. The number of homeless people further grew in the 1980s, as housing and social service cuts increased and the economy deteriorated. The United States government determined that somewhere between 200,000 and 500,000 Americans were then homeless. The number of homeless is reported to have risen since that time. Over the past decade, the availability and quality of data on homelessness has improved considerably, due in part to initiatives by the US Department of Housing and Urban Development, the US Department of Health and Human Services, the US Department of Veterans Affairs, and several nongovernmental organizations working with homeless populations. Improved data collection has lead to a more accurate and complete understanding of the nature of homelessness in the United States.

According to the US Department of Housing and Urban Development, there are over 664,000 sheltered and unsheltered homeless persons nationwide on a single night. Additionally, about 1.6 million persons used an emergency shelter or a transitional housing program. This number suggests that 1 in every 190 persons in the United States uses the shelter system. According to the United States Conference of Mayors, the main cause is the lack of affordable housing. The three next primary causes are mental illness or the lack of needed services, substance abuse and lack of needed services, and low-paying jobs. The causes cited were prisoner release, unemployment, domestic violence and poverty.

Establishing an accurate statistical number for the homeless population in America is complicated at best. Studies from reputable organizations report varying percentages. Homelessness as a subject matter is a contributing factor to this inconsistent reporting. The numbers of homeless fluctuate daily with an estimate of only 56% living in shelters.

Accurate statistics are impossible and can only be estimated based on educated guesses and sample population reporting. The two main types of homeless in America can be generally defined as chronic and transitional. Chronically homeless people make up around 23% of the homeless population and are specifically defined as disabled persons who have been persistently homeless for more than a year or who have been repeatedly homeless within the past three years. The transitional homeless can be defined as individuals and families who are without housing for a specific and generally shorter period of time.

Families constitute around 40% of America's homeless. Of the remaining 60% statistics show that and 40% are veterans and persons with mental illness make up around 20%. One study in Los Angeles determined that women constitute half of America's homeless population. This same study reports that children under the age of 18 represent 40% of the overall homeless population. Homeless statistics are generally based on an average of reporting counties who determine their statistics by the number of homeless living in shelters on a given night. Comprehensive national studies are rare and become dated by the time the results are published. Government reports may be slanted based on partisanship and other factors, while accurate independent information is complicated by lack of organization. Developing a more accurate estimation of the number of homeless living in America should be a priority. Underestimating the homeless population is a mistake that will significantly impact future social services procurement as well as the overall response from the general population. Having one study report that 744,000 persons were homeless in 2005 while another reported that 3.5 million were homeless creates too large a margin for error.

One of the most characteristic and consistent human behaviors over thousands of years is that humans build shelters. Homes offer protection from the elements and from a variety of health hazards and provide basic amenities such as a secure place to eat and sleep, to keep one's possessions, to raise a family, and be part of a community. Housing is a basic human need, yet the Human Development Report notes that more than 1 billion people, one-quarter of the world's population, live without shelter or in unhealthy and unacceptable conditions. Over 100 million people around the world have no shelter whatsoever. The health consequences of this level of homelessness are profound.

Homelessness is a matter of concern anywhere in the world, but it is a particular cause for concern and shame when it occurs in the richest nations in the world. Sadly, homelessness is a significant problem in both the United States and Canada. Accurate statistics on the level of homelessness are hard to come by. In part, this is because definitions of homelessness vary. It includes not only those who are living on the streets or in shelters but also those who are living in temporary accommodation or in housing that is unfit for human habitation. Estimates of the number of people without homes in the United States vary from 230,000 to 3 million, including between 50,000 and 500,000 children. The U.S. Department of Housing and Urban Development estimated in 1999 that "there are at least 600,000 homeless men, women, and children in the United States on any given night," adding that roughly one-third of this population is composed of families with children. In its 1997 position paper on eliminating homelessness, the American Public Health Association (APHA) noted that "as many as 7.4% of Americans (13.5 million people) may have experienced homelessness at some time in their lives." Homelessness increased in the 1990s, and the fastest growing segment of the homeless population was homeless families.

A wide array of factors contribute to homelessness, but they can be thought of as falling into one of two categories: structural problems and individual factors that increase vulnerability. Structural problems include a lack of affordable housing, changes in the industrial economy leading to unemployment, inadequate income supports, the deinstitutionalization of patients with mental health problems, and the erosion of family and social support. Added to this are factors that increase an individual's vulnerability, such as physical or mental illness, disability, substance abuse, domestic violence, or job loss. Reducing homelessness will mean addressing issues such as these.

The health effects of homelessness include higher rates of infectious diseases, mental health problems, physical disorders, disability, and premature death. A United Kingdom report noted that those sleeping on the street on average lived only to their mid-to-late forties. Higher rates of infectious disease result from overcrowding, damp and cold living conditions, poor nutrition, lack of immunization, and inadequate access to health care services. There has been a particular concern with increased rates of tuberculosis (TB), particularly multiple drug-resistant

TB. It has been reported, for example, that 48% of the homeless in Toronto test positive for TB. Another factor leading to increases in TB and other infectious diseases is the higher prevalence of AIDS (acquired immunodeficiency syndrome) in those segments of the homeless population involved in drug abuse and prostitution. The conditions in which homeless people live also make them more prone to trauma. A study of street people in Toronto found that 40% had been the victims of assault in the previous year, while 43% of the women reported sexual harassment and 21% reported they had been raped in the previous year. These street people were also more than five times more likely to have been involved (as pedestrians) in a motor vehicle accident than the general population, and one in twelve of them had suffered frostbite in the previous year.

The increase in homelessness among families in recent years has focused increasing attention on the serious health problems faced by children living in hostels and temporary accommodation. These problems include disturbed sleep, mood swings, depression, and developmental delays, as well as increased rates of obesity, anemia, infections, injuries, and other health problems. Not surprisingly, given all their health problems, homeless people make significant demands on the health care system. A study found that two-thirds of street people had seen a physician, more than half had used emergency rooms, and one-quarter of them had been admitted to hospital. But at the same time, homeless people, both those living on the street and temporary shelters, experience significant barriers in accessing care. These barriers include procedural barriers such as the need to have a home address or a health card, economic barriers in terms of purchasing necessary medications, medical supplies, or appropriate foods, and perhaps worst of all prejudice and rude treatment on the part of health care providers. It is particularly unfortunate that a group that is so vulnerable and has such high needs should suffer further indignity and prejudice from what are supposed to be the caring professions. Homelessness is a significant public health and health care issue. The persisting numbers of homeless people in America are an indictment of our collective failure to make basic ingredients of civilized society accessible to all citizens.

The condition of not having a permanent place to live is widely perceived as a societal problem. Estimates of the number of homeless people in the United States are imprecise. A survey made in 1994 found that 12 million Americans had experienced homelessness at some point in their lives; the vast majority of those who are homeless consists of single men and families with children. The problem exists in all major cities and many smaller communities. The causes range from large-scale deinstitutionalization of mentally ill people to disintegration of the social fabric in minority communities, drug and alcohol abuse, relatively stagnant wages at lower income levels, cutbacks in federal social-welfare programs, job loss, reductions in public housing, and rent increases and real-estate speculation. Some 3,700 agencies and organizations now operate shelters.

No nation is without its homeless. In the United States alone, between 280,000 and 600,000 men, women, and children are homeless each night, according to differing estimates. They are without permanent lodging because of poverty, lack of affordable housing, low wages, substance abuse, mental illness, or domestic violence. In many other countries, however, civil unrest, war, and famines bring about homelessness. At the beginning of the twenty-first century, there were more than eleven million homeless worldwide. Paramount among the problems facing the homeless are poor nutrition and hunger. They can be life-threatening, especially among refugees. Protein-energy malnutrition is a major contributory cause of death among newly displaced refugees. International relief organizations and the United Nations set up refugee camps and make the distribution of nutritionally adequate food rations a high priority. The homeless in the United States often do not experience such extreme food deprivations. However, many are often chronically undernourished. Compared to other groups at risk for hunger, the homeless are at greatest risk, being ten times more likely to go without food for a day compared to the poor. Few are able to obtain three meals a day, and many go at least one day a month without any food.

While many rely on homeless shelters, especially in winter months, a large number find refuge in cars, abandoned buildings, in parks, or other outdoor places. Most have been without a fixed and regular residence for more than one year. Lacking a stable home environment and cooking and storage facilities exacerbates their inability to obtain an adequate, varied, and healthy diet. While it is not uncommon to see a homeless person panhandling or scavenging for food through trash cans, most depend on soup kitchens and shelters for the major portion of their daily nourishment. Soup kitchens and shelters typically serve one meal a day on-site, although some shelters permit their residents to prepare and cook their own meals. Those who are substance abusers or have mental health problems are more likely to resort to obtaining food from trash cans or begging, compared to those without these health conditions. Participation in the Food Stamp Program, the government's largest anti-hunger program, is unusually low among the homeless. While homeless advocates speculate that most of the homeless are eligible, they argue that barriers such as documentation of identity or administrative burdens prevent many from participating. The difficulty of making effective use of food stamp benefits without adequate cooking and storage facilities is also a barrier. While the Food Stamp Program does permit states to contract with restaurants to serve meals at low prices to the homeless, such authorizations are uncommon among states.

There are many major causes of homelessness. The deinstitution-alization movement from the 1950s onwards in state mental health systems, to shift towards 'community-based' treatment of the mentally ill, as opposed to long-term commitment in institutions. Many patients ultimately lost their rooms, didn't get proper community health support, and ended up in the streets. Redevelopment activities instituted by cities across the country through which low-income neighborhoods are declared blighted and demolished to make way for projects that generate higher property taxes and other revenue, creating a shortage of housing affordable to low-income working families, the elderly poor, and the disabled. The failure of urban housing projects to provide safe, secure, and affordable housing to the poor. The economic crises which caused high unemployment. U.S. unemployment insurance does not allow unemployed insurance recipients to obtain job training and education while receiving benefits except under very limited situations. The failure of the U.S. Department of Veterans Affairs to provide effective mental health care and meaningful job training for many homeless veterans, particularly those of the Vietnam War. Foster home children are not given job training in school or at home. Without a means to make money, nearly half of foster children in the United States become homeless when they are released from foster care at age

18. Natural disasters that destroy homes such as hurricanes, floods, earthquakes, etc. Places of employment are often destroyed too, causing unemployment. People who have served time in prison, have abused drugs and alcohol, or have a history of mental illness find it difficult to impossible to find employment for years at a time because of the use of computer background checks by potential employers.

Prison Population

America's prison population topped 2 million inmates for the first time in history in 2002 according to a new report from the Justice Department's Bureau of Justice Statistics. The 50 states, the District of Columbia and the federal government held 1,355,748 prisoners (two-thirds of the total incarcerated population), and local municipal and county jails held 665,475 inmates. By midyear 2002, America's jails held 1 in every 142 U.S. residents. Males were incarcerated at the rate of 1,309 inmates per 100,000 U.S. men, while the female incarceration rate was 113 per 100,000 women residents. Of the 1,200,203 state prisoners, 3,055 were younger than 18 years old. In addition, adult jails held 7,248 inmates under 18.

For the first time since 1997 the number of additional jail inmates grew faster than the number of new jail beds. Nonetheless, local jails were operating at 7% below their officially rated capacities. At the end of 2001, the most recent period for which the data is available, state prisons were operating from around 15% above capacity, and federal prisons were at 30% above capacity. The Justice Department has released a new report showing the nation's prison and jail population reached a record 2.3 million people last year. The report provides a breakdown, noting "of the 2.3 million inmates in custody, 2.1 million were men and 208,300 were women. Black males represented the largest percentage (35.4 percent) of inmates held in custody, followed by white males (32.9 percent) and Hispanic males (17.9 percent)." The United States leads the industrialized world in incarceration. In fact, the U.S. rate of incarceration (762 per 100,000) is five to eight times that of other highly developed countries, according to The Sentencing Project, a criminal justice think tank.

Some of the key factors for the record imprisonment rate includes race and immigration. Black males continue to be incarcerated at an extraordinary rate. Black males make up 35% of the jail and prison population, even though they make up less than 10% of the overall U.S population. Around 4% of U.S. black males were in jail or prison last year, compared to just over 1% of Hispanic males and less than 1% of white males. In other words, black males were locked up at almost six times the rate of their white counterparts. Is it an emerging crime trend or is this the result of more local police and federal targeting of illegal immigrants? Non-U.S. citizens accounted for nearly 8% of the jail population in 2007, the new Justice Department report noted. Locking up these prisoners comes with huge economic costs. The Sentencing Project estimates that cost to be $60 billion per year for federal, state and local prison systems.

Has anyone ever thought of making prisons a place where people really don't want to go? Let's face it for the vast majority of prisoners prison is a lifestyle upgrade. You are housed with violent men whom you can't trust. They cook your food and do the work as do you. There is one TV in a common area that is shared by all and many men fight over it. You have no privacy for urinating or pooping. The States house the mentally ill in the prison because they tend to commit crimes. The guards play games, torture, retaliate, and do their best to cause you misery. No one wants to go who is in their right mind. Once you are in, there is no one on the outside who can get you out. The gates are locked.

Many states, facing budget crises, are struggling to pay for their corrections systems. As a result, many state programs are being slashed, with some states looking to release certain convicts early. No fewer than eight states have recently contemplated releasing prisoners early. Others are planning to push some categories of newly convicted criminals into rehabilitation programs. Kentucky, California, Rhode Island, New Jersey, South Carolina and Vermont are among the states wrestling with these issues.

The unrivaled growth of the United States' incarcerated population over 30 years casts a great burden on this nation. The country's $60 billion prison budget results in less money for education, health care and child services. Communities need the resources to prevent crime by investing in youth and families. In California, the governor had considered a massive plan to release tens of thousands of prisoners, but recently decided against the proposal. Local jail officials continued to reduce the inmate population by approving early releases where appropriate. In Kentucky, where they have been facing a billion-dollar deficit, corrections officials told ABC News they are looking at a variety of measures to reduce their state prison population, including early release of some non-violent offenders and expanding the home incarceration plan which allows inmates to be released for substance-abuse treatment and to seek employment. In Michigan, it costs $2 billion to run the corrections system. An increasing number of state leaders say they really can't afford to pay that kind of money. We spend more on prisons than we do on higher education, and that has got to change. According the News, the Michigan Corrections Department already devours 20 cents of every tax dollar in the state's general fund and employs nearly one in every three state government workers, compared with 9% of the work force 25 years ago.

It's estimated that at least nine million people are currently imprisoned worldwide. However, it is believed that this number is likely to be much higher, in view of general under reporting and a lack of data from various countries. Since the beginning of the 1990s, the prison population in most countries has increased significantly. The United States currently has the largest prison population in the world, with more than 2 million. Both Russia and China, the latter with a population 4 times that of the U.S., also had prison populations in excess of 1 million. As a percentage of total population, Rwanda has the largest prison population as of 2002, with more than 100,000 (of a total population of around 8 million), largely as a result of the 1994 genocide. The United States is second largest in relative numbers with 486 prisoners per 100,000 of population, according to the Bureau of Justice Statistics, also making it the largest in relative numbers amongst developed countries.

Men are over 8 times more likely than women to be incarcerated in prison at least once during their life. The high proportion of prisoners in developed countries may be explained by a range of factors, including better funded criminal justice systems, a more strict approach to law and order through the use of mandatory sentencing, and a larger gap between the rich and the poor. In non-developed countries, rates of incarceration may be a reflection of a tendency for some crimes to go unpunished, political corruption, or the use of other mechanisms which provide an alternative to incarceration as a means of dealing with crime. Currently in the United States, 1 in every 31 adult persons is either in jail or prison or on parole or probation. That amounts to 7.3 million Americans and a cost that exceeds $68 billion annually. The statistical breakdown of the U.S. correction system is as follows; 1 in every 45 Americans is on parole or probation, 1 in every 100 Americans is in jail or prison, 1 in every 11 African American adults is in jail or prison, and 1 in every 27 Hispanic American adults is in jail or prison.

Typically, one thinks of an offender going to prison as a result of a finding of guilt by the court. Although a large number of admissions to prison do result from new commitments, the number of offenders already involved in the corrections system who are returned to or enter prison is on the rise and becoming a more important force in determining the growth of the prison population. The length of sentence of new commitments will be increased as sentencing guidelines and truth-in-sentencing laws take effect, but the length of sentence for offenders already involved in the corrections system is not affected by these new laws. As the number of offenders returned to or entering prison as the result of a technical violation continues to increase, the policies affecting these offenders become important in determining the make-up and growth of the prison population. The number of parole and probation agents, as well as the direction that those agents receive, could become an increasing focus of public policy discussions about the growth of the prison population in the future.

Most offenders under 18 years of age are tried as juveniles and are incarcerated in the juvenile corrections system. However, Michigan allows for certain youthful offenders to be tried as adults and incarcerates these offenders as adults, although they may be segregated within housing units from older prisoners. Correctional facilities operated or contracted by the State are "prisons" and locally operated correctional facilities are "jails". For uniformity of reporting information, eight offenses (murder, rape, robbery, aggravated assault, burglary, larceny, motor vehicle theft, and arson) are reported by law enforcement agencies nationwide. These offenses are referred to as index crimes and, based on the seriousness of the crimes, a change in frequency of their occurrence is an indication of national trends in crime.

Circuit court probation agents are funded through the Department of Corrections budget. Probation, as discussed in this paper, refers to circuit court probation in most cases because the supervision is provided by the State. However, jails or other local resources may be used by both district and circuit court judges and the State interest in decreasing prison admissions may result in funding of programs that target district court probation. Special alternative incarceration is also known as boot camp. This sanction is not community-based, because offenders are removed from the community to a centralized camp. However, at the conclusion of the centralized program, the offender is returned to the community and may receive intensive supervision.

Welfare System

Federally funded and governed US welfare began in the 1930's during the Great Depression. The US government responded to the overwhelming number of families and individuals in need of aid by creating a welfare program that would give assistance to those who had little or no income. The US welfare system stayed in the hands of the federal government for the next sixty-one years. Many Americans were unhappy with the welfare system, claiming that individuals were abusing the welfare program by not applying for jobs, having more children just to get more aid, and staying unmarried so as to qualify for greater benefits. Welfare system reform became a hot topic in the1990's. Bill Clinton was elected as President with the intention of reforming the federally run US Welfare program. In 1996 the Republican Congress passed a reform law signed by President Clinton that gave the control of the welfare system back to the states.

Eligibility for a Welfare program depends on numerous factors. Eligibility is determined using gross and net income, size of the family, and any crisis situation such as medical emergencies, pregnancy, home-lessness or unemployment. A case worker is assigned to those applying for aid. They will gather all the necessary information to determine the amount and type of benefits that an individual is eligible for. The Federal government provides assistance through TANF (Temporary

Assistance for Needy Families). TANF is a grant given to each state to run their own welfare program. To help overcome the former problem of unemployment due to reliance on the welfare system, the TANF grant requires that all recipients of welfare aid must find work within two years of receiving aid, including single parents who are required to work at least 30 hours per week opposed to 35 or 55 required by two parent families. Failure to comply with work requirements could result in loss of benefits.

The type and amount of aid available to individuals and dependent children varies from state to state. When the Federal Government gave control back to the states there was no longer one source and one set of requirements. Most states offer basic aid such as health care, food stamps, child care assistance, unemployment, cash aid, and housing assistance. To apply for a welfare program one must contact the local Human Service Department located in the government pages of the phone book. It may be listed as Human Services, Family Services or Adult and Family Services. An appointment is made with a case worker. The case worker will give a list of required documents needed at the appointment. Common documents asked for are proof of income, ID, and utility bills or other proof of residency. Once an appointment is completed a case worker will review all required documents, applications and information provided at the meeting. They will use this information to determine eligibility.

In the American vocabulary, "welfare" has often had a limited meaning, most commonly associated in public discourse with public assistance to mothers with dependent children. Yet government welfare can also be given a broader definition, as a general social safety net designed to support citizens in need. Under this definition, "welfare" refers to government protections for workers' incomes, which are often threatened by structural economic change under the free market system. In an economy in which workers rely on wages to support themselves, threats to income arise due to unemployment, sickness, old age, and loss of the family breadwinner. In the United States, then, government welfare has been a collection of different programs that includes unemployment insurance, health insurance, old age pensions, accident insurance, and support for families with dependent children.

In the twentieth century, many nations in Western Europe built what became known as the "welfare state," a comprehensive system designed to protect citizens from the hazards of an industrial, capitalist economy. Compared with the European welfare state, the American welfare system is late developing, less extensive, haphazardly constructed, and reliant upon dispersed authority. While European nations instituted programs for old-age pensions and accident insurance near the turn of the twentieth century, the United States did not develop significant welfare programs until the 1930s under Franklin D. Roosevelt's New Deal. Unlike the European welfare state, the American welfare system has never included universal health insurance or guaranteed family incomes. Significant groups of Americans in need have not been covered by government welfare programs. Moreover, the American old-age pension system is based on worker contributions, and thus does little to redistribute wealth. While the European welfare state was consolidated in the coherent programs of social-democratic or labor parties, the American welfare system has lacked a comprehensive structure. It was initially built as a response to emergency, during the economic crisis of the Great Depression. The American welfare system is characterized by dispersed authority. Unlike the nationalized European systems, responsibility for welfare has been shared by federal, state, and local governments, which has often led to wide disparities in welfare eligibility and benefits in different regions of the country.

Throughout its history, the American distribution of government welfare has been closely connected to cultural attitudes toward the poor. Americans have commonly distinguished between the deserving poor, who become needy through no fault of their own and are entitled to public assistance, and the undeserving poor, who are responsible for their own plight and who could escape poverty by developing a strong work ethic. Separating the deserving poor from the undeserving has often proved difficult. Nevertheless, for much of American history, many needy people have been seen as undeserving of public assistance. Because of a deeply held cultural belief in the "American dream," which holds that anyone can achieve economic advancement through hard work, Americans have characteristically attributed poverty to the moral failings of individuals.

In the American welfare system, the distinction between the deserving and the undeserving poor has translated into a division between social insurance and public assistance programs. Social insurance, which includes old age pensions and unemployment insurance, has been available on a universal basis to those who earn it through work. Public assistance, such as aid to dependent children and general assistance for the very needy, is targeted at the poor and requires financial and moral evaluations for applicants to prove their worthiness for aid. The benefits of public assistance are typically less generous than those of social insurance. Recipients of public assistance have often been seen as undeserving of aid because they are not seen as having earned it through work. Public assistance has thus carried a social stigma. There is also a gender and racial dimension to the devaluation of public assistance in comparison to social insurance, as recipients of the former are disproportionately female and minority.

Welfare has, for several decades, been a necessary entity in our society since the broad-scale reforms of Franklin Delano Roosevelt's administration during the Great Depression. The aim was to help "the forgotten man", the stereotypical American man with a job in manufacturing or management that had fallen on hard times. Conceptually, it was an admirable endeavor and for many years truly worked for many. The welfare movement picked up even more steam under Lyndon Johnson and his "War on Poverty" movement. However, this is often overlooked because of the explosive Vietnam War and the fight for civil rights. However, today, the welfare system is in arrears, mainly because of the many ways that the system can be cheated and swindled. Now, it is easier than ever to cheat the government despite the fact that it is fraud, because of the lack of enforcement of welfare regulations.

In an ABC Nightline special that aired in the mid-1990's, a study was done on the social welfare system, primarily Social Security. For the hard-working middle class, a certain portion of our pay, around six percent, goes to the Federal Insurance Contributions Act, otherwise known as the FICA tax. This goes to funding Social Security and Medicare, two programs supported under this government bill. After age sixty-five (or older, as is becoming increasingly common), one is eligible to receive a check to help cover medical expenses and other necessities for older people. In addition, disabled person who can no longer work receive a check for the same things. However, many are taking advantage of the government by claiming disabilities that do not prevent them from working, and then exchange the money for drugs and other substances, sometimes reselling them to make more money than they started with. Then others use it to subsidize their morally-irresponsible lifestyles.

Another abuse of the welfare system is the fraudulent use of Pell grants and other forms of government aid in education. Pell grants in particular are slated for families that make less than twenty thousand dollars a year, which puts many at or below poverty level. One must sign an agreement that the funds will only be used for academic pursuits, yet people still get away with the money. Usually, the person shows up for a few weeks so as to get the money, and then they take that money and subsist on it. The sad part of it is that often, they get away with it on multiple occasions at the same institution.

Now, I don't think we have to completely get rid of social welfare just yet, but I do believe that we should enforce the stipulations already set forth by the government, and I also think that it is time to scale back on government handouts to those who do not exhibit a genuine need for it. We have become a welfare state, where if you choose not to work, it can be rectified by a check, no questions asked, from the government. It is high time that the working and middle classes no longer carry people that choose not to work and criminals. Instead, we need to create a republic where getting and holding a job is preferred to taking the easy way out. However, the only way to motivate people at this point is to curtail what the government gives to whom. Lets advocate helping one's neighbor by things like helping them find a job, not give them a handout, with little or no accountability for what they choose to do with it. This country was based on freedom and opportunity, and it is opportunity that beckons to every constituent. It is time that we help the needy help themselves merely by becoming productive, skillful, and self-sufficient.

The history of welfare programs in the United States is a controversial one. Although many other nations in the world have welfare systems, some of which provide certain kinds of assistance for all citizens, the United States has always been divided in terms of what welfare means and who should receive welfare benefits. The welfare system in America underwent significant changes in the late 1990s in order to reduce the number of people receiving certain types of welfare benefits. This occurred as a result of political and economic changes that caused American society to reexamine the meaning of its welfare programs against a rising tide of concern about and disdain for public assistance.

— 8 —

The Human Race

Perhaps the most important question in life for the human race is not life itself, but what happens to the human being after life? Is there a God and eternal life? Does the Devil, known as Satan, walk this planet? If so, who is Satan? Will we receive the kingdom of Heaven or the fire and brimstone of Hell? What does the Bible really tell us? A human being has the ability to think – past, present and future, or so the current human being thinks so in their mind. Does humans use international terrorists to support their beliefs in God? The prison and homeless populations on our planet tells a good deal about the human race – past, present, and future.

Ideas

My ideas may not all be true, some may be inadequate or misleading. They have all contributed to my current thinking on these issues. We have the human understanding and appreciation of the human condition and creative possibilities. Is there a one God who dwells in all of us? Is there an argument for the development or evolution of man from other animals? Think about the inability of infants to find food. Is there a way of truth beyond the grasp of human understanding? Perhaps there is the way of truth and the way of opinions.

Think about the Constitution of the United States – 1st Amendment from 1791. Congress shall make no law respecting as establishment of religion, or prohibiting the free exercise thereof; or abridging the freedom of speech, or of the press; or the right of the people peaceably to assembly, and to petition the Government for a redress of grievances.

As a citizen of the United States, we have a right to freedom of speech on this planet called Earth. My intent is to exercise my freedom of speech under the 1st Amendment of the Constitution of the United States. As human beings on planet Earth, we may want to rethink our thinking about what we think we know.

The idea of salvation is perhaps preordained. There is nothing specifically that the individual can do to attain salvation. God will make his presence felt in the heart of a particular individual, or he won't. Therefore, under this concept there is nothing we can do, it's in God's hands from day one. Either God exists or he does not. If God does not exist, then we lose very little by believing that he does exist. If he does exist, then we stand to gain an awful lot by believing that he does and lose an awful lot by thinking that he doesn't. Therefore, it is sensible to wager that he does exist and to behave appropriately. What do you have to lose? You can not convince unbelievers of God's existence by rational argument. If a person's future is predestined, why do anything? Just sit back and wait for God to act and show himself that he does exist.

We should and need to understand that we are only a tiny part of this universe that we live in. Moses parted the Red Sea and allowed the Jews to escape their Egyptian pursuers. Miracles such as this were no more than a natural phenomenon. The rational argument is that a man could not part the Red Sea. Therefore, this must be a natural phenomenon which will happen again sometime in the future. If you believe that this did happen as stated in the Bible, if mankind lives for many years on this planet, if the human race does not destroy itself, we could see the parting of the Red Sea once again. If and when this happen, what does this tell us about Moses and his belief in God?

God, the most perfect being, exists. Since God is perfect, it is inconceivable that he might have made things better than he has. Therefore, this world that we live on is the best of all possible worlds. It is possible that there is no best world. In which case, God can only choose from an infinite series of worlds where each is better than the last. The evil which exists in this world rules out the existence of an all powerful, loving, personal God. The argument is that a perfect God would create a perfect world. The trouble is that it is obvious that this world, which we live in is not perfect, there can't be a perfect God.

All we have are the representations and no way to climb outside our skulls and compare them to the ways things really are. How do we know that there is a world out there at all? What if, our minds and the ideas in them are all that exists? Minds are active things that provide knowing, perceiving, sensing, willing, imagining and remembering. Ideas can exist only in a mind. What if the universe is nothing but matter in motion in space? There is not much room for the possibility that human life matters much in the grand scheme of things.

Mankind should be the enemy of ignorance, myth and superstition. Use feeling and thinking which constitute human reason. Look into the larger question of the immortality of the soul. Demonstrating the soul's immortality is beyond the abilities of human reason. However, at the very least, it may be useful that people believe the soul to be immortal. Perhaps, God created human beings with the kinds of moral dispositions necessary for them to live good lives. But this kind of optimistic view is threatened by the presence of evil and suffering in this world. Is this world, created by a rational God, the best of all possible worlds?

Mankind lives with impressions and ideas. Impressions and ideas might be either simple or complex. Simple impressions and ideas cannot be broken down into more simple impressions and ideas; while complex impressions and ideas are composed of more simple impressions and ideas. However, matters of fact depend on more than just thinking. Mankind needs to know how the world is in order to discover truths. Reason alone, has no hand in our belief systems. The future may not be like the past or we could make the argument that the future will be like the past, because in the past the future was like the past. Nothing but human nature underpins our thinking. This is the reason we should rethink our thinking of the things we think we know; but we go about the business of daily living.

Human Reason

Does free will and belief of a God go hand in hand? Human reason in our species is burdened by questions. The very nature of reason itself, mankind is not able to ignore the question of where did mankind come from or where are we going. Mankind is also not able to answer these important questions. The reason to undertake these most difficult of all questions is perhaps self-knowledge. The mind is the mirror of nature. If the mind manages to conform to the way the world really is, perhaps mankind will know something about the world of mankind. Objects must conform to our minds. If mankind can discover where he really came from, perhaps he'll know what's in the future for mankind. Morality is based on sentiment or even the consequences of action. Doing the right thing is not a matter of one's character of disposition or even circumstances. Perhaps all of which are or might be beyond one's control. So if you want such and such, then do so and so. However, mankind is on a quest for true answers due to human reason.

Are people born with equal and natural rights? Mankind does not live as isolated individuals, but rather in societies where they enjoy the benefits of cooperation and sociality. Human beings are far from perfect, both atheism and Christianity. As inhabitants of planet Earth, every person has an equal claim over Earth in its natural state. Were does the vengeful and spiteful God of the Bible come into play on common sense of this world? Mankind has a practical mind. People act in their own interest, which consists of getting pleasure and avoiding pain. What makes an action right or wrong are its effects. It depends on such factors as a person's education, religion and social standing, all of this must be taken into account. Sometimes the only way to bring about a greater balance of pleasure over pain is by one or more of us suffering for someone else. This is not to claim that the poor ought to suffer for the sake of the rich, but take a long hard look at all mankind on this planet for equal and natural rights. Rich becomes richer and poor becomes poorer. The fact that being moral is not easy.

Mankind needs to understand the whole of reality. An individual self-consciousness moves towards self-certainty. Mankind needs belongingness. Along the journey that we travel, we are transformed by the experience of work and come to possess the intellectual tools necessary to progress to a greater self-understanding. The focus is on rationality and understanding. It's about building communities which enable individuals to live out a freedom that is based upon their common ability to reason.

The world we perceive is constituted by the mind. Objects appear to us in space and time. Our sensory experience of the world is not our only access to the world, or at least not our only access to a part of the world. I know my hand just reached for the phone because I saw it, but I would have known anyway, because I willed it. The view that there is just one mind and everything else is a mere appearance. Life is something which ought not to be and this is the very worst of all possible worlds. The life of our body is only constantly preventing dying, a postponed death. Every breath we draw wards off the death that is constantly intruding upon us. We are only a breath away from death. Perhaps we should see life for what it is, the blind craving of a single will. The ultimate state is nothing like a heaven of pure satisfaction and eternal happiness, but nothingness in space and time.

Good acts are those which produce the greatest happiness for the greatest number of people. Acts which produce the greatest happiness for the greatest number are good. Happiness itself is understood in terms of pleasure. We ought to pursue it as an end. Pleasure is actually desired by everyone and something we ought to pursue. The only things visible are things seen and the only things audible are things heard. Actions bring about a greater balance of pleasure over pain. Self development is individuals pursuing their own aims, is among the essentials of human well being. Coming to conclusions about what is best for everyone, good of mankind as a whole. People should be able to do what they like, even jeopardizing their own happiness, so long as they harm no one else.

Emphasize the importance of immediate gratification and living in the moment. The contrast of immediate gratification is built on duty and obligation. Where does a human find true freedom and fulfillment? The religious sphere is constituted by a leap of faith. It is simply not possible to appeal to rational argument or evidence to justify such a belief. God commanded Abraham to kill his son Isaac. This requires behavior which is completely outside the domain of normal morals. Abraham must simply follow a command. Would you kill your son on a simply command of faith? That will have a consequence that is absolutely unthinkable in terms of normal morals. Religious faith then is not an easy option. So why choose it? Why not the aesthetic and ethical modes of existence? Perhaps the answer is that it is only by religious faith that individuals can avoid despair and find their true selves in the freedom which is dependence upon a transcendent being brings. This attempts to achieve objective knowledge of human thought and experience. God and the Christian faith is transparent to reason and rational argument. Mankind must make their judgments about where they stand on particular issues and arguments. Think for themselves with an on going commitment to the importance of individual choice and responsibility; individual freedom and the burdens which it brings. Freedom and passion are important to the human race and a strong factor in the leap of faith.

Self Realization

Humans come to full self realization in the process of transforming the world in their own image. People are alienated when they lose control over the circumstances in which they engage in activity and unable to live a fully human life. Abolish all class distinctions. There will come a day when state power and the government of people will not be necessary. Race, religion, sex and social status will not be a factor in a human life. Civil rights, international marriages and gay rights are transforming the world as we know it. One day in the future, there won't be a skin color of black, white, brown or yellow; only one color, the human race.

Clarity comes by working through the experimental consequences of the content of a thought or concept. How to make our ideas clear and define truth? The idea here is that on any given issue all investigators will eventually come to the same conclusion. We should argue that one should never be committed to the truth of current scientific opinion, but merely accept it as a stage on the way towards the real truth. We should believe the human race is optimistic about the possibility of attaining final answers to particular questions. As long as the questions have genuinely testable consequences, then the truth about them would eventually be known. We should believe that truth is provisional and needs to be constantly reassessed in the light of the results of new information and experiments. What we know to be a truth today may change tomorrow.

What difference could a life make if every action, thought and hope were caused by prior events? What meaning could a life have at all? Think about the conflict between religion and science, and hard facts of scientific information. The sustaining of a thought because I choose to when I might have other thoughts. One might not be able to choose which thoughts come into the mind, but an act of will can focus the mind on some thoughts at the expense of others, thoughts which then determine action. Is mental life and visible bodily life connected? What makes you yourself over time? A kind of activity which consists in one's present thinking makes you become you. Our understanding of truth and meaning controls our life. An idea of X is only a useful idea if it helps one deal with X should X exist. Ideas must be consistent with other ideas to stand a chance of being true.

Evidence can't decide that God exist, therefore, the decision consists of the belief that God will improve life. Belief in God wins because it leads one to a better attitude towards the future and puts some much needed meaning into a life. Can one really just will to believe something like this? Believe that life is worth living and your belief will help create the fact. Mankind knows that he will die and needs something to hold onto giving life meaning. Belief in God makes you believe that there may be some outside chance there's something after death. Somehow, this makes mankind feel better, just believing that there might be a God, true or not.

Religion is worth thinking about. That truth has no value and religion is everything. Perhaps it was possible for human beings once to buy into the idea of complete faith and a basis in something beyond this world; God and the afterlife, but no longer. There is no God and if he did once exist, he is dead. Look at the world around you, how an all powerful God could let this happen. Reveal your beliefs for what they really are and replace them with something better. It's very easy to lose one's way in all of this. The admirable person is a creator of values and truths – no matter where it may take us. Each individual ought to function according to their own truths, right or wrong and perhaps only look after their own interests.

Religions or hopes and illusions in the belief and faith of a God are perhaps fictitious; the belief that consists of obeying the will of a dead God. The will to power is the elementary force underlying reality. We want more than just sense. What we're after is truth, thoughts on how to live, some ideas of what we ought to value, some conception of rightness and wrongness in action of the real truth, whatever it may be. If we are to overcome the herd instincts which motivate this kind of objection, we are going to have to do some thinking for ourselves. What is the foundation for all human knowledge?

Are we listed in God's book of life? If so, will the dead be judged according to their works? Anyone not found written in the book of life is cast into the lake of fire. Are we sinners in need of forgiveness and salvation? Should we take the bible literally? God provided the perfect environment, the Garden of Eden, but sin invaded, then came the faith age, in which Old Testament heroes acted on their trust in God. Jesus died for our sins and all we have to do is trust him and his work on the cross for our salvation. This all sounds pretty simple, all we need is faith.

The organisms and species are ever changing as they interact with their environment. Humans are the product of a lived practice. Thought emerges as people interact with their environment. Does a human have a fixed determinate nature? Humans have adopted the modes of behavior to achieve specific goals in particular circumstances. How we think is perhaps the key. The question is to do with how we can know that the stuff in our minds, our perceptions, corresponds with external reality. What counts is whether our beliefs provide us with rules to interact with the world around us. All beliefs are subject to revision. Approach every situation with a view to construct it in such a way that it offers the best opportunities for human fulfillment. Find out new things about the world. Proper education aims to foster imaginative responses to new information and situations by engaging people in active, cooperative practices of learning.

Think about relations to one another in space and time on the one hand and reality itself on the other. We should tackle the big questions, of God, time and being, head on. The true nature of what it is for something to exist, coming to grips with the nature of ourselves as a being. What is being? Is being at least a component part of nature? Maybe a human being is conceived as only an object like any other in the world. Yet, a human being is a thinking thing entirely unlike other objects in the world, because we can think and reason. Recognizing that one is where one is as a result of some past facts or decisions by own family tree over which one now has no control. It is a simple fact of humanity that we neglect large parts of our nature, our past and future and focus ourselves in the daily grind. We really do measure out our lives one day at a time. The point is that human time in its entirety requires careful consideration if we are to understand the true nature of being. We have to do better than our current preoccupation with the present. In addition to having a past and a present, human time is essentially a time with a limit. One day, our lives will come to an end, then what? We are where we are today due to the facts and decisions made by generations before us. What will be the facts and decisions of our generation for future generations?

Improve human life; serve as a basis for choosing and believing. If we can never know whether or not a theory is true, we have no reason to think it's true. People are condemned to live certain kinds of lives by the events which occur in their past. Individuals are to choose their own lives and morals. Emptiness lies right at the heart of the being. The human being must have something to hold to, the possibility that things might be other than they are. Portray the actions as entirely governed by a binding moral code. A blind leap of faith is our blinding moral code, something that does not stand up to reason. In principle the self is something which can be changed; it can be reconstructed.

There's an awful lot in the universe out there to think about. Outer and inner perception, we need clarity from the start to understand. Picking up an idea and running with it. How power and knowledge interact to produce the human being today. The desire to understand leads to our most personal thoughts, feelings and desires both to ourselves and others. Show how power produces human being and the knowledge that we have. The management and administration of human species or population and control or discipline of the human body is interesting. Look at the interest in issues with gay rights, prison reform, mental health and the welfare of the human race. Human relations are defined by the struggle of power. Perhaps right and wrong, truth and falsehood are illusions. Populations in various ways are surveyed, categorized, disciplined and controlled.

The prison system population on our planet tells a good deal about the human race. Why is our prison system over-populated and why must this population be controlled for our safety? What is our society doing wrong? Our society will be judged by this factor of our prison system population. As the human race we must rethink our thinking on our issues. We have placed a man on the moon, but can not care for the prison system population. Would an all powerful God stand by and watch this happen?

The homeless population on our planet tells a good deal about the human race. Why are the homeless over-populated and why must this population be controlled for our safety? Having many thousands of homeless and high unemployment is a huge problem. Why do we have so many homeless people? What is own society doing wrong? Our society will be judged by this factor of homeless population. As a human race we must rethink our thinking on our issues. Thousands and thousands die on a daily basis; we only stand by and focus ourselves in the daily grind of our personal interests. Would an all powerful God stand by and watch this happen?

Rational Deliberation

Why is it that, in a world created by an all powerful, all wise, and just God, there is sin and suffering? Why do bad things happen to good people, and good things to bad people? Should we believe that the universe was created by a good, wise, all powerful, and all knowing God? But the problem of evil was only one battle in a much larger conflict. Behind it lay the even greater and more important challenge of getting the conception of God right. How does God act? What faculties and capacities has God worked with? To what extent is his behavior, like ours, to rational understanding? Can his ways be explained and justified? Or is God, in many respects, very much like us? Guided in his choices by rational deliberation and acting for the sake of what he believes to be good. Or is God not a rational person and no comparison can be drawn between the way God acts and the way we act? Why is there something rather than nothing? Why is the world as it is, not just physically but morally as well? Why do bad things happen to good people? How can we make sense of suffering and human evil that often seem beyond comprehension?

If only one could discover and properly interpret the core religious beliefs that unite all Christians, then there would be a possibility of reuniting the faithful within a single church. Is it possible for someone to do good works and achieve salvation without God's help? According to the Catholic Church a human being is saved by grace and faith alone, independently of any good works, regardless of the merits of individuals. God has simply resolved to give the supreme gift of faith to some and to allow others to be damned, a resolution made independent of God's knowledge of the actions of those individuals. Is it impossible for even a just individual to carry out the commandments of God without grace? But can we be sure God exists only because we clearly and distinctly perceive this? Before we can be sure that God exists, we ought to be able to be sure that whatever we perceive clearly and evidently is true.

God's activity is always in accordance with the laws of nature. If we accept the good from God, shall we not accept the evil? There is the claim that there is a God and that God is the creator of the world. There is evil in God's creation. There is undeniably imperfection in the world, especially relative to human beings and their well being. Birth defects, natural disasters, criminal behavior and undeserved affliction are all evident features of the world. God can do whatever he wills to do. God knows everything, including the alleged defects in his work. God is wise, just and he wills only the good.

How can the existence of imperfection, disaster, evil and undeserved suffering in the world be reconciled with the belief that the world was created by a just, wise, good God? It can not be said that God knows about the evils and would like to do something about them but is unable to. Nor can it be said that God can and would do something about those evils if only he knew about them. We must entertain the possibility that God knows about the evils and could do something about them but simply does not care to do so. God either wishes to take away evils and he can not, or he can and does not wish to. If he wishes to and is not able, then he is weak, which does not fall in with the notion of God.

The world is not physically perfect; particularly from the perspective of human needs, desires, and ambitions. Humans lie, cheat, steal, murder and wage war, human beings are involved in violations of God's commandments. Why does God allow such things to happen when he can so easily prevent them? God is constantly and intimately involved in the world, actively concurring in all events, including the sinful actions undertaken by human beings. There is the problem that the world God created does not seem to be a very just place. People often lead lives of poverty and pain, while people, precisely because of their vices, such as greed and dishonesty, frequently prosper. Why would a just God permit such injustice?

God, according to Christian Gospels, wants all human beings to be saved. Yet not everyone receives salvation, either because they have not made proper use of the grace given to them by God or because they are not among the elect who are predestined to receive the grace that is necessary and sufficient for faith. Why is grace sometimes given by a just God to people who do not deserve it, and at other times to people who, as God knows, will fail to make proper use of it? God must contend with an independent, equally real and powerful force of evil, Satan.

If one only broadened one's perspective on events and on the world at large, one would see that what appeared to be evil was not in fact evil. The evil was real, but that it formed an essential and necessary element into something larger that was, on the whole, good. If man considered and represented that which exists and know the smallness of his part in it. Now the true way of considering this is that all individuals of the human species are of no value in comparison with the whole that exist and endures. When one takes a long view of history and a wider view of the state of the world, one will see that the number of evils, even within the human domain is not as great as many believe. In fact, it is far outweighed by the number of good things. For you will find cities, existing for thousands of years, that have never been flooded or burned. Also thousands and thousands of people are born in perfect health each year.

Trying to decide whether the number of good things is greater than the number of evils must ultimately lead to an endless numbers game. More important, it leaves the fundamental question at the heart of the problem of evil unresolved. Why is there any evil at all in God's creation? Can a society of atheists be more moral than a society of professed Christians? It is not so much that God is the direct cause of sin, although God appears to cooperate positively in the production of evil, he allows it to occur. According to the doctrine of original sin, all human beings are corrupt and capable only of evil. Grace and faith alone allows one to perform good works. Why then are some saved and others left to damnation?

God has chosen to create this actual world rather than any of infinitely many other possible ones, even though it includes evil and sin, simply because it is the best of all possible worlds. God is infinitely wise and he infallibly knows which world is the best. No matter how good any given world may be, it is always possible for God to make a world that is better. For God to have chosen a world with even one less instance of evil would mean crating a world with less overall goodness. All things are connected and every single aspect of the world makes a contribution. In short there is sin and suffering in a world created by an all wise, all powerful, all good God. God can achieve his will to create the best of all possible worlds only by allowing the sin and suffering it contains to come into existence. God may in a sense be the ultimate physical cause of evil, but is not the moral cause. The sinner is the author of his own sins.

God wants everyone to enjoy happiness and all people to be saved, but all things are not equal and there are other wills in God that are contending for realization. God wants the world to be governed by simple, universal laws that do not allow for exceptions, even when the ordinary course of nature leads to the suffering of individuals. God also wants the world to be populated by free agents who are morally responsible for their actions and who may act in such a way as sin and therefore deserve punishment. While all events are directly caused by God, a miracle is an extraordinary state of affairs that he brings about in violation of the laws of nature. That of all the possible plans of works that God discovers in his wisdom, he must choose the best.

Jesus Christ died or that he shed his blood for all men without exception. God does not will to save all men. God wants to save all men must not be taken literally. It certainly does not mean that God positively wills that each and every human being be saved. Rather, the phrase "all men" refers to all kinds of human beings. The general claim means that while God has elected to save only certain individuals, they are drawn from all sorts of conditions, ages, sexes and nationalities. The rest of humanity is to be left.

Is the universe the most perfect that God can create? There are so many monsters, so many disorders and the great number of people. Does all this contribute to the perfection of the universe? Does God act only for his own glory? God's glory finds its highest expression in creation in the establishment of his church. What makes the establishment of that church possible is presence in the world of Jesus Christ. When we open our eyes to consider the visible world, it seems that we discover many defects. The world is the work of blind nature, which acts without design.

In the actual world, not every person is rewarded nor every wicked person punished. Why then is there evil in the world? Why are individuals born without limbs? Why are there floods and droughts? Why is there sin and suffering? Why do people sometimes suffer while other people prosper? Why are not all human beings saved by the grace of God? These unfortunate events occur because God allows them to occur. God permits disorder but he does not create it. It is no disorder for lions to eat wolves, wolves then eat sheep and sheep eat the grass that God tends to carefully that he has given it all the things necessary for its own preservation. Nature is perfectly well ordered and that is exactly why disorders happen.

This is not the best of all possible worlds. It is a defective world, one full of imperfections, sins and inequities. Look at constrains set by the simplest laws; it is the best God can do. That would seriously put in question God's goodness and justice. God does not want everyone to be saved. God does not get to do everything he wants to do. It is Christ who prays for the salvation of individuals. God does things in the way most worthy of him.

So called evils are really just lesser degrees of perfection that appear to be defects only when we take too narrow a perspective on things and fail to see the contribution they make to the overall goodness of creation. It is not possible for all humans to be saved. God is a rational being who does things for an intelligible and objective purpose. A rational being is one for who reasons matter. He strives to achieve what he does because he recognizes it as good, as desirable in its own right. He selects means toward his desired goal because he believes, with justification, that those means are the most efficient way to it. God does nothing without acting in accordance with supreme reason. This is true for all of God's choices, large and small.

God is determined to choose the best, but this does not mean the choice is not free. There is always a prevailing reason that prompts the will to its choice. The choice is free and independent of necessity because it is made between several choices and the will is determined only by the goodness of the object. Order shows that a soul is more important than a body and a human being more worthy than a dog. God's choices are compelled and there are standards that God is bound to observe, but these standards lie in God's wisdom, and the obligation to obey them comes from his nature alone. He might wish for all things being equal, but he ultimately does not want to achieve, at least not at any cost. God does want to save all human beings.

God's ideas are our ideas and we know truths exactly the same way God knows them. Then we have access to divine wisdom. If God wants a person to have faith and do good works, then he will give that person enough grace to overcome the pleasures of the body. God wills to save all people, but not everyone is actually saved. Nothing happens in the world, be it a leaf or a fruit falling from a tree, the birth or death of an animal except by the will of God applied to each event. Scripture employs a language so extraordinary that it has misled everyone who has read these divine books for thousands of years. All of nature, from the smallest detail to the largest, is a direct expression of God's power.

God orders all things. Only this conception of God's action makes him directly responsible for everything that has and will happen. We believe that God's extends to all things. This is one of the primary truths of the Christian religion. To know how this happens and in what way everything that happens in the world is directed, regulated and governed by the secret orders of this is something that surpasses our intelligence. Why does God not will to save all individual human beings? God has his reasons, but they must remain hidden.

Practical Reason

God is a rational being. Led by practical reason, he deliberates and chooses in a manner to human beings, doing things for an intelligible purpose and selecting that which he recognizes to be the objectively preferable option. Reason matters for God and his actions are guided by his wisdom. Who will dare say that God has created all things without reason? Adam sins by eating the fruit of the tree of knowledge. If the first man had not eaten the fruit of the tree of knowledge, then he would not have been Adam but rather some other individual very much like Adam.

God's first free choices in creation are also his last free choices. For God may have been free to create or not to create Adam. That is, the first human being, whose individual concept presumable includes and thus necessarily implies not just the original sin but everything that succeeds him. This includes all of the human race and everything that happens to it for all of time. God is above all or else a rational being, just like us. These include the nature of truth, the possibility of knowledge and the objectivity of values.

Does God make or do something because it is good, or is something good just because God does it? The Bible says that on each day of creation God surveyed what he had done and that it was good, but did God choose to create what he did because he perceived it to be inherently good? Is what God created good because he created it? With the implication that had God created something entirely different, then that would have been good instead? There are many possibilities that will never be realized but that are nonetheless well within God's abilities.

God cannot change the nature of justice and make what is just unjust. What is right and good is such independently of God's will. God can't make a human that is not a rational being, fire that is not hot or a horse that does not possess all of the essential properties of a horse. There is even greater consensus that God cannot violate the principles of mathematics. God can't make one plus one equal three or make a triangle's interior angles more or less than 180 degrees. Above all, almost everyone agrees that while God can do whatever is possible, he can't do what is logically impossible. God can't make a square be a circle.

If justice was established arbitrarily and without any cause, if God came upon it by a kind of hazard, as when one draws lots, his goodness and his wisdom are not manifested in it, and there is nothing at all to attach him to it. It would make no more sense to ask why God does what is good than to ask why the Devil does what is evil, since whatever the Devil does, by the fact of his doing it is evil. God cannot make what is unjust into what is just, nor can he, through his will alone, reverse all of the values that inform our judgments about what is true, false, good and bad.

God operates just as human beings operate. Through practical reason, confronted with objective values that are not of his making and that normatively serve him in making the choices that he makes. As to order and justice, we believe that there are universal rules that must hold with respect to God and with respect to intelligent creatures. God knows and wills things in the same way that we do. When God knows and wills the good, what happens is not essentially different from what takes place when a human being knows and wills the good.

The individual concept of each person involves once and for all everything that will ever happen to him. Should God create that individual, thus entirely independent of God's will? Adam's actual existence may be the result of a free decree of God. Once God has decided to create Adam, everything that happens to Adam happens with a necessity. If Adam exists, then it is certain that Adam will sin and there is nothing God can do about it, just because sin is an immutable part of his essence.

There is suffering among the innocent, prosperity among the wicked, and eternal damnation of innumerable souls. Where is the justice in that? Such is God's will. There is, quite simply, nothing more to be said on the matter. This is not to be understood as the commonplace demand that one should have faith in God, that he is following some order of justice, one that is well beyond the reach of our understanding. Richard Nixon so revealingly put it, when the president does it that means it is not illegal. So, if God does it, does that mean that it cannot be bad?

Whether or not one believes God to be guided by objective and independent moral principles certainly had implications for how one conceived of the distribution of grace and the true path to eternal salvation. Standing before the God of reason and the God of will, we face a set of questions about the nature of reality itself. Do we inhabit a cosmos that is fundamentally intelligible because its creation is grounded in a rational decision informed by certain absolute values? Is the world's existence the result of a reasonable act of creation and the expression of an infinite wisdom? Or on the other hand, is the universe ultimately a non-rational, even arbitrary piece of work?

Organized Superstition

What if the depiction of the Bible was not of divine origin but a mere work of human literature; religion as organized superstition? God is nothing but nature. There is nothing good or bad, perfect or imperfect about God or Nature, it just is. Therefore, it is what it is, nothing more or less. There is nothing supernatural; whatever is or happens is a part of nature. It comes about with an absolute necessity and as a result of nature's laws and process. Even human beings and their states of mind, their volitions, passions, thoughts and desires are determined by nature. There is no freedom of the will and no uncaused spontaneity anywhere in nature, not even in the human psyche.

Are human beings endowed with an immortal soul? There is an eternal aspect of the human mind, namely the adequate ideas or truths that a person pursuing knowledge acquires in a lifetime. Because these ideas are like all truths, eternal, they do not come to an end with the death of the person. But this eternity of the mind, which is enjoyed and confers benefits in this world, must not be confused with the personal immortality of the soul in some world to come, a superstitious doctrine that only fosters the harmful passions of hope. The life of freedom and happiness is guided by reason and knowledge.

The world and God are but a single substantial thing that God is the substance of all things and that creatures are only modes or accidents. God is not some goal oriented planner, who then judges things by how well they conform to his purposes. Things happen only because of nature and its laws. Nature has no end set before it; all things proceed by a certain eternal necessity of nature. To believe otherwise is to fall prey to the same superstitions that lie at the heart of the organized religious.

The traditional religious conception of God leads only to superstition, not enlightenment. God may be the cause of all things, but this is only because whatever is in nature is brought about by nature. Because nature is all there is, there is nothing outside nature to constrain it to do one thing rather than another. Therefore, God acts from the laws of his nature alone. The existence of God or nature itself is absolutely necessary. Whatever happens in nature, everything that has been or will be, is caused by nature, thus it comes about through natural principles. Things could have been produced by God in no other way, and in no other order than they have been produced. It is the only possible world.

All things exist through the necessity of the divine nature, without any act or choice by God. What is the meaning of existence, the understanding of why things are as they are? God is a supremely moral being and his will alone is what determines right and wrong, good and bad. The view is not simply that God is needed to enforce such values and to motivate human ethical behavior with the promise of reward and the threat of punishment; it is the stronger claim that without God as their source, the values simply would not exist. Why is it morally wrong to kill or steal or lie? Because God says it is wrong. It is always and everywhere wrong for one human being to kill another. To nonbelievers and even to believers, divine moral voluntarism faces some troubling objections.

It is very difficult indeed to accept the idea that if God does not exist, then neither does morality. If there is no God then is everything permitted? Judgments about what is good or bad, right or wrong? Moral principles are discovered, not created. Their truth is independent of what anyone, divine or human, wants or believes. Moreover, it is reason, impersonal, dispassionate, universal reason, not sentiment or divine revelation that discovers them. Reason alone can see whether an action is right or wrong.

We take on the fear of dying. The way to approach death is to give up the love of the body and have faith in God's justice and a firm conviction in the immortality of the soul. Death is terrible only for sinners. The just, on the other hand, desire it, for it is the moment when God will provide to each person the immortality or the punishment due for his time on Earth. God's choice is always directed by wisdom.

Should we take the method which involves questioning assumptions, taking no assertion of faith, and building our understanding of the world on observations rather than tradition? By questioning everything until we reach the fact of the matter? The argument that religion is at the core of the world's problems and only a commitment to individual freedoms and rights, will steer humanity into a better future. If we are heading toward some kind of crisis, it's worth asking ourselves a few basic questions. Modern society, as we normally define it, a culture built around tolerance, reason and democratic values, occupies a rather small portion of the world and there are signs that it is shrinking. Abstract thinking is an excellent and necessary tool, but the loftiest thoughts are rooted in our physical being.

It's human nature to have a kind of doubt, to question some of our most basic beliefs. It affects the very structure of people's thought, the way we perceived the world, the universe and ourselves in it. We associate modern with a nonreligious, non-spiritual, rational and scientific outlook. Are we wrong to think that? While writing this book, I found myself with many doubts. I seemed to have gained nothing in trying to educate myself unless it was to discover more and more how ignorant we are about life. I have determined to explore human reason in this world. I seek knowledge which I might find within myself or perhaps in the greatest of nature. One should conduct their own individual research, coming to their own conclusion and then follow their own instructs about this life that we live in.

Why is there something rather than nothing? As philosophers have pointed out, I think, therefore I am. Thinking is taking place, therefore there must be that which thinks. Therefore the mind and its good sense, that is to say, human reason, are the only basis for judging whether a thing is true. There is so much we do not know. Perhaps atheism is a road leading to the most dangerous of places the human mind could go. The nature of the relationship between faith and reason and also the relationship between the spiritual and physical worlds is a moving target. The battle lines between faith and reason have never been clear cut. Blind faith is the problem that humanity has to overcome.

Death is not something we actually experience and that since we aren't conscious of a nonliving state, it is literally meaningless. So instead of spending our lives worrying about the future we should look at each instant as an eternity. We should live in the moment. Death is the event in life; it is our chief organizing principle. It's why we rush and why we dawdle, why we work our jobs and fawn over our children, why we like fast cars, why we write poetry and why sex thrills us. It's why we wonder why we are here.

When a priest blesses bread and wine during Mass and he repeats the biblical formula, the underlying substances of the bread and wine are swapped for the substances of the flesh and blood of Jesus Christ. To eat the bread is also to unite one's own physical body with Christ's, to become part of the body of Christ, meaning both his physical body and the body of believers. The whole infrastructure of the church, parishes and cathedrals, priests and nuns, real estate, art, revenue, the ability to mold and manipulate heads of state, rested on it. The church had what is believed to be a franchise on salvation.

We can reach truth by using the power of reason. While I don't dismiss the relevance of God, I also don't feel that God necessarily played a role in the relationship between the world and the mind that perceives it. A firm division between faith and reason would lead to the modern concept of atheism. The realization that God doesn't control the universe; that rather the blind forces of nature do, but that many people around the world are still caught in the trap of religion and are threatening with intimidation, to drag humanity down the drain. I continue to believe that reason would function alongside faith to increase human happiness and life span, end disease, reduce suffering of all kind and give people greater power over nature and greater freedom in their lives. Bring an end to traditional religion and end what we believe was the tyranny of superstition in which humanity had existed since the beginning of time.

God exist, but he cannot have human properties and does not perform miracles or otherwise intervene in human affairs. The Bible contains much wisdom, but shouldn't be trusted when it comes to tales of seas parting or water being turned into wine. God is synonymous with nature, meaning not merely the natural world but the totality of all things. God as the one and only substance existing in the universe, everything else was some subpart of God. Einstein, when challenged to state his own religious beliefs said, I believe in a God who reveals himself in the orderly harmony of what exists, not in a God who concerns himself with fates and actions of human beings.

The problem with religion is that it keeps individual humans from exercising their own minds and applying their reason to understanding the world and their place in it. Superstition is more harmful than atheism. Relook the foundation of religion, to ground faith not in a church or a holy book but in the human mind, the world, and the relationship between the two. We must stress the order, harmony and a balance of faith and reason.

Time is nothing but a measure of the changing positions of objects in space. In the beginning, there were no objects in space. A year is a measure of the movement of the earth around the sun. A day is the revolving of the earth on its axis. Since by its own account neither earth nor sun existed in the beginning, the authors of the Bible never meant to say that everything was created in seven days in the usual sense of a day.

Even if we allowed that God might conceivably exist, why on earth should God be like us? Why should God's mind be in any way like ours? Of course there is no reason at all, unless it's the other way around. In other words, the only reason why God's mind might be like ours is if ours was made to be like his, that is, if God made us in his image.

In the hour of our greatest anguish there is no point in crying out to the heavens with any expression of our deepest, most heartfelt feelings, because you will find no answers. The human task is to grow up, to mature, learning to come to terms with this. This universe has nurtured us through the millennia, cradled us, helped the unique thing that is human consciousness to evolve and guided each of us as individuals towards the great moments in our lives.

The Human Mind

Everything that goes on inside your body and every interaction you have with the outside world is controlled by your brain. It allows you to cope with your everyday environment. It is capable of producing breathtaking athletic feats, works of art and profound scientific insights. It also products the enormous range of emotional responses that can take us from the depths of depression to the heights of euphoria. Yet its weight, on average is only three pounds. Considering everything the brain does, how can this relatively small mass of tissue possibly be the source of our personalities, dreams, thoughts, sensations and movements?

The human mind is still the focus of the cosmos and responding to its needs. At some point in childhood we all wonder whether a tree falling really makes any sound if it takes place in a remote forest where no one is there to hear it. Is life all just a dream? Could we ourselves be in such a simulation? What we think is the universe is really some sort of vault of heaven rather than the real thing? Should we question the things that we believe to be real? It is a natural human impulse to wonder if life has a meaning. Sometimes things go wrong and life seems pointless. So the big why questions – why life? Why the universe? Today we are encouraged to put aside the big questions of life and death. Why are we here? What is the meaning of life? Such questions are strictly meaningless, we are told. Just get on with it. So we lose some of the sense of how strange it is to be alive.

Once again, the ideas may not all be true, certainly many of them are inadequate, if not false or misleading, but they all contributed to our modern mind, the way we think, human understanding and the appreciation of the human condition. Are space and time illusions? Look at the creative possibilities. Is their one God who dwells in all of us? It could be argued the development or evolution of man from other animals on the basis of observations of the natural order and the inability of infants to find food for themselves. What is the truth? Is the beginning of mankind beyond the grasp of human knowing? Do we want the truth or the way of our opinions?

We must articulate our thoughts with clarity. Perception and truth are related to the experience and judgment of the individual. One can not with certainty either affirm or reject the existence of God. There are two opposing arguments on every subject. We should try to see and understand all sides of an issue. There could be a myth regarding the beginnings of things. Could human beings have a social impulse that blinds them and the civilization as a whole? The secret of human survival is all members of the community, although they have different roles, work together for the good of the whole. Every person has the right to express an opinion and all opinions should be given consideration.

The individual measures truth by their experiences. For the individual, what is true is in his or her judgment. We need to understand that all things are constantly changing, like a flowing river. Nothing stays the same over space and time. Does God exist and what is his form? God exists for those who believe that he exists, but not for others that don't believe. What are the theories for your thinking? The point of intellectual inquiry is to search after the essence of things. Our thought in its attempts to deal with the complexities by the interplay of both invisible and the visible; spirit and matter, over space and time. We have a faith in God and power of the mind, and a never ending concern for human improvement.

A life where the intellect does not pursue truth is, for him, a life not worth living. Every person must care for his soul. The soul is that which is able to be foolish or wise, good or evil. The soul is at the heart of personal intelligence and character. We seek to make it as good as possible. Happiness does not depend so much on physical or external goods, but on knowing how to act right. Education is to enable one to reach his or her true aim in life. What shall it profit a man if he gains the whole world and loses his soul? What is the purpose of life? For every true thinker, everything must be examined. Take the view that the world is in a state of constant flux. What is the nature of real being? There is a nature of change, development and growth. What we see, hear, taste, feel or smell is subject to constant change. Opinions can be shaken by criticism or by conflicting evidence, while true knowledge can not.

Only in the light of the intellect that reality can be seen for what it is. Look at the source of light in which the eye of the mind sees everything. Justice is based on the inner nature of the human spirit. Is the human soul grounded in the rule of reason and the obedience of desire to rational ends? It is the problem of true knowledge. We rest on knowledge of the true standards of life. What is taught to children by way of stories has a profound impact on the child's soul and education is a lifelong process. A society needs spiritual values that produce unity and happiness. The quality of human life comes down to what one thinks and what one does. It's a matter a framing ideas and then challenging them. Things come into existence, develop, decay and pass out of existence.

By nature, we pursue pleasure and avoid pain. The natural goal or end of life is the pursuit of pleasure and avoidance of pain. The good life must consist in the pursuit of pleasure. The natural goal of life is the pursuit of happiness, true happiness is found only in the mind. The mind is of a higher order of reality than the body. We perceive change in the world. Therefore, change must be real; it can not be an illusion. We perceive that everything in the universe can change. A clear view of an object yields truth. We live with myths and superstitions that enslave our lives and the idea that God controls or manipulates our world. If God exists, does he interact with the world? Can the individual take control of his or her life?

One understands what is in one's control by understanding the nature of the world and the human individual. Freedom is not the power to do anything one pleases. Freedom is found in understanding the limits of one's power and accepting them. Not everything in nature is rational. The rational governing principle in each human individual allows him or her to achieve knowledge of the physical world. This individual rational principle is also what each individual shares with

God. God could be above or beyond nature. The ability to understand the nature of the world requires the individual to exercise his understanding. The individual must let reason be his guide. Understanding nature as a whole is to understand the world as the best possible world. To be rational is to understand the difference between things that are in one's power and things that are not. The point is that what counts is the individual's choice or intent, not the result of an action. The only thing in one's power is one's attitude toward it, that is, acceptance or rejection. How we think about something after the fact, for instance the loss of a loved one; is in our power, but changing the fact is not.

The universe is governed by reason. Are we fragmented in our thoughts? Is there a practical approach to life? The universe is governed by law or that the order of things is the revelation of reason. The universe is rational throughout to keep one's will in harmony with nature. When someone treats you badly, you should accept the ill treatment because it can not harm you if you do not let it do so. Jesus said "Forgive them for they know not what they do". It is our duty to accept life and perform the functions required to the best of our abilities. Do your best and God will do the rest. For the rational human being, death is nothing to be feared. Since death is an event of nature, it can not be bad. On the contrary, it's in the goodness of every natural event. At death we simply cease to exist. As rational beings we are governed by a higher law, the law of nature. Under the law of nature we are all equals. It doesn't matter if you are a man or woman, rich or poor, smart or dumb, black or white; nature makes us all equal.

With respect to any question there are appearances, judgments, and objects of weight on both sides of the question. Neither affirms nor denies that things are in fact one way rather than another. A distinction between how things seem to us or strike us and how things in the world are as a matter of fact is in question. We are constrained to lead our lives in a way that things appear to us.

What is the truth, the immortality of the soul, the resurrection, human free will, the existence of the Devil and his angels, the creation of the world? The plan of creation existed in the wisdom of God from the beginning. In the beginning, nothing was essentially good or essentially bad. All rational creatures, angels, demons, and human beings possessed free will. Even the sun, moon, and stars, undergo change. They probably have received commands from God, just as human beings do. Certainly angels operate on instructions from God and receive rewards according to their merits.

God holds the entire universe together. The God who is the Father of Jesus is good but not just. The God of the Old Testament was just but not good. Christ had a soul and all rational creatures have souls. When saved, souls become something like fire and light. Rational animals have the ability to choose between good and evil. The fact that God requires a good life of human beings proves they have free will. The final goal is to become as much as possible like God. Most human beings fail to understand the Bible because they try to interpret it literally. Not everything is the Bible has a literal meaning. It's about the connection of the soul to the body.

What is the relationship between faith and knowledge? Those who reject the eternal light will turn toward darkness. Mankind will fall by disobedience and become subject to death of both body and soul. A bad person lives according to the flesh like the Devil; the good person loves God and other human beings. The former will perish; the latter will reach their immortal home. Christians believes that eternal life is supreme good and real only when one believes in God. Salvation depends on living an upright life and punishment if they do not repent. The reward comes only after death and God is believed to do the impossible.

The age old question of why bad things happen to good people. Minds are incapable of understanding God's infinite intention. Everything that happens in this world must be to a good end, despite appearances to the contrary. What it means to be human, a part of the creation that, along with all matter, will find its true end and fulfillment when it returns to the creator. Wealth, power and fame can not lead to happiness if it is true that happiness is the highest good and that anything that can be taken away can not be the highest good. Bad fortune often teaches the valuable truth that a man's life is far better spent in the pursuit of more lasting values. The pleasures and possessions of this world are simply not the source of true happiness.

All persons, both good and evil, desire good. Only the good can achieve the good. The more one contemplates the mind of God, the freer one is. The more one descends to the flesh, the more enslaved.

God looks out from eternity upon all persons and arranges rewards according to their merit. How can human beings have free will if God has foreknowledge? How can human thoughts and actions have freedom if the divine mind, in foreseeing all things, binds them? People get confused because we comprehend according to own ability to know. True intelligence belongs only to God and must not be confused with the powers of reason that belong to the human race. God with his knowledge of all times remains a spectator of all things from on high.

Bring reason to bear on the problems of faith so as to give understanding. Reason can give understanding to faith, realized that something more than reason is needed when unbelievers can not be moved even by the best of reasons. Do not seek to understand in order to believe, but believe in order to understand. Prove the existence of God through the use of reason alone. Nature could not have been caused, nor could it have come from nothing. Supreme Being is without beginning or end. It exists at all places and at all times. It is also true that the Supreme Being exists in no place nor anytime.

The nature of God is such that it is evident from an understanding of nature that a being of that kind must exit. God must exist because whatever exists must have a cause and God is that cause. God gives the power to show, through the use of reason alone, that God exists, just as faith affirms. Human beings were created by God to live and be happy, but man, through Adam, sinned. For that sin man must be punished. Some will scoff at the Christian faith and regard it as a foolish simplicity. It is fitting that Jesus, out of his mercy and kindness, would be willing to die on the cross as a human being, and freely choosing to pay for man's sins. Man could not be saved without being punished for his sins.

The conduct of good men is generally motivated by error and ignorance. Human goodness is quite apart from human intention. All that is necessary is that men act with good intentions. Even the crucifiers of Christ can not be considered evil men, as they were simply carrying out their orders in support of what they considered to be a just system of government.

The Human Journey

Humans were first made in the image and likeness of God. The first step in our return to God and to our true selves is to know ourselves. If we truly know ourselves, we will be humble and fear God. This is the beginning of wisdom, the opposite of pride. We are first caught up in self-love. Then we begin to love God because we perceive how good he is to us. This complete unity of will with God is the human journey back to its true self.

Reason can provide meanings that remain hidden from the untrained mind. Faith is the existence of God and is subject to rational proof. God created the universe and is the cause of everything that exists. The priority of God means that he is without limits to time and space. There can be no relation between God and time or space.

God knows all about what it is to be a human being, no doubt, that at any given time there are a lot of us. God knows nothing about any individual human being as distinct from any other. He can not watch over individuals, or care for them, or separate those who should be rewarded from those who should be punished, or bring about any particular historical event. Moral responsibility requires that people make choices and know, as individuals, what they are doing. What if there is no afterlife? Lack of an afterlife could under mind the possibility of influencing people's behavior by rewards and punishments. Perhaps the existence of God in not self-evident to reason alone, anyone who understands the idea of God but denies God's existence is involved in a contradiction.

The union with God is to be sought within oneself. All things come from God and to God all things eventually return. God is the ultimate purpose of the human being. Any person must become detached from everything else, even from the idea of becoming detached, if we are to gain the immediate experience of God. The person must turn away from everything but his or her own soul, what is within. Thus one must let go, in one way or another, of external things. There is no physical or fleshly pleasure without some spiritual harm. The desire of the flesh is contrary to those of the spirit and the desires of the spirit are contrary to those of the flesh.

In order to attain happiness in this life, reason must prevail.

Ultimately happiness depends on the love for God that opens up the possibility of everlasting life, which is the destiny of humankind. Reason reveals the ultimate end of life. Try to transform from seeing life in bits and pieces to seeing out of a vision of unity. Try building an understanding of the world through a process of selection and analysis. We are a creature destined to love our creator. Paradise as a vision of human destiny fulfilled. Try making yourself pleasing to God through the exercise of reason and discipline of the senses and higher thinking. Our soul conforms to the will of God.

Logic seeks to organize and clarify human thought. God is known by faith, not by reason examining his creation. Reason, as it strives to reach the essence of things, is in harmony with a faith that accepts the revelation of God. Both the creation and the Bible have the same source. We seek closeness to God, the source of all truth and the end of all human longings. We know through our senses and by making judgments on what is directly experienced in the world or in ourselves. Logic is the arrangement of these ideas in order to obtain clarity of thought and an organized body of truths. Truths about God could not be demonstrated by reason alone, but rather by faith. To know God is to have faith.

Should mankind live his life cultivating his mind for a rational program of action and the heart for generosity and tolerance? The illusions allow our society to function as we age in this life; as old men and women, aging bodies, pursuing the pleasures of the young. Who in their right mind, the mind in accords with the values of worldly wealth, power and prestige, would choose poverty, suffering, and self sacrifice? If men and women are to embrace Christianity, they must do so with heart rather than mind, becoming foolish in the eyes of the world. Prizes for the Christian do not come in the form of money or high office, but there is in this lifetime a supreme reward, which is a kind of madness.

Human nature is such that individuals will seek gratification of their lusting for power, pleasures and profit. My thoughts are based upon my years of experience and my continual reading. The behavior of the rich and the powerful led me to view that humanity is corrupt. Men and women will, when given the chance, always turn toward evil and self gratification. Human beings are always the same in their nature. All men are born, live and die in the same way, and therefore, resemble each other. All are animated by the same passions, the same desires and the same impulses. A King must never be deceived into thinking that his subjects will not, at the earliest opportunity, seek their own self interest. Men always commit the error of not knowing when to limit their hopes. Our passions are endless, our desires bottomless. What is necessary to be successful in a corrupt world? It is the situation at the moment that determines which actions are necessary. The goal is success. Political activity is like a game of chess with its rules. The master player knows how to exploit the weaknesses and blunders of his opponents to maximum advantage. The goal is finding the best move, the move that wins. The religion of ancient Rome helps to maintain the strength of the army, binding it by loyalty to an oath. History teaches that exactly the same acts at different times yield different results. The success of every act depended on the relationship between it and its times. It was good fortune if there's a good relationship, bad fortune if it's not. One view is that religion is a childish toy and there is no sin but ignorance and a system of ethics where the ends justify the means.

Christianity was merely an update of ancient cults of sun worship. Look to human reason and human progress, stripped of religion and superstition. The idea is driven home to you that reason alone is an empty vessel. At least some of the problem that the Western world confronts today, as it grapples with such forces as militant Islam, have to do with the fact that the modern Western world has a split personality. It is confused and divided over the relationship of reason and faith. This brings a scientific perspective to bear in polities, economics and education, to reform all of society around the principle of reason. Primary and evident truths which we can discover by observing the operation of the human mind is open.

We believe in the idea of progress. That with each generation, each passing century, humanity is evolving upward, toward happiness, freedom, equality, a higher state of civilization. Man himself must make or has made himself into whatever, in a moral sense, whether good or evil, he is or is to become. Either condition must be an effect of his free choice. Otherwise he could not be held responsible for it and could therefore be morally neither good nor evil. In any analysis, common sense has a part to play in one's reflections.

It might be too vast a problem for the mind to grasp. It does not seem that the human mind is capable of forming a very distinct conception of both soul and body. To do this, it is necessary to conceive them as a single thing and at the same time to conceive them as two things and this is absurd. The view that the physical or material world is the real world and that nothing exists outside of it and a lot of scientists and philosophers ascribe to some form of it. Some people, who declare they are atheists and say that what they believe in is science or the physical world, are adopting a stance.

Human Consciousness

Human consciousness is the well from which we derive much that is most meaningful to us. This is the problem that people have today, usually religious systems and replacing them with a good firm scientific way of understanding. With Darwinism and, in particular, the idea that humans are descended from apes. Each person is endowed with certain strengths and weaknesses and that is was possible, through hard work to improve. Debate on whether the growing mountain of scientific data from all fronts contradicted biblical accounts of the origin of life. Is science destroying the moral foundations of social order? Are activities of the soul only functions of the brain and there is no independent soul?

During this writing, there are over thirty wars being fought on our planet Earth. We are on the verge or over the verge of irreversible environmental damage. There are epic confrontations brewing that transcend national borders, which have to do with clashes of religious, economic and political systems. We are a probing, analytical culture and a certain amount of baggage comes with this. Are we being caught up in hopelessness because certainty does not exist in the real world? Like children outgrowing fantasies, we are supposed to realize ultimately that there is no such thing as certainty, but we want it anyway. We probe the world and our past. Who was Jesus and how do intelligent Christians answer the supposed miracles with our understanding of the physical world? We are all detectives. Sifting clues and making deductions is in our blood, or perhaps better to say in our brains. The bottom line we crave closure.

Religion is a force of chaos and darkness. Are we saved by the fact that it succeeded in separating faith and reason? Our government is built on human reason, with all its fallibility. Faith assumes infallibility and that is the danger. Man is capable, guided solely by the light of reason and experience, of perfecting the good life on earth. The first essential condition of the good life on earth is the freeing of men's minds from the bonds of ignorance and superstition. Is there really a march of progress, with each generation building on the work of the last and moving forward toward some brighter future? Throughout the world we find religious revivals. Religion, including Christianity, has most of the time hindered that development. The scientific and religious worldviews aren't truly inconsistent but that perceived conflicts have to be sorted out. We distrust anything that contradicts science or outrages reason. I think that we have to find an intelligent way not to tolerate religious intolerance.

Today we may wonder how we come into the life that we have. It seems to have little or nothing to do with me as a person. Today many Christians believe that God is present in the blood and wine at the climax of the Mass. Today often seems that we search and search for a genuine spiritual experience but are seldom sure we've had one that genuinely deserves the name. Science and religion agree that in the beginning the cosmos moved from a state of nothingness to the existence of matter. If a human eye had been looking at the dawn of history it would have seen a vast cosmic mist. This gas or mist was the Mother of all living carrying everything needed for the creation of life.

The Bible refers to many disembodied spiritual beings, including the gods of rival tribes, angels, archangels, as well as devils, Satan and Lucifer. The Garden of Eden could not go on forever. If it had, humanity would never have evolved. The story of Genesis is a subjective account of the way humanity evolved. Without Lucifer's intervention, humanity would not have evolved in what we call life today. We can often believe what we want to believe.

The God of the Old Testament is a jealous, angry and warlike God. The old order always tries to stay on beyond its allotted time. Characteristic of human life, its crowning achievement and also the crowning achievement of the cosmos, is the capacity for thought. The brain is the most complex, the most subtle, altogether the most mysterious and miraculous physical object in the known universe. Cycles of life, death and rebirth, cycles in which creatures must die in order to make way for a new generation. Fathers must die to make way for sons, where the king must die to give way to a younger, more vigorous successor.

In the biblical story, the great flood, was intended to destroy the greater part of humankind, because the development of humankind had gone wrong. One day Noah heard a voice that warned him of a rainstorm that would wipe out mankind. Build a boat, he was told. Noah and his family set about building a great vessel, Noah's ark. Legend has it that the only animal missing was the unicorn, which therefore became extinct.

You can't take it with you, goes the popular saying. Religion has had a negative, even destructive effect on human history. People who believe in idealism as a philosophy of life have always tended to believe in spirits, gods and angels. Human spirits should attain individuality, should be able to think freely, to exercise free will and to choose who to love. But look at the life of Christ Jesus, born to a carpenter and a virgin, walking on water and feeding five thousand from a small basket, performing healing miracles, raising from the dead and ascending to heaven.

If you politely turn a blind eye to the supernatural content of the story of Jesus Christ and the rise of Christianity, you still have to accept that something extraordinary happened which needs explanation. Its effect on the history of the world is unparalleled in its breadth and depth. It gave rise to the civilization we now enjoy, a civilization of unprecedented freedom, prosperity for all, richness of culture and scientific advance. What was unique to Christianity, planted by Jesus Christ, was the idea of the interior life.

The nomadic Mongolian tribes were united under a great leader, Attila the Hun. Attila was not the ravening monster of popular imagination, it is nevertheless true to say that if he had succeeded in overrunning the Roman Empire, this would have been disastrous for the evolution of human consciousness. The great terror striking uproar of a Hun army going to battle was made up of the howling of dogs, the clanking of weapons and the sounds of horns and bells. All this was intended to summon the battalions of the dead, the ghosts of the ancestors, to fight alongside them. They were also calling on the group souls of carnivores, the wolves and the bears, to enter into them and give them supernatural powers.

A child called Mohammed was born in Mecca. At the age of twenty-five, he married a wealthy widow of Mecca and became one of the richest and most respected citizens of that city. Mohammed was dissatisfied. He saw a people interested only in making money, gambling and getting drunk. Mohammed became convinced that Arabia needed a prophet, someone like Jesus Christ, who could purge the people of superstitions and of corruption and could unite them in one cosmic purpose. Mohammed was sitting in the hills surrounding Mecca when an angel appeared before him, saying "I am the angel Gabriel". Later Mohammed went into town and preached what Gabriel had taught him. He would summarize his creed in these terms: Allah is the one God, Mohammed is his prophet, do not steal, do not lie, do not slander and never become intoxicated. Alcohol would be forbidden in Islam. The angel who dictated the Koran to Mohammed was Gabriel.

If the Old Testament was the Age of the Father, which had called for fear and obedience, and if the New Testament was the Age of the Son, the age of the Church and of faith, then it suggests that a third age is coming, an age of the Holy Spirit. Gospels recommended a life of poverty, devoted to helping others. Poverty is to have nothing, to wish for nothing, yet to posses all things in the spirit of freedom. The things we posses have a hold on us and threaten to rule our lives. At the same time, logic shows Christianity to be absurd. Will logic eat up religion, all true spirituality?

When we are in love we choose to see the good qualities in the one we love. Our good-heartedness helps to bring out these qualities and make them stronger. The reverse is also true. Those we despise become despicable. We good-heartedly decide to believe in the essential goodness of the world. Despite tendency in things that seems to contradict such spiritual beliefs and make them look foolish and absurd.

Jesus Christ revolutionized human consciousness yet left almost invisible traces on the contemporary historical record. The great thing about science is that it works. It produces testable, reliable results and tangible, life changing benefits. The contrast with religion, why is it that miracles always happen only in remote times and places? The result of all this was that physical objects became the yardstick of what is real. The best way to keep something is to try your hardest to do so and never give up. You cannot transform the world by wishful thinking; you must do something about it.

Modern science is killing off wonder, by telling us that we know it all. Modern science is killing philosophy, by encouraging us not to ask the big why questions. These questions are strictly meaningless, they say. Just get on with it. Today's scientists try to insist that theirs is the only way to interpret the basic conditions of human existence. They like to dwell on what they know. In their view, the known is like a vast continent occupying nearly everything there is. Let us sow seeds of doubt. Science is not certain. It is a myth like any other, representing what people in the deepest parts of themselves want to believe. Take a fresh look at the basic conditions of our existence and ask the question why. We only know what we know.

With the current state of the economy, the ongoing wars that rage across the globe, the unsettling changes to the earth's climate, questions about the role of God and religion in world affairs have never been more relevant. Many of us are searching for a place where we can find not only facts and scientific reason but also hope and the moral courage needed to overcome such challenges.

Approximately half of all Americans say they would refuse to vote for a well qualified atheist candidate for public office. In other words, one of every two Americans admits to being prejudice against fellow citizens who don't believe in God. It is not easy to live a good life or be a good person, with or without a God. The fact is that life is hard. Living well and being a good person are difficult to do. Fair minded people of all religions or none do not dwell on the question of whether we can be good without God. If you don't believe in God, you're not sure you believe in God, or if you think you believe in some kind of higher power but you know you don't fit into any organized religion, you're not alone. Over a billion people around the world today feels that way. All the major studies of world religious demographics, indicate that there are somewhere around one billion people on earth who define themselves as atheist or nonreligious. Nonreligious is the fastest growing religious preference in the United States. Mark Twain, Bill Gates, Warren Buffett, Einstein, Darwin and more than a billion people worldwide are nonbelievers.

The fact that being a human being is lonely and frightening. Take one look at a world in which the lives of thousands of innocent children are ripped away every year by hurricanes, earthquakes, and other acts of God, not to mention the thousand other fundamental injustices of life. We must become the superintendents of our own lives. Taking charge of the often lousy world around us and working to shape it into a better place, though we know we cannot ever finish the task. The desire to live with dignity, to be good. A warning that we cannot afford to wait until tomorrow or until the next life to be good, because today, the short journey we get from birth to death, womb to tomb, is all we have. Therefore, believe in life before death.

Faith in God means believing absolutely in something, with no proof whatsoever. Science has the best tool humans have for understanding the world around us. Science can teach us a great deal, like what medicine to give to patients in a hospital. But science won't come and visit us in the hospital. For many people, fear that without religion there is simply no reason to live, or at least no reason to live morally and ethically. We can and must live our lives for a purpose well beyond ourselves. What really matters is whether we live according to our values, and that takes hard work and a hundred hard choices every day. Do good work together and build something positive in this world, the only world we have. If you ever meet anyone who tells you his or her religion can offer all the answers, run away, or at least hide your wallet.

One view, death is not the end of you. Death is not your termination, but your transition into eternity, so there are eternal consequences to everything you do on earth. Every act of our lives strikes some chord that will vibrate in eternity. While life on earth offers many choices, eternity offers only two, heaven or hell. Your relationship to God on earth will determine your relationship to him in eternity. If you learn to love and trust God's son, Jesus, you will be invited to spend the rest of eternity with him. Just like Santa Claus, marking whether we have been naughty or nice. On the other hand, if you reject his love, forgiveness, and salvation, you will spend eternity apart from God forever. In carrying out the Holocaust, Hitler wrote "I am acting in accordance with the will of the Almighty Creator - by defending myself against the Jew, I am fighting for the work of the Lord". The Nazi army's belts were inscribed "God is with us".

Intuitions

What we do not understand frightens us. The billion of stars and trillions of big and small rocks that surround us in this universe do not care about us. They do not hear our prayers. The only guidance for which we have ever seen evidence is human guidance. The only purposes we've ever been able to understand are the purposes we have created and chosen. It is now time for us to open our eyes and take responsibility for our future. The scientific method, while imperfect, is the most reliable tool human beings have ever known for determining the nature of the world around us. We question everything, including our own questions, and we search for as many ways as we can to confirm or deny our intuitions.

A lot of people say they believe in God, but what they means by God may not be all that relevant to their lives or to the world. God is the most important, influential literary character human beings have ever created. Faith is the state of being ultimately concerned, to live with dignity, to treat themselves and others with respect. Better education, including science and the scientific method as our most important tool for determining the truth. God was not the universe, but the positive forces in the universe as far as humans are concerned. The idea that God is personal empowerment, strength and the ability to make a difference.

Religious and nonreligious people alike are in for a lifetime of unresolved debate and often meaningless discussion if we continue to convince ourselves that what is really important about religion is whether or not we say we believe in God. If there is a creator or manager of the world, he does not run things in accordance with the human moral agenda, rewarding the good and punishing the bad. We cannot prove or disprove that God existences. But the golden rule is golden because it's a simple, easy to understand reminder that there are many reasons to be good. Beyond God, and in fact, God may not even be the real motivating force behind the good behavior of many people. We are evolved creatures, and much of our goodness, along with our constant struggle to bring it out, comes from the way we evolved. Simple put, it feels good to give to others, whether we get back or not.

If there is no God, why is the belief in God so universal? We must be wired to believe in God, the claim usually runs, or why would such a huge majority of human beings hold such a belief? It is true that most people, even a great many who call themselves nonreligious say they believe in some kind of supernatural God. Why? Was this notion implanted in our brains somewhere, whether by nature or by God himself, so that we would go forward faithfully, no matter how many natural disasters, religious wars, and abusive preachers gave us reason to doubt?

Causal reasoning is a self explanatory term. Our minds evolved to look for the causes of things, not eating causes hunger, watering plants causes them to grow, and so on. If we did not understand that actions have consequences, it would be very difficult to get anything done. This pattern of causal thinking is so strong, it even outlasts belief in a traditional God. We just don't like randomness, so we look everywhere around us for little signs that the mysteries in the universe have a purpose and that the strange things that happen to us every day were caused by some sort of watchful force. We evolved over millions of years to look for causes, whether they exist or not, because if we hadn't, the world would look even more confusing to us than it does now.

The world is not all good. The moral values we find in human beings are not all good. Much of the world we live in is absurd. Ignorant, selfish fools prosper while innocent babies are slaughtered. Is there a all powerful God? We can neither prove it nor disprove it. We have no right to steal clean air and water and the diversity of plant and animal life that we know future generations will desperately need. After all, slavery was once considered morally acceptable by almost all religious people, including Christians. No war can be justified by the fact that the one true God is on our side. This notion of absolute morality favoring one side of a conflict has been used to justify almost every war ever fought. Shouldn't we be slower and more hesitant to ship our sons and daughters into bloody battle?

There are certain mysteries that will remain mysteries forever. What did come first, the chicken or the egg? Because as long as we humans have believed, we have also doubted. Who really knows? The gods came afterwards, with the creation of this universe. Perhaps the universe formed itself. Perhaps not, the one who looks down on it, in the highest heaven, only he knows. Or perhaps he does not know. No one has ever been able to prove that he or she has witnessed a miracle. No man or woman has ever risen from the dead. No god has ever appeared on earth to explain how or why he created the basic elements. Those who beg us to believe, that is, to believe the unbelievable, almost always have their own self serving agenda. If God created the world, where was he before creation?

As a statesman, Jefferson promoted and defended religious freedom, helping to build our nation, as an example to the world, what he called a "Wall of Separation" between church and state. He designed the University of Virginia as the nation's first truly institution of higher learning, a temple of knowledge and human reason. Later, in retirement, he rewrote the New Testament, cutting and pasting its pages to remove all contradictions or miracles, leaving only stories of Jesus as a human philosopher he greatly admired. The Life and Morals of Jesus of Nazareth or the Jefferson Bible. Jefferson, the great leader and champion of democracy, honoring his religious and cultural heritage while refusing to accept it at face value without applying to it his own critical intellect and all the wisdom he could muster.

Marx came to see religion as a projection of human hopes and needs onto a supernatural realm that did not exist. He insisted that we transcend all such projections, overcoming our inadequacy as religious believers. He was in search of a better life for all people. There are no utopias. No utopian vision, godly or godless, must ever be allowed to justify violent repression or the coercion or conscience, no matter how noble the ultimate goals.

Lets engage with another old familiar question. What is the meaning of life? Perhaps meaning of my life has nothing to do with the meaning of your life? What if I discover that the meaning of my life is exploiting you? Indeed, the meaning of life is only really worth thinking about if we start with the premise that a meaningful life is a good and ethical life. Jesus couldn't possibly have been born of a virgin and resurrected from the dead. Life can sometimes seem meaningless, like a never ending defeat. The man without a purpose is like a ship without a rudder. We need to choose our own purpose in life.

There are many meaningful and difficult choices we must make every day of our lives, even if the universe doesn't spell them out for us. Which of them are really worthwhile? Most people in the world say they believe in God. But whether they do or not, faith in God is not what drives the vast majority of people. But you still have to take responsibility and decide what you are. I can't do that for you. No one else can. What drives most people in this world? I suspect, whether they admit it or not, is get, get, get as much as you can. Get really rich, get really powerful, get the nicest cars, the nicest women, the nicest jobs, whatever. What if our lives are driven by little more than the desire to win, to acquire things or people or status? The problem with the rat race is that even if you win, you are still a rat.

Ambition is a healthy part of life if set in the service of worthy goals. But when it becomes the entire point of life, there is no way to satisfy it, because there will always be another battle, another potential conquest. When is this going to be enough? The person who works and works and works toward a goal he can never attain, or who attains it and then realizes, I can strive all I want but it's to no end. I worked all my life to get a great job. I got the job and I was bored, it didn't full fill me. I worked for years to get the best education. I studied for years and years, and when I graduated I wasn't sure if I was any wiser than when I began. No amount of success can calm the emptiness we are pone to feel. When we are driven by nothing but victory, no victory can quench our thirst for yet another. No matter how much you win.

It's impossible to eliminate all desire, and even if it weren't, some desire and striving is healthy. The question is - what are we striving for? It is good to desire and it is good to care. The questions are, what do you desire and what do you care for? Be passionate about things that are worth being passionate about. So what are these things that are most worth being passionate about? Much of our time and energy today, in every society, is devoted to obeying rules, rebelling against them, or trying to come up with new rules to replace them. Happiness is the most obvious value one might choose as the goal in life. Who doesn't want to be happy? I believe that the most important purpose of human life is for every individual to strive for and attain self fulfillment, to become what each is capable of and to help others do the same. The United States Army created an advertising campaign "Be All You Can Be".

The idea of making a difference, being of service to one's fellow human beings and working toward the welfare of humanity. You have to strive to be selfish half the time, because more often than that is no good, but if you think you're being selfish less than half the time, you're probably lying to yourself. The general idea of being of service to others, are a reminder that free people, no matter how generous, will want to choose a purpose that also affirms the value of their own individual lives. Working toward the welfare of humanity is a crucially important part of life. Being of service to others is very important. Remember that just as a loving parent in an airplane whose cabin pressure has destabilized must put on her own oxygen mask before attending to her children. When we explain why we ought to give and to help others, we must begin with our individual needs, and then move to others' needs, not vice versa. We've know since Aristotle that everyone lives according to purpose. People are living to achieve and to succeed.

The first thing we have to be in order to be a good person is learn to look inside ourselves, understand what we love and hate, and use this information when deciding how to treat others. The golden rule is embarrassingly important because it is humiliating to think about how often we ourselves often buzz right past our kids or our spouse or our best friends, eyes distracted, focused on some goal or fantasy we have about how our day ought to be going. Forgetting that these people too are struggling not only with petty everyday problems but with their own fears about aging, sickness, and death. While the golden rule may be simple, it is hard to follow. Religious and secular people alike fail at it all the time. Then we wonder why our lives and our countries are such a mess. Do unto others.

When people are killed, we seek the best ways to remember their lives and legacies. If they were mainly good, beloved people, we try our best to carry on the good things they did. We remind ourselves, again and again if necessary, and it usually is necessary, that we are capable of making a positive difference, even if a small one. With the size of the universe, it can feel as if we make no difference. But each time we offer just one gentle word to a loved one in pain we make a great difference indeed. None of us will ever be all things to all people, or to ourselves, but we can identify which areas we're particularly strong in and cultivate those talents, surrounding ourselves with friends, loved ones, and coworkers whose strengths complement ours.

In the long run, winners don't punish. Nice guys do finish first, because winners are not bitter, and bitter people are not winners. This is a message truly worth teaching to our children and to each other. When you are slapped, you don't necessarily have to turn the other cheek to be slapped again, but neither should you slap right back. You can walk away. You can work hard to move forward without wasting your own precious energy making sure that those who cause your suffering suffer in turn. Let the impulse go.

To be healthy, you must balance work, play and rest. The average American is lucky to have more than a couple measly weeks of paid vacation per year. We Americans weren't always such workaholics. As recently as the 1900s, Europeans worked longer hours and took less vacation than we did. How much do you sacrifice in relationships in order to succeed in career goals, etc… We often forget that until approximately ten thousand years ago, humans had not yet invented agriculture. For most of the time that humans have walked the earth, we got our calories exclusively from hunting and gathering, so life was a day-to-day experience. Nearly everyone needed to be devoted to the enterprise of basic survival. Slowly, this began to change when we leaned techniques for producing our own food.

We accept with enthusiasm the modern proposition that all people must be free to make basic choices about the shape of their family life; whom to love, whether to have children, how to structure a family. Americans like to talk about family values. We have decided to do more than talk, we use our tax revenues to pay for family values. It isn't possible to feel the same way about one person for your entire life. Novelty, variety and mystery will always be tempting. That is the scary news. The good news is that our need for companionship, touch, compassion and trust does not change. These are things we can best enjoy by maintaining long term partnerships. We choose partners because we feel a sense of excitement around them, a thrill to be near them, but we also recognize that these feelings are not magical. We cannot stress too much the importance of plain old fashion honesty in every walk of life. The good is that which facilitates human dignity and the health of the natural world that surrounds us and sustains us. The bad or evil, is that which creates needless human suffering. We can all agree that we want to reduce needless human suffering.

For fourteen billion years of random, purposeless, unguided evolution, matter floated around, formed stars that lit up and were extinguished. Those stars eventually formed the material that formed you and me. Why would we expect any perfection? How are we supposed to figure out how to fix a serious problem if we're confused about how and why it started? We focus not on who wronged us, but on what we can do, what we can build, how we can grow, to make our lives better. As long as we're alive, we're always growing. We're all going to die. No one can do anything to change that. As long as we are alive we can all still grow. We can still use that time constructively.

We can grow tremendously in our abilities to understand and to feel. We can build up those around us, and we can build a better world. Recognizing the difference between magic and reality. Then bring people together to help each other get on with the work of growing and building. A good life in the twenty-first century may value simplicity. We can choose to focus more energy on those few things we do need, and let the rest drop away. Ordering and guiding of our energy and our desires, a partial restraint in some directions in order to secure greater abundance of life in other directions. It involves a deliberate organization of life for a purpose. Of course, as different people have different purposes in life, what is relevant to the purpose of one person might not be relevant to the purpose of another. The degree of simplification is a matter for each individual to settle for himself. Especially in a world with an economy build almost entirely on tempting you to buy products you don't really need, with money you don't really have. We cannot hide from global climate change, the proliferation of nuclear and chemical weapons, and the recent global financial crisis fueled by fear that we have massively overextended our entire economic system.

There is no question that religious people have killed too many in the name of their God. One in five young people in America now considers themselves nonreligious. We should teach our children creeds and customs, prohibitions and rituals, texts and music, and when we cover the history of religion, we should include both positive and negative. One should always challenge oneself to understand all perspectives on religion. Reason requires us to acknowledge that religion is here to stay. We human beings may not be if we do not find the collective moral motivation to beat back climate change, rein in terrorism before it realizes its most destructive hopes, and prevent the erosion of our democracies as economies shift and hopes are dashed.

We all need to be ambassadors for our community and for the planet Earth. Separation of church and state must be absolute. This benefits all people, religious or not. We need to build consensus with other groups in order to find solutions that works for all people. At its heart, it's grassroots educational process in which the goal is to gain knowledge about individuals and their beliefs in a way that lessens fear. Simply open your eyes and minds and see if there is something more. What's right in your heart is right in your heart and people are in different places in life.

Religion is the creation of human beings and not a God. Human beings are nothing if not adaptive and adaptable, religious institutions have always found new ways to thrive in response to criticism, rather than merely wilting away at the first sign of withering theological critique. Life in general, and religion in particular, is not as simple as deciding that I believe or I'm an atheist. Your relationship with religion, whether you're religious or not, is about more than which God you profess to worship or deny when asked in some census. It's about how you live life every day, how you respond to a thousand situations that are impossible to fully predict or prepare for.

The old joke that there are no atheists in a foxhole. The message is that in a foxhole, even the Soldier who is least religious under normal circumstances can't resist the urge to pray to an unseen God; help me, protect me, save me from the bullets and bombs. It's also a metaphor, there are no atheists when the chips are down, when you're in danger, whenever you want something so badly that all you can do, it seems, is close your eyes and pray for it. Our emotions and behaviors are profoundly connected to our thoughts, so by changing your thinking, you may be able to positively affect your future thoughts and actions.

When confronted with problems we don't immediately know how to solve or respond to, a specific and very old biological response kicks in. It's call the "fight or flight" mechanism because our early ancestors, when they encountered a potential predator or other such danger, would quite naturally either fight or run. Our fear of death is not only normal, it is part of the motivation we feel to live a good life now, while we still have time. But when the moment comes for someone we love to die, there are almost never good answers for our questions. Why? The raw feeling of these unanswered questions are so strong because they are the sign that we care about life. Without our ability to care, sometimes to the point of great pain, we could perhaps continue to walk and speak, but not really live.

It's a time to recall the significance of the life that has ended, no matter what it may be, to share stories and memories, meaningful readings and songs, and to express love in the form of laughter, tears, hugs and just sitting. It's amazing that just sitting in the room with a grieving person, neither running away nor wishing their pain away, is the single best thing we can do. Death needs courage. It is so overwhelmingly final that it fills our lives with dread and anxious fear. Courage is the power to confront a world that is not always fair. It is the willingness to accept what cannot be changed. Courage is loving life, even in the face of death. It is sharing our strength with others even when we feel weak. It is embracing our family and friends even when we fear to lose them.

We must act together for our own good and for the greater good. We are so fortunate to have evolved and been nurtured to possess reason, compassion and creativity. It is what we do with those qualities that will determine everything. But goodness is a choice. It is the most important choice we can ever make. We have to make it again and again, throughout our lives and in every aspect of our lives. We have to be good for ourselves. We have to be good for the people we love and care for. We have to be good for all the people around us, be they friend or foe. Let us go out and make a difference now.

It's not even hard to understand why highly intelligent people can believe so easily in an invisible God. After all, when a child's mother leaves the room, he has to be able to learn that she still exists even though she is invisible to him. She'll come back, he internalizes. From there, it's not too much of a stretch to think that God, the being who created our mother and the whole world, is only invisible for now and will return soon too. If mother can be mother even while not present physically, how much more so with an allegedly all powerful father. Is God like a fairy tale or Santa Claus? At best we are confused.

Our minds are what they are, we did not choose for them to evolve this way. It makes little sense to say that logic, reason, and science should eliminate or replace all religious beliefs. When that same scientific approach tells us these beliefs have taken millions of years to evolve and are deeply enough ingrained that they will be with many of us in some form for a long time to come. There are many individuals who do just fine and live perfectly good lives without God, but perhaps society as a whole would break down if we didn't have a godly foundation for our public values.

At the end, only you can choose to be a believer or nonbeliever. By using both faith and reason, what will you do? One day, death will come to us all. Upon our death, what happens? In the meantime, choose to be a good leader. We live every moment in a universe of seemingly eternal thoughts and ideas, yet simultaneously in the constantly churning and decaying world of our bodies. We are graced with a godlike ability to transcend time and space in our minds but are chained to death. The result is a nagging need to find meaning. Everybody wants to go to Heaven, but nobody wants to go now.

— 9 —

Leadership Principles to Live By

Effectiveness - Leadership ability determines a person's level of effectiveness. If your leadership rates a 10, then your effectiveness will never be greater than a 9. If your leadership rates a 5, then your effectiveness will never be greater than a 4. Your leadership ability, for better or worse, always determines your effectiveness and the potential impact of your organization.

Influence - If you don't have Influence, you will never be able to lead others. Is management and leadership the same? Are those that possess knowledge and intelligence leaders? Are those that are out front leaders? It's not the position that makes the leader; it's the leader that makes the position, leadership is influence, nothing more, nothing less.

Process - Leadership develops daily, not in a day. There are four phases of leadership growth: I don't know what I don't know; I know what I don't know; I grow and know and it starts to show; and I simply go because of what I know. To lead tomorrow, learn today the secret of success in life is for an individual to be ready for their time when it comes and champions don't become champions in the ring, they are merely recognized there.

Navigation - Anyone can steer the ship, but it takes a leader to chart the course. The secret to navigation is preparation. A leader is one who sees more than the others see, who sees farther than others see and who sees before others do.

People Listen - Being in power is like being a Noncommissioned Officer in the US Army. If you have to tell Soldiers who you are and who you are not, you will have issues. The proof of leadership is found in the followers. People become real leaders because of: Character, who they are; Relationships, who they know; Knowledge, what they know; Intuition, what they feel; Experience, where they've been; Past Success, what they've done; and Ability, what they can do.

Solid Ground - Trust is the foundation of leadership. When it comes to leadership, you just can't take shortcuts, no matter how long you've been leading your people. You may fool your boss, but you can never fool your colleagues or subordinates. To build trust, a leader must exemplify competence, connection, and character. How do leaders earn respect? By making sound decisions, admitting their mistakes, and putting what's best for their people and the organization ahead of their personal agendas.

Respect - People naturally follow leaders stronger than themselves. When people respect someone as a leader, they follow them. The more leadership ability a person has, the more quickly he recognizes leadership, or its lack in others. The greatest test of respect comes when a leader creates major change in an organization.

Intuition - Leaders evaluate everything with a leadership bias. Who you are dictates what you see. There are three levels of leadership intuition: those who naturally see it; those who are nurtured to see it; and those who will never see it.

Magnetism - Who you are is who you attract. The better leader you are, the better leaders you will attract. If you think the people you attract could be better, then it is time for you to improve yourself. If you think your people are negative, then you better check your attitude.

Connection - Leaders touch a heart, before they touch a hand. People do not care how much you know, until they know how much you care. To lead yourself, use your head, to lead others use your heart. The stronger the relationship and connection between individuals, the more likely the follower will want to help the leader.

Inner Circle - A leaders potential is determined by those closest to them. Get the right people in your inner circle. Potential value; those who rise up themselves, every leader must have the ability to lead and motivate themselves. Positive value; people that boost morale in an organization are invaluable and a tremendous asset. Personal value; those who rise up leaders, it's lonely at the top, so you better take someone with you. Production value; those who rise up others, value people who can rise up others. Proven value; those who rise up people who rise up other people, the greatest value to any leader is someone who can rise up other leaders. Never stop improving your inner circle.

Empowerment - Only secure leaders give power to others. The people's capacity to achieve is determined by their leader's ability to empower. A key to empowering others is to have high belief in people.

Reproduction - It takes a leader to rise up a leader. People cannot give to others what they themselves do not possess. Followers simply cannot develop leaders.

Buy In - People buy into the leader, then the vision. People don't at first follow worthy causes. They follow worthy leaders who promote worthwhile causes. People want to go along with people they get along with.

Victory - Leaders find a way for the team to win. Successful leaders feel the alternatives to success are totally unacceptable, so they figure out what must be done to achieve success, and then they go after it with everything at their disposal. An organization doesn't become successful if its people have different agendas.

Momentum - Momentum is a leader's best friend. Leaders always find a way to make things happen. If you can't make some heat, get out of the kitchen.

Priorities - Leaders understand that activity is not necessarily accomplishment. The three priorities are: What is required? What gives the greatest return? What brings the greatest reward? Everything has a purpose based on priorities.

Sacrifice - Leadership means setting the example. When you find yourself in a position of leadership, people follow your every move. When you become a leader, you lose the right to think about yourself. The higher the level of leadership people want to reach, the greater the sacrifice they will have to make.

Timing - When to lead is as important as what to do and where to go. Timing is everything. The wrong action at the wrong time leads to disaster. The right action at the wrong time brings resistance. The wrong action at the wrong time is a mistake. The right action at the right time results in success. If a leader repeatedly shows poor judgment, even in little things, people start to think that having him as the leader is the real mistake.

Explosive Growth - To add growth, you must lead followers and to multiply, lead leaders. It is your job to develop people that are going to build the organization. The only way to experience an explosive level of growth is to lead the way.

Legacy - A leader's lasting value is measured by succession. Leadership is one of the things you cannot delegate. You either exercise it, or you relinquish it. Just as in sports a coach needs a team of good players to win, an organization needs a group of good leaders to succeed. A legacy is created only when a person puts his section into a position to do great things without him.

Source Notes

I consider myself a Free Thinker. An individual whose opinions are formed on the basis of an understanding and rejection of tradition, authority or established belief. A philosophical viewpoint that opinions or beliefs of reality should be based on science, logic and reason. Ideas should not be derived from religion, authority or governments. A Free Thinker should not reject nor accept any proposed truths of organized religion, established norms, media, etc... They should determine if the belief is valid based on their own knowledge, intuition, research and reason. Just because other people believe in it, doesn't mean it's right. Use your own judgment and think critically. This is a collection of my notes, experiences, learnings and readings over my lifetime as a Husband, Father, Leader and Member of the Human Race.

Lightning Source UK Ltd.
Milton Keynes UK
UKOW04n0704301217
315251UK00002B/35/P